"一带一路"

THE BELT AND ROAD INITIATIVE
A BRIDGE TO THE FUTURE

与我们的未来(二)

董叙含　张思齐　宋政翰　等◎著

中国经济出版社

CHINA ECONOMIC PUBLISHING HOUSE

·北京·

图书在版编目（CIP）数据

"一带一路"与我们的未来．二/董叙含等著．
—北京：中国经济出版社，2020.3
ISBN 978-7-5136-5445-6

Ⅰ.①一⋯ Ⅱ.①董⋯ Ⅲ.①"一带一路"—国际
合作—青少年读物 Ⅳ.①F125-49

中国版本图书馆 CIP 数据核字（2020）第 024558 号

责任编辑　夏军城　郭国玺
责任印制　马小宾
封面设计　任燕飞工作室

出版发行　中国经济出版社
印 刷 者　北京九州迅驰传媒文化有限公司
经 销 者　各地新华书店
开　　本　710mm×1000mm　1/16
印　　张　14.75
字　　数　228 千字
版　　次　2020 年 3 月第 1 版
印　　次　2020 年 3 月第 1 次
定　　价　68.00 元

广告经营许可证　京西工商广字第 8179 号

中国经济出版社 网址 www.economyph.com 社址 北京市东城区安定门外大街 58 号 邮编 100011
本版图书如存在印装质量问题，请与本社销售中心联系调换（联系电话：010-57512564）

世界是我们的教科书

何　雷[①]

"知行合一"。当代中学生不仅要读好万卷书，还要行好万里路。面对学习压力，如何行好万里路？参与"一带一路"研学便是一种很好的选择。其重要意义主要体现在以下几个方面。

一是时代之需。"一带一路"倡议和建设，旨在运用"丝绸之路"这一历史符号，传承"天下大同"的文化思想，坚持和平发展与互惠互利，主动发展与沿线国家的经济合作，与世界各国建立友好关系，共同打造政治互信、经济融合、文化包容的利益共同体、命运共同体和责任共同体。习近平主席提出"一带一路"伟大倡议6年多来，已有150多个国家和国际组织积极响应和参与，与中国签署了共建"一带一路"合作协议。"一带一路"倡议的提出和实施，既创造了难得机遇，也面临着严峻挑战；不仅有利于国家之未来、世界之未来，而且事关当代青少年个人前途命运。当代青少年应该顺应时代发展之势，及早做好准备，参与研学实践，积累知识、经验和能力，"取得真经，修得正果"，锻造成为"一带一路"建设的有用之才。

二是成长之需。习近平主席指出，"青年人要立志做大事"。中国人民大学附属中学师生们紧跟时代前进的步伐，以积极的行动响应党和国家号召，一批热血青少年报名参与"'一带一路'与我们的未来"研学项目，学校从中遴选出课题组成员。12名高中生既仰望天空，又脚

---

① 何雷，中国人民解放军军事科学院特聘首席专家，中将军衔。

踏实地，从 2017 年初开题，在一年多时间里，认认真真研学，扎扎实实思考。通过学习研讨、实地考察等，将青春与理想诉诸文字，属文成章，书写出有价值、有意义的研究报告，为"一带一路"建设做出了自己的贡献。

值得欣喜的是，第一批课题组成员多数考入清华大学、北京大学、浙江大学、南京大学以及美国常青藤大学等名校。课题组组长李续双同学现就读于浙江大学竺可桢学院，她的研究是从"一个中国人如何获得非洲酋长身份"的设问展开，通过学科交叉研究，以 L 公司等为代表的中国投资企业为例，探讨中国企业"走出去"展开跨文化合作的挑战、经验及推进途径等，从青少年视角探讨跨文化合作问题，为"一带一路"建设人才培养和文化融合提供了有参考价值的建议。另一名课题组组长宋子玉同学现就读于北京大学光华管理学院，他的研究以"从 20 世纪 90 年代以来哈萨克斯坦能源输出角度简析其外交政策发展"为题，梳理了哈萨克斯坦外交政策发展过程，分析其确定独立外交地位、以周边外交为重点以及全面独立自主外交三个阶段，总结了哈萨克斯坦力图摆脱俄罗斯的影响，追求自主性、独立性、平衡性的努力，并提出推进中哈两国合作的对策建议：一是实现"一带一路"政策与"光明大道"新经济计划的对接；二是在"平等互助"原则下，深入开展交流与合作；三是坚持将能源输入作为推动中哈双边关系发展新的突破口；四是利用中国软实力的提升，推进双方民众交流。课题组成员杜闻馨同学目前就读于南京大学，她以中国食文化为大背景，采用文献分析、问卷调查与案例分析等研究方法，以兰州牛肉拉面为例探究了中餐在"一带一路"沿线国家的跨文化认同与推广作用，得出"一带一路"沿线除部分信仰佛教的国家与地区外，人们对中华饮食文化有较强的认同感，对兰州牛肉拉面具有一定的跨文化认同，兰州牛肉拉面具有较强的推广价值。

三是教改之需。来自中国人民大学附属中学等学校的十几名学子以"一带一路"为研学内容，从青少年视角研学世界这本取之不竭、用之不尽的教科书，从不同专业和领域开展研究，创新了研究方式、研究内容和研究视角。课题组自 2016 年下半年开始筹备，2017 年 1 月正式成立，3 月顺利开题，5 月进行了中期报告和研讨，12 月以中英双语报告和论文形式圆满结题。他们获得了学校、专家、家长以及社会各界的大力支持、关注和称赞。素质教育是当代中国教育改革的方向，中国人民大学附属中学"'一带一路'与我们的未来"课题研学实践进行了有益的尝试和创新，为素质教育提供了可借鉴、可复制的宝贵经验。

四是社会之需。在"一带一路"建设过程中，当代青少年的参与是有效的社会动员方式。"影响了一个孩子就能够影响一个家庭，而一个一个家庭又能够影响社会。"课题组成立以来，无论召集会议还是外出调研采访，家长们都给予了大力支持。有的家长拍照、摄像，有的家长收集资料，还有的家长联系调研采访单位……"一带一路"研学不仅成为青少年研学的重要课题，也成为家长们关注乃至参与"一带一路"建设的重要活动。

星星之火，可以燎原。第一期研学成果已经产生了强有力的辐射效应，迅速扩散。2018 年 10 月，在浙江宁波，又迎来了一批高中生积极参与"一带一路"研学活动。2018 年 12 月 31 日，"'一带一路'与我们的未来"第二期研学项目开题报告会在中国人民大学附属中学成功召开，截至 2019 年 6 月，这些高中生的研究成果还在紧锣密鼓地修改与完善之中。立志做大事、成大业，正被广大青年学子接力接续、善作善成。

时代的发展，技术的进步，给当代青少年更多的机遇和挑战。当代青少年是幸运的。学校、家庭乃至全社会都要想方设法地调动他们敢想、敢干、敢创新，敢于走前人没有走过的路、敢于做前人没有做过的事的勇气和积极性，发动他们对感兴趣的"一带一路"建设重大问题展开研究与交流，积极探索国际合作与全球治理的新途径、新方法、新模式，为国家政策决策等提供有价值的建议。

青少年是世界的未来、社会的未来，也是"一带一路"建设的未来。衷心祝愿当代青少年在"一带一路"建设的道路上，贡献聪明才智，早日成人成才。

"一带一路"上的诗和远方

张 磊①

转眼间，"一带一路"研学项目第二批成果已经出炉了，我作为最早的参与者之一，又惊又喜。

犹记得 2017 年底，中国人民大学附属中学的李续双、宋子玉等同学提议同学们聚焦"一带一路"倡议，通过研学方式，进行一系列小课题研究，既能增长自己的知识与能力，又能为国家倡议做出贡献。这一想法得到了家长们的大力支持，也得到了翟小宁校长和学校各位老师的关注，竟从设想转化为行动。于是，我和一些高校教授应邀参加了这个项目，与项目总策划李春霞教授一起，指导他们完成研学项目。孩子们的想法充满创意，既有"中国企业在'一带一路'沿线国家的形象"这样高大上的题目，也有"牛肉拉面与'一带一路'旅游发展"这样接地气的课题，有诗有远方，指导过程充满了趣味。

2018 年 5 月，第一批研究成果全部完成，并由商务印书馆正式出版发行。国家发展改革委社会发展司司长欧晓理教授、加拿大西蒙菲莎大学国家讲席教授赵月枝等应邀作序撰文，对课题成果给予充分肯定，使成果有了理论高度和深度。

如今，第一批参与"一带一路"研学项目的同学陆续毕业，并进入高校深造。李续双同学进入浙江大学竺可桢学院就读，宋子玉同学进入北京大学光华管理学院就读，而我当时指导的郑汪涛同学更是负笈海

---

① 张磊，中国传媒大学教授、国家传播创新研究中心研究员。

外，到美国的西北大学求学。

第二批研学项目不仅继续吸引了中国人民大学附属中学的同学积极参与，还吸纳了宁波几所中学的同学。浙江是中国对外开放的桥头堡之一，拥有多个辐射海外的制造业、商业和运输业中心，有众多侨乡，是"海上丝绸之路"的重要起点，这使得研学项目更趋多元化、更具对话性，研学成果令人耳目一新。

如今，第二批研学成果即将汇集成书，我想谈谈这一项目的特色和它所具有的社会价值。

第一个特色，研学兼备。

以研究促进学习，以学习完成研究。在研学过程中，课题组成员通过大量阅读、广泛调查和认真思索，积累拓展了知识，学会了各种研究方法，得到了学术规范训练，这为他们今后的深造奠定了良好根基。处于知识爆炸、信息海量的时代，在终身学习型社会，研究能力不仅是以学术为志业的人所必须具备的素质，也是所有人安身立命之本。研学兼备，使中学生们站在了更高的起点上。

第二个特色，知行合一。

王阳明曾经说："知者行之始，行者知之成。"知行合一，一向是处理学习与实践关系的指导原则。研学过程中大家坚持将之贯彻到底，参与者不囿于书斋，走向广阔的实践田野，而且把研学"一带一路"建设的心得体会应用到与外国友人的交往中，把自己的思考与研究成果反哺到实践中去。学生们从书本走向社会，从动脑转向动手，从线上走向线下，为自己拓展了成长的新维度。

第三个特色，前后相继。

一方面，青少年参与这个研学项目，可为其在个人成长的关键阶段留下浓墨重彩的一笔；另一方面，这一研学项目持续不断地开展，将一届又一届中学生联系了起来。长期的积累会带来历史性变化，无论对于个体还是集体，都具有重要意义。

第四个特色，内外互通。

"一带一路"倡议是中国走向世界、融入世界的新设想，它的核心理念是"共商、共建、共享"。2019 年"一带一路"研学项目的参与者来自北京、宁波两地，指导教师则来自海内外多所知名高校，调研活动所涉及的企业、机构与个人更是来自全世界。作为中学生的研学项目，该项目拥有开阔的视野，被纳入全球背景，成为全球化的一个小样本。它面向世界，具有鲜明特色。

由于具备研学兼备、知行合一、前后相继、内外互通等特点，"一带一路"研学项目具有丰富的社会意义和社会价值。

第一，它对于参与项目的青少年具有重要意义。通过这一项目，孩子们增长了见闻，学习了知识，培育了能力；同时，熟悉了社会，结交了朋友，这些朋友既包括参与项目的同学，也包括作为调研对象的国内外人士。更重要的是，这个项目能够促使他们以全球的视角来思考问题，在人生的关键阶段经受内心反思，从而成长为胸怀天下的有志之士。

第二，它对于中国的发展具有一定意义。随着中国经济实力的增强和社会文化的发展，国际影响力在不断扩大，这对中国在树立国家形象、处理国际关系和赢得全球声誉等方面提出了新要求。要想真正实现中国与世界的相互理解和共赢，就需要每一个公民从自己做起，在各个方面践行交流互鉴的精神。

第三，它对于世界同样具有意义。今天的世界局势比以往任何时候都要复杂，逆全球化与新版全球化此消彼长，既有的国际主流价值观受到挑战，双边矛盾和冲突不断发生，部分热点区域成为问题之源。在这种情况下，中国作为崛起的大国，既要主动承担责任，贡献中国方案和中国智慧，又要抓住机遇，推动全球迈向更好的未来。"一带一路"倡议和"全球命运共同体"理念互相融合，形成有力驱动。因此，这样的研学活动可以为全球发展做出贡献。

青少年代表着国之未来，"一带一路"代表着世界之未来，孩子们的思想与成果虽然略显稚嫩，但却不乏勇气和创新精神。正如费孝通所言："各美其美，美人之美，美美与共，天下大同。"期待研学成果能够成为新的起点，推动中国青少年走向全球，与全世界青少年携起手来，共塑人类美好明天。

目录

Contents

"一带一路"上的旋律

——中国与匈牙利音乐人才培养模式比较研究

董叙含①

摘要： 音乐是每个民族文化不可缺少的部分。本文选取"一带一路"沿线国家匈牙利和中国做比较分析，从中国和匈牙利音乐人才培养现状入手，进而分析中匈两国音乐人才培养体系的不同，形成自己的思考与见解，最后对我国音乐教育事业的发展提出对策建议。

关键词： 音乐教育　柯达伊教学法　柯达伊　高等音乐院校

一、引言

李斯特曾说："音乐既表达了感情的内容，又表达了感情的强度，它是具体化的、可以感觉得到的我们心灵的实质。"② 音乐教育是文化传承的方式之一，是对音乐文化的继承、传递和创新。匈牙利作为世界音乐教育的模范国家，在音乐人才培养模式、课程理论和实践应用水平等方面居世界前列，培养出了如李斯特等众多优秀的音乐人才。因此，借鉴匈牙利培养音乐人才的成功经验，探索我国音乐教育的发展规律，已成为当前教育创新框架下一个新的时代命题。

基于上述目的，本文将匈牙利音乐人才培养体系与我国音乐人才培养体系进行比较，为我国音乐人才的培养提供对策和建议。

---

① 董叙含，女，宁波科学中学高中二年级。

② 邹力宏. 让道德素质在欣赏中提升——论戏曲艺术与德育的关联 [J]. 江西财经大学学报，2005（6）.

二、中国和匈牙利音乐人才培养现状分析

(一)中国音乐人才培养现状分析

中国音乐院校的教育和培养目标在不同时期随着社会经济体制的变化而不断调整，我国的专业音乐教育体系和模式基本上遵循苏联的高等专业音乐教学模式，同时借鉴欧美先进的教学理念，在原有教学方法和制度改革的基础上继续发展。[①] 以中央音乐学院为例，从其不断调整的专业音乐教育人才培养目标中，可以探究我国高等音乐院校对专业人才培养的发展轨迹与脉络。

（1）从 1955 年到 1958 年，中央音乐学院的培养目标为，要培养具有较高音乐教育水平的音乐专业人员，需要培养音乐教师。因此，中央音乐学院在各专业均开设了教育学、教学方法和教学实践课程。

（2）1964 年 3 月，中央音乐学院将教学培养目标确定为：发展欧洲传统音乐流派、风格、技术，结合中国民族特点，培养专业的创作型、表演型人才，首次为普通中学和教师提供专业音乐教育培训，并首次提出将普通中学和师范学校的教师培训纳入专业音乐教育培养目标中去。

（3）1977 年，在改革开放初期，中央音乐学院确立了一个新的培养目标：培养音乐专业人才，全面发展学生道德、智力和体魄。

（4）1988 年《中央音乐学院 1988—1992 年工作计划》提出："培养较高层次的专门人才，即'培养的目标不是片面的追求技术畸形发展的人才，而是既具有坚实的技艺根基，又具有较深厚的音乐素质，有更大后劲的更全面的人才'。"目前，中央音乐学院的培养目标为具有国际视野的高层次音乐人才。[②]

截至 2016 年，全国公立专业音乐院校共 11 所，分别是上海音乐学院（1927 年）、沈阳音乐学院（1938 年）、四川音乐学院（1939 年）、西安音乐学院（1949 年）、中央音乐学院（1950 年）、武汉音乐学院（1953 年）、

---

① 杨洋.中高等专业音乐教育人才培养模式比较研究——以帕德莱夫斯基音乐学院与天津音乐学院为例［J］.肇庆学院学报，2018，39（3）.

② 李鸣镝.高等艺术教育体系中有关问题的借鉴与反思［J］.河南师范大学学报（哲学社会科学版），2004（6）：142-144.

星海音乐学院（1957 年）、天津音乐学院（1958 年）、中国音乐学院（1964 年）、哈尔滨音乐学院（2013 年）和浙江音乐学院（2016 年），其中中央音乐学院是唯一一所被列入国家"211 工程"重点建设的艺术类院校。11 所音乐院校在学科和专业设置、教学体系结构、教学人员、组织与管理等方面不断优化和调整，共同承担着培养高水平音乐人才的任务。

（二）匈牙利音乐人才培养现状分析

在匈牙利，人们普遍认为，良好的音乐教育使人们一生都受益，音乐教育与人类自然的非世俗精神要求相对应。因此，儿童音乐教育将使人们保持良好的情感，使人们纯洁，超越思维。匈牙利的音乐教育体系是根据音乐教育家柯达伊的教育理念建立的。

柯达伊教学法是以"儿童的自然发展"为基础，即课程的顺序是根据儿童在其成长各个阶段的自然发展所形成的生理和心理能力来安排的。音乐教学由以往的方式向逻辑有序的音乐理论体系转变，改变了传统教学模式的主题顺序，使课程的各个阶段都能让儿童、年轻人参与其中。[①]

柯达伊教学法集世界音乐教育众家之长，它倡导从世界各国音乐教学的优秀成果中合理汲取营养，并根据匈牙利的实际情况对其进行改造和结合，使之成为具有匈牙利特色的教学框架。节奏字母中的符号是很好的示例。它根据英国的首调唱名法、柯尔文手势唱名法、法国的节奏时值读法和意大利的字节音名修改和组合而成，从而成为一个新的音乐教学工具。它反映了柯达伊的感性焦点和教学重点，在训练晦涩的教学理念过程中，为孩子们指明了一条笔直而平坦的通往音乐殿堂的道路，这反映了柯达伊的难点分散的教学方法。

从柯达伊的课程思想和实践过程可以概括出以下六个特点：

（1）回到音乐的起源。音乐的起源是音乐的声音形式，因此，柯达伊强调音乐教育应该以听觉训练为起点，以体验为起点。这一思法贯穿于他的音乐课程。他把孩子们从公认的音乐中解放出来，也就是说，从音乐中

---

① 马磊. 柯达伊音乐教学法的启示［J］. 甘肃科技，2003（12）：166-167.

直接感受音乐，而不是从枯燥的概念和语言解释中识别音乐。① 因此，柯达伊认为，音乐理论的目的不是传播特殊的术语和概念，音乐阅读和写作不应是抽象的理论学习，而是实践、听觉能力的发展，以及使用音乐来思考和培养创造性能力的能力。

（2）主母语音乐，强调匈牙利民间音乐的使用。匈牙利的音乐教育是以匈牙利民间音乐为基础的，这对其音乐课程来说是不可或缺的。柯达伊声称，音乐是他的第二个母语，他说："在音乐方面，就语言而言，只有一开始就以匈牙利为中心，我们才能进行一种合理的教育。音乐学习如果不是以简单而严格的系统为基础，音乐概念将被混淆。简单而严格的系统将为其他方面和更高的发展水平奠定基础。"②

（3）强调基本训练，这是柯达伊音乐的另一个特点。柯达伊的音乐基础训练强调体感训练、听觉感知训练和心理感知（唱）训练三种训练。因此，以匈牙利民间音乐为主体的音乐体验、听觉训练、音乐读写训练和歌唱训练出现在柯达伊音乐课程中。

（4）培养学生的音乐能力。1945 年，在柯达伊的领导下，音乐课程和教学任务被确定为：自觉地使学生掌握音乐的母语；激发学生的歌唱兴趣；培养和引导学生的音乐爱好；培养学生的音乐能力；培养以民间歌曲为基础的音乐素养。柯达伊音乐教学的核心是：以匈牙利民间音乐为出发点，通过激发和培养学生对音乐的兴趣，进而更好地学习音乐，培养学生的音乐素养。

（5）培养听众和音乐人。柯达伊音乐课程的另一个突出特点体现在它的目标和评价上，即培养音乐家和听众。在人们的心目中，普通音乐教育和专业音乐教育相距甚远，但柯达伊音乐的辉煌和成功在于它成功地把两者放在了一个共同的基础上，结果证明，他的课程不仅为匈牙利音乐教育提供了一个共同的音乐基础，而且为他们提供了一个共同的文化基础。

（6）拯救机械化时代的人们。在 20 世纪中叶，匈牙利的工业化浪潮

---

① 马磊．柯达伊音乐教学法在农村幼儿音乐教育中的应用研究［D］．兰州：西北师范大学，2004.

② 李方元，吴祖英．论柯达伊音乐课程思想与实践［J］．中国音乐，2002（3）：25-31.

刚刚出现，但是文化伴随着机械化自然地影响了人们的精神生活。庆幸的是，柯达伊已经敏锐地意识到工业时代对人们精神的负面影响，也看到音乐教育在消除这种影响方面可以发挥的积极作用。1966年，他在为山德尔·伏瑞基什编写的《匈牙利的音乐教育》一书书写的前言中说道："现在出版的这本书证实了音乐教育在匈牙利是沿着正确的轨道运行的。它的目的不仅是培养音乐家，也要培养听众。如果有人试图用一个词来表达这种教育的实质的话，它只能是'歌唱'。在我们这个机械化的时代，终将沿着使人们自身成为机器的道路走去，只有歌唱的精神可以把我们从这种命运中拯救出来。"①

三、两国音乐人才培养模式的比较

（一）中匈音乐人才培养模式的相似之处

中国和匈牙利在音乐人才培养方面有着类似的目标，也就是说，教师专门接受针对普通初中和高中音乐教育的培训。因此，两个国家在音乐教育本科层次人才培养计划上存在许多相似之处。两个国家在人才培养方面的相似性表现在以下几个方面：

（1）所有学生都要通过专业素质考试，培训期为四年，学生必须具备一定的基本素质和专业素质，经过四年的学习和培训，达到初中和高中音乐教育专业水平。

（2）培训课程基本相同，注重提高音乐教育人才的综合素质。课程包括声乐、乐器、音乐学、音乐理论、音乐教育、彩排和实践等，注重学生音乐理论、实践和素质的培养、训练和熏陶，注重学生综合能力的培养。②

（3）两国在人才培养中注重"一专业、多才能"，使学生在毕业以后具备多种素质和能力，并具备专业音乐技能。

（二）中匈音乐人才培养模式的差异

"中西方文化的确有差异，但是音乐没有国界，它可使中西方文化相

---

① 王丹琴. "回归人的本性"——柯达伊合唱教育思想对我国音乐教育的启示 [J]. 中国科教创新导刊，2009（2）：99-100.

② 王贞贞. 中德音乐教育学专业（本科）人才培养比较研究——以曼海姆音乐学院和泉州师范学院对比为例 [J]. 黑河学院学报，2017（2）：32-35.

结合，贯穿古今，直达心灵最美之处。"钢琴演奏家郎朗如是说。具体而言，中匈两国在教学课程设计及考试等方面存在以下差异：

（1）人才培养专精程度的差异。例如：入学选拔考试难度不同；入学选拔考试音乐理论知识门槛要求不同；主副专业培养方案和课程设置不同；主副修课程教学强度不同。

（2）教材选择的灵活性和课程内容开放性方面不同。例如，在教材选择、辅助教学资料、教学形式多样性方面均存在一定的差异。

（3）课程的充实程度不同。在彩排和声乐课程上，国内高校并不像匈牙利音乐学院那样丰富。例如，彩排课程、乐队编排、乐队指挥、室内乐合奏和爵士合奏极大地提高了学生的多重能力，锻炼了多方面的专业技能。声乐语音保护课可以使学生更清晰、科学、客观地掌握和使用声音。语言课程的建立（德语、意大利语和法语）大大提高了学生的语言水平和对外国艺术歌曲、歌剧和其他作品的解释水平。

（4）测试灵活性和严格性方面的差异。在匈牙利，音乐学院学生不需要参加所有课程的考试。一些课程只需参加讲座，可由教师提供。该评估系统可以为学生提供更多的机会和更多的时间来专注于他们感兴趣的课程，而不必花费过多精力。特别是声乐、钢琴、乐器音乐专业，仅有两次考试——中期考试和毕业考试。相比之下，中国的音乐学院学生通常在每学期期末都有考试。为了取得良好的成绩，中国学生把整个学期都花在一个或两个歌曲上，忽视了基本技能的训练。同时，训练渠道数量有限，导致音乐视野狭窄。

据了解，匈牙利音乐学院对毕业考试非常严格，体现在三个方面：第一，应届毕业生必须举行一场 60 分钟的独奏或独奏音乐会，以衡量学生能否进入论文答辩；第二，论文主题由考试委员会和学生协调确定，必须在确定主题后 6 个月内完成。第三，为培养学生的音乐能力，激发学生的学习积极性，激发了大量不同方向、不同形式的实践性课程。

（5）课程学习时间的选择。在国外，学生可以根据自己的条件确定某些课程的学习时间，提前申请免修某些课程和提前毕业。例如，如果学生经由专业教授组成的评定小组测试达到标准，可以免修该课程。学生也可以提前申请举办毕业音乐会，只要教授书面确认学生已经提前完成了毕业音乐会。这些措施针对每个学生自己的专业课程表，而不是严格的教学安排。对于选修课的要求，虽然学校为学生提供了足够的空间以便于学生选择自己喜欢的课程，但学生需要在教学大纲规定的学期内完成课程，并且限制选修课的数量。

四、推动我国音乐教育事业发展的对策建议

通过比较可以看出，匈牙利音乐学院在培养音乐教育人才方面具有诸多优势，这对我国音乐教育改革很有借鉴意义。

事实上，从 20 世纪 50 年代开始，我国的音乐教育就采用了柯达伊的教学方法。21 纪初以来，为引进这一教学方法，先后出版了大量的导论著作和教材。但是，这些著作主要介绍柯达伊教学法的概念及其在匈牙利的实施概况，并没有结合我国的实际情况给出建设性建议。一些翻译成中文的教材内容非常贫乏。例如，由于不懂匈牙利语，加拿大学者洛伊斯·乔西（Lois Choksy）在他的第二部著作《从民歌到经典》中，竟然把匈牙利小学音乐教科书《歌唱与器乐》（Enek Zene）当作教科书编著者的名字，认为所有教材都是由这个所谓的"埃内克译内"编写的。在他强调的西欧古典音乐方面，存在巨大的偏差。这本书在匈牙利音乐界被当作一个笑话，却被我们作为一本优秀的教科书译本出版。当然，也有一些教材是很好的，如匈牙利专家撰写的《音乐的读与写》，介绍了科尔文手势、第一声调唱法、节奏阅读法等教学方法。好的教科书对我们有很大的参考价值，但是，我们必须使柯达伊教学方法中国化、本土化，才能使其在我国产生更大的影响和发挥更大的作用，以下是一些对策和建议。

（一）充分发挥人才优势，培养专业音乐教育人才

重视教学人才的培养，充分发挥教学人才的才华和优势。作为未来的音乐教师，我们需要有很强的音乐专业素养。例如，对钢琴有好悟性的学生可以集中精力来训练钢琴演奏技能，挖掘学生的潜能，做到因人而异，因材施教。一些拥有音乐天赋的学生由于得不到足够的培训而失去了自身的优势，这不利于音乐教育和音乐教学事业的发展。因此，建议国内音乐学院借鉴匈牙利"一科多才"的教育方针，将"一门专业"贯穿全校各专

业的教学中，注重学生专业技能的培养，使人才培养更加准确、更加专业化。

（二）丰富和完善课程内容设置

音乐课程可横向拓宽音乐知识学习，学生接触的音乐领域越广泛，就越有利于提升其学习兴趣，拓展其思维能力。

音乐教育是一门实践性很强的学科，其理论体系来自音乐教育的实践，反过来也指导音乐教育实践。因此，建议中国的音乐院校可以在不同的方向上提供大量实用课程，如匈牙利地方音乐学校采取不同形式，发展学生的音乐能力，促进学生自主学习。

（三）进行研讨式教学，丰富教学形式

研究教学课程的发展，使教学形式更加多样化。这样，既避免了教学形式单一、教学效率不高的问题，又促进了教学和科研共同进步，并能够以自主探索精神培养音乐人才。

（四）提高教材的利用率，避免教材选择的单一性

国内音乐学院应该借鉴匈牙利音乐学院的教材，不断引进新的教学内容，更新陈旧的教材和教学案例。图书馆馆藏，国外音乐图书、音像等资源的增加，对学习和教学有很大的益处。

（五）改革考试制度，兼顾灵活性和严谨性

匈牙利音乐学院坚持"严格进入，严格退出"的教学理念，同时注重灵活性，注重学生对知识的灵活掌握和应用，而不是死记硬背知识。这种考试制度确保了毕业生的高素质，使其能迅速适应新的工作。国内高校可以借鉴这一考试制度，兼顾灵活性和严谨性，把毕业生的整体水平提到一个新的高度。

（六）重视音乐素养的培养，重视学校的艺术氛围

艺术氛围直接关系到学生的学习热情，在艺术氛围浓厚的学校，学生一般具有较高的审美水平和艺术鉴赏水平。匈牙利大多数音乐学院都为学生提供免费音乐交流课程，每年邀请著名音乐家参加大师班、音乐周表演等活动。这些具有巨大国际影响力的活动在提高学生的艺术素养和视野方

面发挥不可估量的作用。在过去的十年里，国内的音乐交流活动越来越频繁，例如，中央音乐学院每年举办音乐周、器乐展览、大师班等免费开放和交流班，以拓宽学生的视野，推广艺术。因此，国内音乐学院可以在这方面进行有益探索，营造学校的音乐艺术氛围。

五、结束语

通过对本课题的研究和探索，笔者对于中国与匈牙利音乐人才培养模式有了一些思考和心得体会。

当今社会越来越强调文化多元化，因而对他国的文化学习越来越有必要，就音乐教育来说也是如此。在国内外学者的推动下，中国接触了国外四大音乐教学体系。对于新体系的学习可先从未来的教师即主修音乐教学的大学生入手，通过对未来教师的培养将这些新的教学法运用到教学实践当中；但很多毕业生在实践中一味照搬国外的方法，结果不尽如人意。

查阅很多资料之后，笔者产生了一些想法，有反思、想象，也有学习、感悟。反思中国当前的音乐教育，想象中国未来的音乐教育；学习柯达伊教育思想和匈牙利的教学体系，有感中国的音乐教育落后于世界水平太多，我们可以通过借鉴匈牙利音乐教育体系来改变现状。

之所以将匈牙利音乐教育模式作为范例，是因为中国的音乐教育与匈牙利过去的音乐教育状况很相似。我国是一个历史悠久且有着丰富民族音乐文化的国家，但现在很多人喜欢西方的音乐，忽略中国本土音乐文化的学习。从身边的情况来看，很多孩子从小就学习钢琴、小提琴等，耳濡目染的是国外音乐，意识上忽视民族文化的重要性，以至于现在很多家长在给孩子选择学习乐器时，重西洋轻民族。我们的民族音乐文化是中华民族几千年智慧的结晶，作为中国人，我们有义务学习并传承。

同时，笔者认为，加大中匈两国音乐人才培养方面的合作力度十分有必要。2015 年至今，上海音乐学院与全球四所顶尖音乐学院进行联合办学——"上音—英皇联合学院""上音—伯克利现代音乐学院""上音—李斯特—肖邦音乐学院联盟"。[①] 这些高端国际合作平台，为推动音乐表演学科发展、培

---

① 阚政.中国好声音：上音奏响时代音符［J］.新民周刊，2017（46）：18-23.

养顶尖音乐表演人才提供了更大可能性。

以"上音—英皇联合学院"为例，该学院以"导师管总，大师引领，以演促学，以赛促练"为培养理念，采用"短中长"个性化教学方式，周末集中授课。教学团队中，首席教授包括上音团队 8 人、英皇团队 10 人，全部为顶级教授。

而在"上音—伯克利现代音乐院"，一同招进来的学生毕业时双方可以一起评分，这就建立了同样的质量体系，同时毕业生可以获得双方的文凭。该项目负责人、上海音乐学院音乐工程系主任陈强斌教授表示，目前上海音乐学院的课程设置已获得伯克利方面的充分认可，实现了学分互认。

2017 年，上海音乐学院还与匈牙利的李斯特音乐学院、波兰华沙的肖邦音乐大学建立了中欧三方联盟。该联盟将以系列音乐节和国际巡回演出为契机，将古典音乐创作、表演推向世界一流水平，进行全方位的国际交流与合作。

"顶尖音乐人才需要量身定制、个性化的培养，若能得到大师级音乐家手把手的教导，更是如虎添翼。"上海音乐学院党委副书记刘艳如是说。事实的确如此，只有不断开展合作，才能立足国际视野，融会贯通，创新中匈文化交流模式，开展一系列中匈艺术交流活动，为更多爱好艺术的孩子搭建更大、更广的展示平台。只有携手并行，才能力促教育共赢。我们必须向好作品敞开大门，不管它们来自哪个国家，它们都会使我们的文化更加丰富。

"一带一路"给金融全球化带来的创新研究

张思齐①

摘要： 美国等发达国家主导的全球化本质是资本全球化，金融全球化是其表现形式，带有不平等的性质；"一带一路"推动新型的全球化，目的是实现全球经济的均衡发展，构建更加公平的全球化体系。"一带一路"倡议建立在中国小康、世界大同的伟大理想之上，是全球化的中国方案，旨在破解资本主义逆全球化这一难题。"一带一路"向世界传达了善意，向沿线国家伸出了援助之手，反映了全世界人民的共同愿望。与资本主义世界的全球化体系不同，"一带一路"以国际主义精神，坚持成果共享、和平发展与互惠互利，推动沿线国家政治互信、经济融合、文化包容。金融全球化是"一带一路"的根本课题，只有解决好资金融通的问题，才能推动"一带一路"沿线国家的各项建设，商业、贸易、文化、人才、技术交流才能得以发展。"有道之士，贵以近知远，以今知古，以所见知所不见。"② 本文基于此，分析"一带一路"给金融全球化带来的模式创新。

关键词： "一带一路" 金融全球化 资本主义 创新

一、前言

2013 年，习近平提出了"一带一路"的伟大倡议，2014 年 12 月，中央将"一带一路"作为重点建设项目，并且设立 400 亿美元的丝路基金给予支持。"一带一路"推动了沿线国家贸易和投资的便利化，丰富了国际公共产品服务，改善了各国的基础设施，有助于沿线各国人民脱贫致富。同时，通过发展互联网金融，构建开放式金融平台，实现共融共通，在新

---

① 张思齐，男，浙江省余姚中学高中二年级。
② 引自《吕氏春秋·慎大览·察今》。

的金融全球化体系下改善发展中国家的国际分工处境，让"一带一路"沿线国家实现自立自强。除此之外，"一带一路"致力于探索解决当前全球化困局的有效方法，构建互利共赢合作分享机制，打造人类命运共同体。但是，也必须看到"一带一路"沿线国家众多，① 文化背景不同，经济发展不平衡，各国人民信仰和习俗差异大，以传统的产业全球化模式推动"一带一路"周期较长，困难较多，需要克服的困难多。但是采用金融全球化创新手段进行推动，是一个有效的创新思路和切入点，可以加快"一带一路"的实施。另外，金融发展是推动"一带一路"的必要条件，只有融资渠道畅通，才能保证项目的顺利实施。只有资金充足，建设才有保障，才能实现宏伟蓝图。

本课题在研究方法上有所创新，力图在政治经济学框架内分析"一带一路"和金融全球化问题。与西方经济学倡导的以计量模型为基础的问题探讨模式不同，本文认为，经济问题不仅要专注于经济领域，还应该深入把握地区深层次的文化、道德和哲学问题，以更加开阔的视角来探究问题的根源。因此，本研究更多地从政治经济学的角度结合经济发展规律进行创新性思考。

传统资本主义国家主导的金融全球化通过构建不平等的国际分工体系，持续从发展中国家掠夺财富，将国内矛盾转移到发展中国家，造成全球收入差距的持续扩大。中美贸易摩擦就是一个典型案例，美国害怕中国发展壮大，在贸易和技术上对我们进行封锁。"一带一路"构建新的金融全球化秩序，通过基础设施建设等发展中国家急需的金融支持，真正帮助发展中国家解决现实问题，让广大发展中国家实现自立自强，摆脱对欧美发达国家的依附，实现对金融全球化模式的一系列重大创新。

---

① "一带一路"沿线国家涉及东亚、南亚、中亚、西亚和中东欧地区的 65 个国家。

二、问题的提出

1. 资本主义国家通过金融全球化建立了新的剥削体系

首先，资本主义金融全球化让发展中国家经济陷入恶性循环。资本主义全球性金融危机和主权债务危机本质上是因为全球贫富差距，通过全球化，资本主义国家把风险和矛盾转移至发展中国家。资本主义国家主导的金融全球化，无论是人口还是财富都不可能无限积累，只有"一带一路"推动的新型金融全球化才能够解决这一问题。

图 1　资本主义金融全球化的恶性循环

如马克思所预言的一样，经过资本原始积累，利益被少数资本家独占，① 同时，欧美国家日益累积的社会问题转移至发展中国家。资本主义国家之所以看似规避了马克思主义理论推演的结果，没有出现系统崩溃，是由于其通过全球扩张的方式将国内的矛盾转嫁至发展中国家。通过国际经贸合作，发达国家一边将高污染的产业、过剩的产能和通货膨胀转移至发展中国家，一边从发展中国家掠取资源类产品，同时遏制其往产业链上游移动，如当前美国从中国低价进口稀土资源，同时对高科技产品征收关税，以芯片为手段遏制中国科技产业发展。近年来，以美国为主的发达国家经济景气度呈现下降态势，就业压力凸显，为了创造足够多的实体就业岗位，美国通过加大征收中国出口商品关税来缩小贸易逆差，甚至扬言中国对美顺差剥夺了美国本土的就业岗位。与此形成鲜明对比的是，中国丝路基金给"一带一路"沿线国家的劳动人民，包括广大妇女创造了大量的就业岗位。

其次，资本主义国家内部各界对传统金融全球化日渐不满。在资本主

① 叶险明. 世界历史理论的当代构建 [M]. 北京：中国社会科学出版社，2014.

义几百年的发展历史上，社会各界对资本家的批判不绝于耳。在哲学界，康德指出，历史是由恶而开始的，因为它是人的创作，[①] 本质上揭露了食利者的贪婪。在文学界，对于食利阶层的批判，以巴尔扎克为代表，其笔下的多个人物都有着鲜明的特征，最著名的就是欧也妮·葛朗台这个人物，形象地刻画了食利者嘴脸。即使是在金融发达的美国，关于资本的争论也从未停止。美国独立之初，杰斐逊等多数立国者都否定资本主义，富兰克林一生都在批判个人的资本积累，《独立宣言》对英国政府打击美国制造业只字不提。在资本主义国家，劳苦大众和底层人民对金融资本是深恶痛绝的，他们对资本家的不满由来已久。

最后，金融全球化继承了殖民时代的体系。从某种定意义上来说，在当代资本主义金融全球化发展过程中，能够看到殖民时代的影子。《资本论》认为，第一次全球化在殖民扩张时期就已经开始。马克思提出，欧洲列强利用战争和殖民方式掠夺美洲的资源、非洲的劳动力，实现资本血腥积累。没有工业发展，就没有现代金融强权。换言之，今天的金融全球化起始于地理大发现的资本主义殖民时代，意味着资本主义全球扩张的开始。资本主导全球化从未摆脱殖民意识和剥削思想，一生向往小农场主理想的杰斐逊拥有 600 多个奴隶，他的民主农业理想国是建立在蓄奴基础之上的。杰斐逊禁止输入奴隶，是因为奴隶的后代终身为奴，比购买奴隶的成本更低。托马斯·皮凯蒂[②]在《21 世纪资本论》中指出，1770 年到 1860 年南方奴隶数目从 40 万增长到 400 万。南北战争之前，奴隶的市场价格是自由劳动力 10 倍以上，1860 年，一个奴隶主需花费 2000 美元才能购买一个青壮年奴隶，而同期工资水平是一年 200 美元。实际上，奴隶主支付给奴隶的近乎为零，只需要提供他们最低的生存需求就足够了。

2. 资本主义金融全球化的系统性缺陷

首先，资本主义的核心矛盾在于资本收益大于劳动报酬。资本所有者不需要劳动，坐地收租，劳动者一生的价值积累不如大资本家的一日利

---

① ［德］康德. 历史理性批判文集［M］. 何兆武，译. 天津：天津人民出版社，2014：66-67.

② ［法］托马斯·皮凯蒂. 21 世纪资本论［M］. 北京：中信出版社，2014.

得。这在房地产和采矿业等资源型行业最为明显，资本家凭借的是其对这些资源的占有权。在殖民时代，资本游走于全球。殖民者到了美洲，就把墨西哥的金矿据为己有，在非洲则抓捕奴隶，从事罪恶的三角贸易。他们宣称对这些资源的占有权，光明正大地进行掠夺，墨西哥金矿、北美种植园里的奴隶在鞭挞之下工作。今天，当资本以金融工具的方式活跃于全球，很多社会底层民众在负债中度过他们的一生，每月的辛勤劳动所得多半用于偿还昂贵的贷款，次贷危机就是因为资本泡沫的破裂。而金融危机一旦发生，就会危及全球的经济体系，1929 年的大萧条和 2008 年的国际金融危机都验证了这一点。

其次，工人和机器一直在做斗争，但是很少有人意识到，工人其实是在和机器背后的资本做斗争。2014 年数据显示，一个机器人可以替代 12.24~14.37 个人，对采矿业、制造业、水电气供应、建筑业影响很大。新机器让劳动力的重要性不断降低。资本主义社会的过剩金融资本在全世界范围流动，利用先进机器设备剥夺了发展中国家民众的工作岗位，造成这些国家的产业贫困。

最后，金融资本收益不可能无限积累，资本越大，资本收益率越低。资本家为了保持自己的收益水平，就要进一步压低工人工资或者恶性竞争。资本家在全球设厂，用过剩资本压榨发展中国家的工人，形成了金融资本的剪刀差。

3. 资本主义的金融全球化保守而封闭

贸易战表明，发达国家试图利用资本和技术限制发展中国家，造成全球经济和社会发展机会的不平等。如工业革命早期，即使是制度温和的英国，输出纺织技术也是违法行为。知识和技能的扩散削弱了资本积累带来的不平等，而全球化过程中知识共享则是打破科技封锁的关键。从本质上说，美国维持世界霸权靠的不是创新和技术，而是资本对技术的垄断。中国崛起让美国感受到挑战，《纽约时报》指出，过去 10 年美国专利所占份额跌至原来的 52%，诺贝尔奖获奖人数跌至原来的 51%。哈罗德·埃文斯等在《他们创造了美国》一书中指出，真正创造美国历史的是各行各业的小人物。这些发明家和创新者以其救赎的道德意识和近乎疯狂的创造动力，致力于让社会大众享受过去只有上层社会才能够享受到的商品，但是资本家却利用这些发明成果为其谋取垄断利润。资本主义金融资本对创新有压制作用，即使是拥有 1093 项专利的托马斯·爱迪生，也曾告诫助手："我们必须拿出成果，不能像有些德国教授那样，毕生研究蜜蜂身上的绒毛。"① 美国很多发明家和创新者往往毕生都穷困潦倒，约翰·菲奇就是因为没有资金推广蒸汽船而绝望自杀。弥留之际，他预言资本家将会从他的发明中获得名声和财富，而贫穷的他将会被历史遗忘。② 正如惠特尼的轧棉机强化了南方奴隶制度，今天美国主导的逆全球化本质是建立技术壁垒，以便实现其垄断地位。

4. 小结

资本主义的金融化是服务于资本家的，而非服务于劳苦大众；资本家通过金融的全球化手段将大众的财富掠夺走，实质是将国内矛盾转移到发展中国家。一位来自巴基斯坦的朋友向笔者讲述，这些年来巴基斯坦的债务危机实质上是美国等发达国家金融掠夺的结果，而"一带一路"提供的金融支持正逐渐帮助巴基斯坦从经济困境中解脱出来。因此，现在每一个巴基斯坦人都感谢中国，而多数人对美国的金融资本持反感态度。

三、"一带一路"构建了新型金融全球化体系

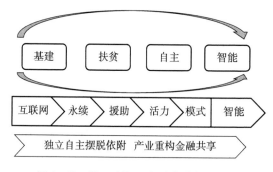

图 2 "一带一路"下金融全球化的特点

---

① ［美］哈罗德·埃文斯，等. 他们创造了美国［M］. 北京：中信出版社，2013.
② 同上。

如图 2 所示，"一带一路"通过支持欧亚非发展中国家的基础设施建设、扶贫工作、产业独立和技术创新，通过构建互联网信息设施、完善交通设施、创新金融模式、建立共享机制、精准援助，为这些国家经济注入活力，让沿线国家实现产业重构和金融共享。

因此，"一带一路"是医治资本主义金融全球化桎梏顽疾的良方。一方面对传统资本主义全球化产生的问题开出处方；另一方面，构建了新型金融全球化体系，确立了新型金融全球化体系的优势。

1. 中国经济高速发展推动"一带一路"倡议实施

我国经济的高速发展为"一带一路"奠定了基础。1978 年，我国人均国民生产总值只有 385 元，2018 年这一数字是将近 6 万元。1978 年，农民一天只赚一角多钱，而 2020 年，中国将实现全面脱贫，部分地区农民收入比 1978 年增长了上万倍。过去 10 年，我国超越日本成为世界第二大经济体，超越德国成为全球最大出口国，超越美国成为第一大贸易国，在专利技术申请量方面也已经超越美国位居世界第一。我国企业数量世界第一，"世界 500 强"企业中有 120 家是中国企业，前 10 名中有 3 家中国企业，全球盈利能力最强的 10 家公司中，中国有 4 家。在公共产品供应方面，中国电力供应能力持续增强，电力市场化水平不断提高。我国移动电话数量位居全球第一，信息通信能力不断增强，铁路、公路等交通设施不断完善，私家车保有量与日俱增，农村科教文卫等公共产品的供应能力持续增强。过去几十年，中国政府不仅带领中国人民实现脱贫致富，而且积极援助贫穷国家。在"一带一路"建设中，中国通过金融全球化来增加国际公共产品供给，提升服务全球能力。在过去 40 年里，中国取得了资本主义世界几百年才实现的奇迹，这是一个前所未有的成就。在经济全球化背景下，"一带一路"倡议通过金融支持与发展中国家共享发展成果，和资本主义国家推动以掠夺发展中国家资源为目的的金融全球化有着本质的区别。

2. "一带一路"是医治资本主义金融全球化的良方

保罗·巴兰和保罗·斯威齐早就提出金融资本扩张是资本主义生产陷入停滞的结果。换言之，资本主义积累体现了金融全球化的特征，"经济活动重心从产业领域（甚至是服务业）转向金融领域"。① 在互联网金融时代，金融资本积累比产业资本积累更有优越性，金融资本可以在全球范围内实现瞬间积累，数以亿计的资本在伦敦、纽约、东京、中国香港等国际金融中心之间随心所欲地流动，不受时间和空间的限制。例如，通过西联汇款就可以将美元汇到"一带一路"沿线国家，支持那里的事业。后凯恩斯主义学派把货币借贷者作为食利者进行分析，认为食利阶层是推动金融发展的主要力量。当前，发达国家正在扮演这一角色，其让发展中国家身陷债务陷阱。正因如此，经济金融化趋势已经凸显。② 正如弗朗索瓦·沙奈所指出的，"当今资本主义最深刻的变化发生在金融领域，经济全球化和经济金融化则导致资本主义发展进入了一个新的阶段"。③ 在此背景下，中国以金融引领对"一带一路"沿线国家和地区的投资，带动相关产业发展，全面推进各项经济文化活动，促进新兴经济体形成其经济体制，实现全球经济再平衡。

在逆全球化浪潮此起彼伏，中美贸易摩擦再起波澜，美国修建边境墙以邻为壑，英国脱离欧盟自顾，全球政治经济环境趋于动荡的背景下，发达国家选民开始通过投票表达他们对政府的不满。在金融全球化过程中，发达国家面临三个问题：第一，占领华尔街等事件表明只有金融寡头在全球化中获利，而99%的民众不但没能从金融全球化中获益，甚至还遭受金融资本的损害。第二，在金融全球化过程中，实体经济遭到破坏，影子银行和泡沫经济不断把经济推向虚高，而真正需要金融支持的基础设施、科技创新、产业孵化领域却不能得到应有的发展。第三，在全球化过程中，发展中国家得不到金融支持，金融成本较高，撒哈拉以南非洲地区和发达国家的经济差距持续增大。这是由资本的逐利性决定的，金融资本倾向于那些能够最快获得回报的领域，而对不发达国家投资风险大，利润小，回报慢。从种种事件可以看出，资本主义主导的金融全球化正在遭遇困境，

---

① ［美］约翰-贝拉米·福斯特. 资本主义的金融化［J］. 国外理论动态，2007（7）：9.

② ［美］戈拉德·A. 爱泼斯坦. 金融化与世界经济［J］. 温爱莲，译. 国外理论动态，2007（7）：14.

③ ［法］弗朗索瓦·沙奈. 金融全球化［M］. 齐建华，胡振良，译. 北京：中央编译出版社，2001：4-6.

在全球范围内受到抵制。而"一带一路"倡议推动的全球化金融，本质上是支持发展中国家，帮助其从贫困中解脱出来；同时抵制逆全球化浪潮，让世界人民共享发展利益，切实解决发展问题，而不是给少数金融资本家提供暴富的机会。

3. "一带一路"倡议给金融全球化带来的创新

首先，"一带一路"沿线国家和地区庞大的基础设施建设催生了金融需求。在亚非一些国家，阻碍经济发展的根本原因就是基础设施建设不完善，极度落后的交通基础条件和严重匮乏的电力让经济增长失去了动力。以非洲拥有 5000 万人口的坦桑尼亚为例，只有 10% 的家庭可以使用电，这不仅给民众生活、学习和工作带来了极大的不便，还使其发展现代科技困难重重。国家开发银行行长郑之杰提出，"一带一路"沿线国家和地区资金缺口巨大，2030 年，基础设施建设需求将会达到 94 万亿美元，其中 20% 无法得到有效支持。众所周知，基础设施建设是一项投入巨大、回报慢的项目，在亚洲和非洲很多不发达国家，政府无力承担基础建设费用资金，很多非洲国家民众还住在简易的原始草木屋中，道路、水利、电力、通信、卫生条件非常不完善，空中交通更是无从说起。作为东非最发达的国家之一，埃塞俄比亚许多城市的房屋还是用黏土和石块砌成的，很多地区连食物都得靠中国游客援助，"一带一路"项目的支持对改善他们的生活发挥了巨大的作用，尤其是在道路交通方面。有了中国的金融支持和技术援助，埃塞俄比亚老百姓也坐上了轻轨，再也不需要为交通烦恼了。此外，撒哈拉以南非洲国家每年用于基础设施建设的公共支出仅仅占国民生产总值的 2%，为世界最低标准的 3%。"一带一路"倡议构建的新型金融全球化体系能够给各国的基础设施建设提供数以万亿美元的资金支持，帮助各国从基础设施落后、教育文化贫困、经济发展停滞的恶性循环中解脱出来，真正实现自立自强，对提升非洲国家的教育水平发挥了巨大作用。

其次，金融支持向不发达国家倾斜。在传统国际分工中，不发达国家处于产业链低端，发达国家制定的国际金融和贸易规则始终向发达国家倾斜，导致全球贫富差距过大。"一带一路"倡议致力于打造人类命运共同体，让全世界人民共享金融全球化的成果，开辟世界发展新阶段，将资本家金融改革为普惠金融，重构国际分工体系。和传统金融全球化不同的是，"一带一路"推进的金融全球化着眼于那些不发达国家，通过基础设施建设将没有参与全球化的国家联结起来，打造一个新型全球化体系。中国帮助安哥拉、埃塞俄比亚等非洲国家进行基础设施建设，推动当地科教文卫事业发展，改善卫生医疗和教育环境，免费建设医院学校，给穷人看病，降低文盲率。这些国家已经从沉重的债务负担中解脱出来，不再任由西方国家垄断其工业产业，摆脱资本主义金融资本家的控制。在"一带一路"项目提供的金融支持下，逐渐走向自立自强，并逐步发展民族工业，真正服务于工人和广大群众。"一带一路"下的新型金融全球化和资本主义国家金融全球化最大的不同在于：一方面，新型金融全球化出于善意和无私，而非老牌资本主义国家的贪得无厌。另一方面，"一带一路"项目提供金融支持以提升沿线国家经济自主能力为目标，让这些国家逐渐实现独立自主，降低负债率，实现可持续发展。

最后，有利于改善发展中国家的国际分工处境。过去，发展中国家用资源换取发达国家的技术，极度珍贵的自然资源以很低的价格流入欧美国家，同时欧美国家利用发展中国家的低价劳动力进行掠夺。而美国在国际上的金融统治地位来自其对国际货币的垄断地位，各国大量购买美国国债，使资本回流美国，客观上形成了美国低成本融资模式，导致美国民众高消费、低储蓄的现状。美元霸权地位与其金融强权密不可分，从布雷顿森林体系确立以来，美国通过对外输出数以万亿的美元纸币，换取了同等价值的商品。这种金融手段在金融全球化过程中被称为剪羊毛，美国通过让美元成为全球流通的结算货币，达到从其他国家掠夺财富的目的。

现有的国际金融秩序便于发达国家通过资本全球流通来掠夺发展中国家的资源。在这种分配体系下，发展中国家和发达国家之间的差距越来越大，正如今天我们所看到的全球贫富分化。"一带一路"倡议改变了这种现状，构建新的金融体系和秩序，切实帮助和支持贫穷国家获得金融支持。

在"一带一路"体系下，发展中国家可逐渐实现独立自主，不再依赖欧美资本和技术，独立进行技术研发；各国通过产业互补合作，依托自身的比较优势，实现价值链中高端化和产业升级。尤其是在当前国际贸易保护主义势力抬头的背景下，"一带一路"倡议有利于开创发展中国家的大市场，让产品和技术不再依赖发达国家市场，实现发展中国家的内部流通，改变过去产业垂直化分工和产业承接转移的方式。"一带一路"倡议通过提供金融支持，为发展中国家建立一套独立的科研和生产配套体系，推动区域性地位的跃升。通过提供金融支持，使发展中国家不再依赖出口低端附加值产品赚取外汇，改变其长期处于"微笑曲线"底部的局面。

四、"一带一路"金融全球化创新面临的挑战和建议

1. "一带一路"金融全球化创新面临的挑战

如图 3 所示，"一带一路"金融全球化创新面临着巨大挑战，发展中国家在经济上和西方发达国家差距较大，短期内还难以撼动其领导地位。同时，全球经济面临一定下行风险，发达国家企图把经济风险向发展中国家转移，金融风险加大。中美贸易摩擦加剧，美国加大对华为等中国高科技企业的封锁，企图遏制中国崛起。国际形势风云突变，大国间矛盾冲突加剧，这对我国推动金融全球化形成了挑战。

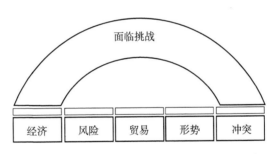

图 3 "一带一路"金融全球化创新面临的挑战

首先，金融危机让欧美国家经济持续低迷，全球经济下行压力加大，美国加大对中国的遏制，以转嫁改善国内的经济危机。其次，发达国家将其制度的不平等扩散到全球，不仅让发展中国家沦为其低端制造工厂，还造成发展中国家政治动荡和两极分化等问题。本质上，发达国家将国内的环境污染、经济剥削、生态破坏等问题转移给了不发达国家。再次，美国等发达国家打着"国家主义"旗号，行种族主义之实，实质上是为了维护利益集团的利益最大化，重拾单边主义和贸易保护主义，这与"一带一

路"倡议的人类关怀思想严重冲突。随着国际形势剧变，欧债危机，英国脱欧，发达国家内部右翼势力的崛起，右翼政党对移民、难民和外来贫困人口持敌视态度，反对分担解决难民问题的成本和提供救济援助。特朗普上台以来推行美国优先战略，指责发展中国家剥夺了美国人的工作岗位，为修建边境墙，美国政府创造了史上最长的停摆纪录，美国还退出多个国际组织，逆全球化思维正在抬头。最后，中国取得的历史性成就让美国感到威胁，而非机会，美国为了维护其国际分工地位，阻碍中国技术进步，致使中美发生史上最大的贸易摩擦。特朗普政府已经宣布对我国2000亿美元商品加征关税，由10%提高到25%，并且威胁对剩余的3000多亿美元产品加征关税，特朗普政府奉行单边主义思维，给"一带一路"建设带来了不利影响。

2. "一带一路"金融全球化创新的原则

首先，要以共享发展为原则，改变传统剥削思维。金融资本和产业发展应该是互利互惠的关系，绝非掠夺与被掠夺的关系。在为发展中国家提供金融支持时，要实现优势互补，解决当地资金短缺问题。因此，要推动金融资本支持沿线国家的基础设施建设，加强基础设施建设让当地民众共享发展成果。例如，建设医院、学校、公路等设施，让当地民众能够享受到更好的教育、医疗和生活服务。再如，华为公司对巴基斯坦提供了广泛的援助，在当地建设发展基金，为巴基斯坦培养技术人才，改善当地民众的生活。

其次，运用社会主义思想指导金融全球化发展，改善"一带一路"沿线国家的贫困局面，推动精准扶贫。马克思早在其中学毕业论文《青年在选择职业时的考虑》中就指出，资本主义世界会因为争夺工作机会而导致职业的相互冲突。他提出，一种利益不应该消灭另一种利益，人类应该为别人的幸福和完美而工作。"一带一路"倡议推动的金融全球化就是基于这种思想，金融资本要为人类的幸福而工作，而不是吸附于劳动。因此，要赋予金融资本以活力，切实让金融支持应用于生活改善、扶贫帮困、科技创新和教育文化等。中国给发展中国家提供金融支持，是为了缩小发展中国家的贫富差距，绝非为了金融掠夺和剥削，是基于成果共享精神。例如，中国对尼泊尔提供了广泛援助，扶贫基金会给当地学生送去书包，改善他们的学习条件，并向学生提供餐食、奖学金。

再次，帮助"一带一路"沿线国家实现独立自主，改变传统金融国际化中的不利局面，支持当地金融资本参与竞争，让资金流入当地最需要发展的领域，同时在技术创新和产业发展上给予支持。例如，中国企业不仅开拓巴基斯坦市场，而且在当地建立本土化企业，支持其技术研发；同时建立实验室、科技园等研发机构，加快科技合作基地的建设，支持技术转移，孵化创新创业平台，支持当地产业发展。

最后，创新金融全球化的方式，如改变金融资本的扩张方式。发达国家的金融全球化，通过金融资本对产业工人实施掠夺，通过使用新机器剥夺工人的工作岗位，而收益全都归资本家所有。在技术革新过程中，"一带一路"倡议推动的金融全球化，劳资双方共享所有权，工人也享有一定的权益。创新金融共享方式，打破资本垄断，建立信用发展体系，提升信用共享额度，让穷人在起步之时就能获得发展的资本，改变金融资本只流向大企业的沉疴。

3. "一带一路"金融全球化创新的建议

首先，在"一带一路"倡议践行过程中，大力传播和分享知识技术。将中国的先进文化、技术传播到沿线国家，促进沿线国家和地区的产业升级和技术进步。在传统金融全球化下，发达国家掌握最尖端技术，技术进步不断提高资本密集程度，导致技术越发达，密集度越高。由于发达国家对专利技术保密等原因，导致技术向发展中国家外溢机会非常少，发展中国家产业升级速度缓慢。而"一带一路"倡议推动新型金融全球化，以加快科学、知识和技术的传播来打破资本垄断技术导致的不平等，帮助各国实现自主知识产权和科技的发展，增强企业的竞争力；从而有利于企业以更低的融资成本获取资金，扩大规模实现跨越式发展。要提升沿线国家的经济发展水平和人民幸福指数，就要加大文化交流和知识共享力度，促进开放。要通过知识产权转让，开设技能培训机构，建立学校等方式实现知识和技术普及，同时培养创新型人才，实现创新型驱动发展。

其次，"一带一路"建设要与金融创新相结合。创新大数据和区块链等技术应用，搭建新型金融平台，在架构、治理和逻辑上去中心化，打破资本主义发达国家对全球市场的垄断，在规则制定上形成共识机制。美国主导的金融全球化，是由金融强权和寡头操纵全球金融市场。迈克尔·道格拉斯在《华尔街》中精彩的表演揭露了资本贪婪的本质，盖葛毫不掩饰地提出要保持美国头等强权地位。今天，欧美发达国家利用其拥有的金融强权地位，在国际资本市场上通过规则制定权、地位垄断权和信息优先权攫取发展中国家的财富。因此，要构建去中心化的新型金融体系，实现金融平等，促进金融资本自由流动。以人民币为支撑，以微信和支付宝金融平台为载体，实现小额快捷结算。通过这种方法，一方面，可以解决人民币兑换难的问题，构建外币兑换网络。美元作为世界贸易货币，在"一带一路"沿线国家占据统治地位，我国应加大人民币自由兑换力度，在"一带一路"沿线国家构建人民币支付体系。另一方面，微信和支付宝具有安全便捷、简单易用、即时到账、成本低廉的特点，可为"一带一路"沿线国家提供快捷跨境支付和兑换支持。当前，电汇、信汇、票汇等传统金融结算手段已经无法满足"一带一路"建设过程中跨境中小企业资金往来频次增多、交流日益频繁的现实需求。因此，要开发互联网跨境支付，减少资金流通障碍。推动互联网金融创新，参考微信和支付宝等成功经验，在"一带一路"沿线国家发展便捷金融支持服务，提供小额贷款和信用支持，推动金融共享；利用互联网的长尾效应，打造精准化服务，在金融消费、支付、云共享等诸多领域向大众化领域倾斜。

　　最后，出台"一带一路"金融全球化创新的保障措施，绝不能让老牌资本主义发达国家把高能耗、高污染、破坏生态环境的产业转移至发展中国家。中国是全球最大的工业制造国，是世界工厂，但是近年来产能过剩已成为制约经济发展的核心问题；同时，"一带一路"沿线国家的工业生产能力严重不足，有效需求得不到满足。因此，中国要积极向"一带一路"沿线国家提供产品服务，提供金融支持帮助沿线国家建立自己的产业。利用大数据和人工智能打击金融犯罪，规避金融全球化的负面效应，为金融全球化创建良好的环境。同时，通过大数据和人工智能技术建立完善的信用评估体系，加大对穷困人口的金融支持，促进小微金融的发展。以新型金融全球化改变当前资本主义的社会结构问题，革除资本主义社会的弊端，不仅要改革税率、使用高额累进税率等方式，而且要从根本上改革资本主义的结构性问题。因此，要通过推动共享金融等方式，改变发达国家对全球金融资本的垄断，让小额资本和分布式金融发挥更大的作用。通过"一带一路"建设，让金融资本流向经济弱势领域和实体经济，改变金融流向和贫困人群相背离的状况。如在非洲国家，广大民众迫切需要金融支持来改善当前教育、生活和工作条件，"一带一路"倡议推动的金融创新要充分发挥小额资本的作用，在这些国家设立助学贷款、小额生意启动资金、疾病保险等服务，动用富余资本去帮扶非洲各国人民。

五、结论与展望

大道之行，天下为公，"一带一路"倡议推动的金融全球化重大创新改变了过去由发达国家垄断金融市场的局面，真正让金融创新服务于基础设施落后、教育水平低下和科技能力薄弱的发展中国家，有利于创建长效共享的国际金融新秩序和体系。金融全球化是一个宏大课题，笔者之所以选择这个课题，是遵从习主席的教导，"只有立大志，才能成大事"。本着胸怀祖国，放眼全球的精神，笔者进行"一带一路"金融全球化创新研究。受知识储备以及理论修养的制约，表述或有不当，但笔者坚信，随着世界各国广泛参与"一带一路"建设，新的全球金融体系必将建立。

义乌小商品市场在"一带一路"建设中的大作用

宋政翰①

摘要：作为浙江省的一个县级市，义乌从"手摇拨浪鼓磕开致富路，用鸡毛换糖换出大市场"。义乌小商品市场是世界公认的"小商品的海洋，购物者的天堂"。作为参与"一带一路"建设的重要基地之一，义乌是中国商品走向世界和世界商品进入中国的重要平台，义乌成功践行了通过"贸易畅通"促进"民心相通"的伟大构想。

关键词："一带一路"　义乌小商品　中欧班列　国际贸易

一、引言

2013 年 9 月至 10 月，中国国家主席习近平访问哈萨克斯坦和印度尼西亚，先后提出共建"丝绸之路经济带"和"21 世纪海上丝绸之路"的倡议构想。几年来，以政策沟通、设施联通、贸易畅通、资金融通、民心相通为主要内容的"一带一路"倡议，正在世界各地演绎中国式和平建设与发展方案。"一带一路"建设涉及沿线国家约 44 亿人口，占全球总人口的 63%，沿线国家的经济总量约 21 万亿美元，约占全球经济总量的 29%。

浙江省经济发达，特别是民营经济发展迅猛，义乌市的小商品批发市场目前已成为世界最大的商品市场。"无中生有，无奇不有，点石成金"，这是时任浙江省委书记习近平对义乌的评价。义乌与世界多个国家和地区有着贸易往来，促进了沿线各国民心相通。本文通过对义乌小商品市场参与"一带一路"建设情况进行分析，探寻中国企业如何在"一带一路"建设中发挥更大的作用。

---

①　宋政翰，男，宁波惠贞书院高中二年级。

二、义乌小商品市场概况和特色

40 年前，义乌破冰市场经济，小商品市场正式开放，并逐步发展为全球最大的小商品批发市场。随着国际贸易综合改革试点和国家"一带一路"倡议的提出和建设的加快，义乌小商品市场昂首阔步，挺立在全球小商品贸易之巅。

如今，义乌小商品市场拥有 550 多万平方米的超大经营面积，早已超越被西方称为"世界第一市场"的荷兰鹿特丹市场。义乌小商品市场 23.8 万持证经营人员，销售 20 多万家企业生产的 180 万种海量小商品，被称为"小商品的海洋，购物者的天堂"。"如果在义乌小商品市场每个商位前停留 3 分钟，按每天 8 小时计算，需一年半的时间才能逛完市场。"义乌市地方志负责人施章岳如是说。

当年实至名归，如今更上一层楼。2005 年联合国、世界银行和摩根士丹尼公司等世界权威机构联合发布的《震惊全球的中国数字》报告认定，义乌为全球最大小商品批发市场；国际某著名经济学家称赞道，"对于生意人来说，义乌是最理想的地方。在这个巨大的批发帝国，你几乎能找到任何说得出名字的日用消费品"。相比以往，今日的义乌小商品市场不可同日而语。这里除了能找到任何说得出名字的日用消费品，还能找到说不出名字的日用消费品。它不仅超越纽约、迪拜、巴黎、伦敦、中国香港、米兰、东京、洛杉矶被"全球八大购物天堂城市"任何一个日用消费品市场，还是全球日用消费品贸易的枢纽，并以"大众创业、万众创新"的新路径，帮助欠发达国家和地区脱贫解困，打破贸易壁垒、践行自由开放的市场规则，把增进民之相亲、拓展国之交往的新举措和共享财富、迈向富裕文明之路的新使命，展现在世界面前。

（一）义乌小商品市场的发展史

时任浙江省委书记的习近平，曾十下义乌。他说："义乌依靠兴商建市……义乌是改革开放以来浙江县域经济发展的典型，也是当前全省经济社会发展的一个缩影。"

历史上，义乌是个人多地少、仅靠农业的地区。由于土壤酸性重，农作物收成不佳，当地农民长期使用鸡毛充当肥料来改善土质。然而，由于鸡毛有限，农民便把本地所产的红糖制成糖饼，去外地串村走巷，用糖饼换鸡毛。人们把这些从事以物易物的生意人称为"敲糖帮"，这可以追溯到明末清初。随着时间的推移，"敲糖帮"的糖担里，逐渐增加了针线、发夹、手帕、头巾之类的日用小商品。

义乌小商品市场首批经营者冯爱倩这样描述市场建立时的情形："当年我家很穷，母亲和我以及我的五个小孩一起生活。母亲给别人洗衣服挣钱，我工作一天也只能挣2分工，值4分钱。那时的生活没保障，我没办法，就去找当时的领导，提出要做生意。那时做生意被视为搞资本主义，是投机倒把行为，摆摊卖东西是要被抓的，有坐牢的危险。我们只能和市场管理人员打游击，看到他们来就马上跑。"后来，当时的领导顶着巨大压力，默许她摆摊经营。最终，她成为义乌小商品市场的"元老"。

1980年，当地政府恢复对"鸡毛换糖"经营活动的登记许可，并发放了营业许可证7000余份。一些换糖人开始专门采购小商品并长途贩运；同时，自发摸索加工小商品，在集市上交易。如此一来，小商品市场逐步形成。

1982年9月，义乌县政府正式开放稠城镇小百货市场并投资9000元，为露天市场铺设水泥板摊位700个，当年小商品市场成交额高达392万元。1984年，义乌县委县政府提出"兴商建县"的方针，放宽企业审批政策，简化登记手续。随之，义乌全县掀起经商办工厂的热潮，当年底，个体户突破1万户，小商品市场的成交额达2321万元。

然而，随着摊位数量的不断上升，产生市容不佳、交通阻塞等问题。为了解决这些问题，1984年义乌县政府决定兴建小商品市场，在原来的稠城镇小百货市场基础上，进一步完善基础设施，使小商品市场环境更加成熟。1986年义乌小商品市场成交额突破1亿元，辐射范围从周边县市延伸到浙江全省甚至省外。1986年，义乌第三代小商品市场竣工开业，固定摊位扩大到4096个，市场内还配有综合商业服务以及工商、税务、邮电、金融等管理服务大楼。其后，经过多次扩建，到1990年底，第三代小商品市场发展成为拥有固定摊位8503个、临时摊位1500多个的全国最大的小商品专业批发市场。

1991 年，义乌小商品市场的成交额首次突破 10 亿元大关。1993 年，义乌小商品市场走上股份制发展道路，成立了中国小商品城股份有限公司。而第四代市场中国小商品城的摊位增加到 2.3 万多个。进入 21 世纪后，义乌小商品市场走上国际化发展道路，建设完成了第五代专业市场——中国义乌国际商贸城。

义乌小商品市场经过 5 次飞跃发展，已经脱胎换骨。义乌商贸业稳定增长扩大，走出了一条新路子——义乌模式。如今，这种模式正在向外扩散：义乌小商品市场在全国 20 多个省市建立了 30 多个市场；在南非、乌克兰等国家设立了 5 个分市场；12 万义乌经商大军中有 5 万人分布在全国各地。①

（二）义乌小商品市场的企业结构与人才政策

对于义乌小商品市场众多经商户和厂家来说，谁的创新能力更强，谁就能吸引更多客户，占领市场。目前的义乌小商品市场，几乎每天都有新产品上市，新产品更新换代的速度在全国乃至全球的小商品市场都是最快的。

义乌小商品市场产品更新速度快的原因，在于市委市政府重市场、引人才、搭平台、优服务等方面的持续政策支持，从而打造了一大批贴近市场需求机制灵活的企业、研发团队和各类人才。近几年，义乌市政府推出"义乌英才"计划，对于入选"义乌英才"计划的创业创新人才，最高可给予 5000 万元的奖励资助；对于举办创业大赛、创业沙龙、论坛等活动的，给予最高 100 万元的补助；对于缺少初创资金的，给予最高 30 万元的个人贴息担保贷款；同时，还有最高 200 万元的人才住房保障补贴、人才子女入学等优惠政策。至今为止，全市吸引了包括 46 名国家、省级专家和 14 位柔性引进的两院院士在内的 25.9 万名人才。一大批专业设计研发团队和科技创新型工业企业在义乌涌现。现在，义乌有省级科技型企业 98 家、省级以上研发中心 31 家、国家级高新技术企业 49 家。义乌市政府每年在科技创新方面的财政投入近 3 亿元，在浙江省各县市处于前列。位于义乌工业园区的浙江英特来光电科技有限公司，是一家集 LED 产品研发、

---

① 吴献华. 世界商贸之都［J］. 人民画报·2017 义乌特刊，2017：10-14.

生产、销售于一体的企业，公司每年在技术创新方面投入近 1000 万元，已申请各类专利 97 项，先后被评为"浙江省科技型企业""国家级高新技术企业"，是国内少数几家拥有照明和显示屏独立研发、制造技术的企业之一。① 同时，通过对接新兴产业、创造新的商业模式、实施品牌多样化等途径，围绕市场各个环节建立工业设计、创意文化、电商培训等各种载体，为创业者搭建更多就业平台。

（三）义乌小商品市场的发展现状

近年来，互联网裹挟着巨大的信息流、商流等呼啸而来，义乌小商品市场并没有拒绝和排斥，而是主动迎合时代发展趋势，以优质的全方位市场设施为基础，构建电商全域化发展格局，使虚拟的网上小商品市场与有形的实体小商品市场相伴相生、融合发展，为创业创新者提供新的就业机会。他们的主要做法是构建齐全的电商产业平台。义乌现拥有 113 个淘宝村、9 个淘宝镇和 30 个电商园区。淘宝村数量居全国第一，淘宝镇占全省 11.5%，电商园区建筑面积超过 200 万平方米，形成了电子商务园区—专业市场—专业楼宇—示范村平台体系。全市网拍店铺 200 余家，网拍摄影师近千人，面积在 500 平方米以上的摄影机构近 10 家。一个离义乌小商品市场 6 公里、人口不足 2000 人的江东街道青岩刘村，聚集了来自全国各地的创业者，他们开网店、办公司，成立以淘宝为代表的公共电商平台。2015 年，新村民超过 1.5 万人，开办网店 3200 余家，销售额达 45 亿元。2016 年，网店增至 3500 家，销售额达 50 亿元。2017 年，新村民达 2.5 万多人，网店 4000 多家，销售额突破 60 亿元，被国务院总理李克强称为"中国淘宝第一村"。自 2014 年起，义乌连续 4 年位列"中国电商百佳县"榜首。为了让更多白手起家的创业者及电商企业安家落户，义乌市财政每年安排 5000 万元，设立电子商务专项资金，成立财政资金不少于 1 亿元的电子商务产业引导基金，建立电子商务贷款风险补偿机制，并在土地、金融、税收、住房、子女就学等问题上予以政策倾斜。如今，在义乌可以做到电商无断点，创业零成本。哪怕是刚毕业的大学生，也只需拥有一部手机就可以来义乌创业。

---

① 施章岳. 义乌市场的新名片——义乌国际商贸城现状调查［J］. 中国房地产，2009.

义乌先人一步，组建了中国（义乌）商城集团所属的浙江义乌购电子商务有限公司（简称"义乌购"）为核心的义乌电商市场大平台，让传统的小商品专业市场成为全国网货的主要供应地，成功助力全国网商创业创新。如今，义乌小商品市场 7.5 万个商铺都已入驻"义乌购"平台；同时，主动发力、多方发动，对接阿里巴巴、亚马逊、京东商城、敦煌网等国内知名第三方平台，使义乌电商账户达 27.8 万个，其内贸网商密度位居全国第一，外贸网商密度仅次于深圳，位居全国第二。义乌小商品市场的电子商务交易额年年大幅跃升，2015—2017 年，分别达到 1511 亿元、1770 亿元、2220 亿元。①

三、义乌小商品市场在"一带一路"建设中的作用

（一）义乌小商品销往全球，充分发挥了"贸易畅通"作用

40 年前，义乌破冰市场经济；2011 年，国家战略——国际贸易综合改革试点花落义乌，义乌又一次扛起了改革大旗；如今，"一带一路"倡议让义乌再一次站到了新起点上。

"手摇拨浪鼓磕开致富路，用鸡毛换糖换出大市场"，义乌被称为"新丝绸之路的起点"，在"一带一路"建设中，义乌具有无可比拟的优势。义乌是中国商品走向世界和世界商品进入中国的重要平台。这里汇集 7 万多个商铺，经营着 180 多万种商品，日客流量达 21 余万人次，商品出口到 210 多个国家和地区，年出口标准集装箱超过 77 万个。义乌是全球最大的圣诞用品集散地，全球三分之二圣诞用品产自义乌。义乌海关数据显示，义乌向全球近 200 个国家和地区出口圣诞用品。

1. 开通中欧铁路，货物流通便捷

历史上，穿越亚欧大陆的古商道，因为中国的丝绸产品长期是商贸的主要对象而被称为"丝绸之路"，驼队是活跃在丝绸之路上的主要运输工具。如今，飞驰列车的轰鸣声，替代了回荡千年的声声驼铃。

2014 年 11 月 18 日，世界运输旅程最长的货运班列——义新欧班列开

---

① 施章岳. 义乌市场的新名片——义乌国际商贸城现状调查［J］. 中国房地产，2009.

通，班列一头连着全球最大的小商品集散地浙江义乌，一头连着欧洲最大的小商品集散地西班牙马德里。满载着 82 个义乌小商品集装箱的"义新欧"首趟班列从义乌出发，经 21 天的长途跋涉，行驶 13052 公里，最终到达西班牙首都马德里。

一家民营企业，一个 30 多岁的小伙子，是如何借着一条国际铁路线，主动参与"一带一路"建设，助推全球经济一体化的？

冯旭斌，1979 年生人，话语中已有"40 岁成功男人"的稳重与睿智。虽然年轻，但冯旭斌有着丰富的从商经验，他看好国际物流行业。2010年，冯旭斌筹备成立中欧班列运营公司，2012 年获批。然而，通过铁路货运专列把义乌和欧洲联系起来，这是一般人想都不敢想的事。途经那么多国家，经过那么多海关，中途还要换轨，其难度可想而知。碰了几次壁后，冯旭斌也曾想过放弃。2013 年，习近平主席在哈萨克斯坦纳扎尔巴耶夫大学演讲时，提出建设"丝绸之路经济带"的倡议，再次燃起了冯旭斌的斗志。他决定分步实施，首先争取开通中亚五国，再通中欧班列。

2014 年 1 月 20 日，从义乌始发，开往哈萨克斯坦、乌兹别克斯坦、吉尔吉斯斯坦、土库曼斯坦和塔吉克斯坦的"义乌—中亚五国"班列正式启动。消息很快传到西班牙马德里的华商耳中，他们纷纷打电话给冯旭斌，希望班列可以延伸到西班牙马德里。然而，运作中欧班列，难度非一般人能想象。

中欧班列全程 13052 公里，经新疆进入哈萨克斯坦，再经俄罗斯、白俄罗斯、波兰、德国、法国、最后到达西班牙马德里，穿越 7 个国家，几乎贯穿整个欧洲。中途不仅穿越俄罗斯寒冷地带，还有 6 次通关、3 次换轨，费时费力，只要一个环节协调不到位，班列便不能正常行驶。为此，冯旭斌组建了一支 30 多人的精干团队，与各国政府、铁路、海关等相关部门协调。2014 年，这支团队"飞"了 106 次 13 万多公里。

中欧班列要正常运行，必须有很强的组货能力和合作伙伴，否则运输成本会很高。因为同样的距离，传统的海运需要 30~50 天，铁路运行为 12~14天，价格是海运的 2~3 倍，且班列途中换轨通关检查难免会有一些损耗。有些货主宁可走海运，也不走铁路。冯旭斌为此专门物色了两个合作伙伴，一位是浙江盟德进口有限公司董事长周旭峰，另一位是多年在义乌开展货运业务的中远国际货运代理有限公司董事长林辉寰。三个年轻人志同道合，分工协作，冯旭斌负责运营，周旭峰负责组织班列往返货源。

作为国内唯一一条民营线路，掘路之初，客户说什么价就什么价，条件很苛刻，途中风险和责任都由他们承担。从义乌发往西班牙的小商品大都不怕冻，但回程的橄榄油、红酒均是玻璃瓶包装，在低温下可能会爆裂。于是，在回程班列上他们改制了两个恒温大柜，4个标准集装箱，虽然成本加大，但安全有了保障，信誉慢慢建立，与客户的合作条件逐渐合理起来。

"义新欧"开通后，西班牙华侨一片欢呼，有40多家贸易商上门洽谈合作，搭乘这趟班列。[1]

"义新欧"中欧班列的开通和成功运行，赋予了义乌有别于以往更多角色。义乌因此成为"丝绸之路经济带"的起点、"新丝路"沿线国家的地区商品进入中国的桥头堡、长三角经济圈与"新丝路"沿线国家和地区陆上货物主通道；同时，义乌成为我国与"丝绸之路经济带"沿线国家（地区）实现政策沟通、道路联通、贸易畅通、货币流通、民心相通的重要平台。

2011年，义乌获批成为国际贸易综合改革试点城市，成为中国商品走向世界和世界商品进入中国的重要平台。目前，在泰国、阿联酋、俄罗斯、罗马尼亚等10个国家和地区，义乌小商品市场设有境外分市场或配送中心。

与其他中欧班列相比，贯穿"丝绸之路经济带"的"义新欧"班列创下了几个第一：它全程13052公里，比"苏慢欧"班列长1850公里，是所有中欧班列运输线路最长的；途径7个国家，几乎横贯欧洲；境外铁路换轨次数最多，除和其他中欧班列一样在哈萨克斯坦、波兰两次换轨，"义新欧"班列还需要在法国与西班牙交界的伊轮进行第三次换轨。这是我国加快建设"丝绸之路经济带"，打造向西开放"黄金通道"的重要举措。

2014年9月26日，国家主席习近平会见西班牙首相时表示，中欧货

---

① 施章岳，朱庆平．义乌商帮［M］．杭州：浙江大学出版社，2018：267-269.

运班列发展势头良好，"义新欧"铁路计划从浙江义乌出发，经新疆抵达终点马德里，中方欢迎西方积极参与建设和运营，共同提升两国经贸合作水平。

2015年6月28日，"义新欧"班列从义乌出发，首次在波兰华沙、德国杜伊斯堡和法国巴黎等沿线重要城市停靠，实现多站点上下货。这意味着，班列服务的客源和货源将越来越广。随着多站点停靠的实现，"义新欧"班列运输的货物也由之前全部都是义乌小商品转变为包含电子配件、名牌服装、高档面料等价值较高的产品，吸引了上海、杭州、嘉兴、湖州、绍兴等地的客商选择"义新欧"班列作为货运工具。

截至2016年8月，运出义乌小商品市场的日用品、五金、纺织、手机配件等，运来西班牙的红酒、木地板、果汁、橄榄油等货物的"义新欧"班列已往返运行72次，共运输了5176个标准集装箱，实现每周一趟常态化运行。①

义乌直达中亚、欧洲的国际铁路联运物流大通道开通，方便了中亚、欧洲各国客商到义乌采购商品，为义乌商品进出口提供了一条安全、便捷、全天候、大运量的绿色通道。笔者2019年2月24日到义乌小商品市场实地考察时，碰到两位加拿大商人，马塔集团CEO罗杰先生和他的兄弟，目前他们公司的业务主要在黎巴嫩和加拿大，这次特地到义乌考察市场，寻找商机。他对义乌小商品市场商品的多样性和贸易的全球化给予了很高评价。

2. 拓展海外市场，做好全球生意

义乌有句口头禅："革命人，打天下；读书人，知天下；生意人，闯天下。"这形象地道出了义乌人"心怀天下"的胸襟。在义乌人看来，哪里有市场，哪里就是他们闯荡的"天下"。商场没有国界地域之分，没有民族、种族之异，只要有人的地方就会有商机。义乌人不满足于国内的小有成就，他们毅然漂洋过海，闯荡异国天地。

义乌市场模式是义乌人的一个创举。义乌人凭借小商品市场的品牌优势，不仅把小商品市场理念和模式推广全国各地，还把小商品市场创办到

---

① 吴献华. 世界商贸之都［J］. 人民画报·2017义乌特刊，2017：23-25.

海外很多国家和地区，南非、韩国、俄罗斯、瑞典、越南、美国、智利、哥伦比亚、阿联酋、波兰等地都留下了义乌人的印记。

义乌人赵贤文经商多年，1991年开始闯荡海外市场，参加马来西亚吉隆坡国际博览会。1992年他到越南胡志明市做生意。1998年，他把目光转向了非洲，先后赴非洲10多个国家考察。在尼日利亚考察期间，恰逢几次停电，这让他看到了商机，决定在尼日利亚开设发电设备厂。随后，他考虑尼日利亚是非洲人口最多的国家，日用产品十分缺乏，需大量进口，便决定成立义发尼日利亚有限公司。同时，借鉴义乌小商品市场发展的成功经验，他又筹建了尼日利亚中华商城等项目，得到了尼日利亚总统奥巴桑乔的接见和赞扬。后来，赵贤文参加南非共和国举办的世界博览会，发现南非经济发达，最大城市约翰内斯堡虽被人称为"南非的上海"，交通便捷，但工业基础薄弱，日用产品基本靠进口。国内1元人民币的商品在约翰内斯堡一般能卖到1美元，中国的家电轻纺、鞋类等产品物美价廉，商机无限。于是，赵贤文决定在约翰内斯堡市创办"中华门"中国商品批发零售中心。经南非政府和中国政府的大力支持，1999年4月，赵贤文拿到了国家经贸委的批复文件，成为在境外兴办大市场的第一人。①

1970年出生的王芳茂，摆过地摊，在上海投资过彩印厂，承包过多家媒体代理权，经营过音像产品，还创办过物流公司、合办市场以及跨境电商企业，现为易镭公司董事长。他指出，"海外仓在海外集货和控货方面发挥的作用不容小觑，跨境电商企业如果没有海外仓，意味着在货源和操作上没有话语权，对电商企业而言也就没有了货源和价格的核心竞争力。"他认为，海外仓是跨境电商发展的新风向，正在成为中国跨境电商行业竞争越来越重要的"砝码"。

2012年，王芳茂整合多家物流企业，合伙创办了义联物流股份公司，把散布于各货代物流企业的集装箱整合起来，形成箱量后，为义乌企业争取最大优惠的货运价格；再与多家国际知名公司合作，取得了一级代理权。

最初的跨境电商卖家都是销售小商品，售价低，毛利薄，而市场竞争

---

① 施章岳，朱庆平．义乌商帮［M］．杭州：浙江大学出版社，2018：267-269.

十分激烈。王芳茂发现，如果建个海外仓，不仅能对冲高昂的物流成本，还能做双边贸易。使用海外仓，卖家的产品品类可以无限扩张。有些产品使用期长，不属于"快消品"，但市场需求量大，放在海外仓销售非常合适。海外仓对产品没有特别限制，商家完全可以在国内接订单，在国外的仓库发货。去掉多层中介后，利润空间大了很多。

建立海外仓，可以和对方以货换货，彼此见货见心，还能规避汇率风险。这种以货换货的方式是义乌"鸡毛换糖"的复制。经过曲折的探索和挫折，王芳茂先后在澳大利亚、韩国、英国、美国等地建立了海外仓，把国外的产品充实到义乌市场，又把义乌商品推介到国外，外国人不出家门就能买到货真价廉的中国产品。互惠互利，达到了资源共享的目的。①

目前，义乌跨境电商企业已经初步建立遍布全球各地的海外仓网点，涵盖美国、澳大利亚、德国、西班牙、俄罗斯等 13 个国家 22 个地区，服务范围覆盖世界各地，特别是"一带一路"以及"义新欧"沿线国家。义乌已然成为新丝绸之路的起点，义乌人为实施"一带一路"倡议，做了生动的演绎。

（二）通过义乌小商品促进"民心相通"

随着义乌国际贸易城的影响日益扩大、涉外服务水平的不断提升、国际交流层次的纵深推进，义乌在国际上的知名度越来越高，"国际化"这张名片越发亮丽。义乌的朋友遍布全球，"朋友圈"迅速扩展，截至 2015 年底，义乌市已与 18 个国家的 24 个城市结为"姐妹城市"。

义乌市地方志负责人施章岳介绍说：目前，义乌小商品市场不仅吸引了包括港、澳、台在内的全国 31 个省市、56 个民族 130 余万外来创业者，还吸引了世界各国宾朋。与世界上 210 多个国家和地区有贸易往来，到义乌采购的境外客商年均达 55 万人次之多。截至 2017 年底，义乌市外资主体总数达 6806 家，其中外资合伙企业 2577 家，外企常驻义乌代表机构 2355 家，外资公司 1874 家。世界各国常住义乌经商创业者 1.5 万余人。小商品市场周边的江东街道鸡鸣山社区生活着来自 58 个国家的 1100 多位外国商人，福田街道楼西塘村本村居民仅 500 人，而入住该村来自中东、

① 施章岳，朱庆平．义乌商帮［M］．杭州：浙江大学出版社，2018：267-269.

西亚等地区 28 个国家的外国商人超过 400 人，这些社区、村庄被称为"联合国社区"。

义乌小商品市场的经营者懂得，他们与外国人之间不仅仅是围绕小商品进行交往，同时也在进行着文化的交流。外国商人经历过生孩子时医生要其出示"准生证"的尴尬，也经历过在银行办理业务时，一些人不把"一米红线"当回事，与其比肩而立的不安。他们理解外国商人希望有自己的摊位、自己的住房、子女能上学的迫切愿望，努力让交易中的矛盾通过合理的途径得以化解……在政府的引导与助力下，义乌小商品市场经营者会从人性化角度恰当地把握外国商人不同的民族心理、思维方式、服务需求。义乌市委、市政府与市场管理者秉持开放与包容的胸怀，不仅办理了第一张中国香港、澳门、台湾居民个体工商户营业执照，而且还给外国人办理营业执照。外国人在义乌买房可以按揭贷款，子女入学可以先进语言过渡班，邻里交流语言不通不碍事，社区里配备有多种语言翻译。宗教信仰自由，生活丰富多彩，市场周围 30 多条异国风情街，汇集了来自世界各地的美食。即便有贸易纠纷，也可以通过由来自亚非拉等 15 个国家在义商人组成的义乌市涉外纠纷调解委员会来解决。义乌市政府还规定，外国商人可以参加市级先进工作者评比，可以旁听市人大、政协代表大会报告。正是这种对外国商人的优待，使义乌小商品市场成为世界各国商人追逐的创业创新热土。一位来自塞内加尔的商人苏拉，一年中就介绍了 200 多位朋友来义乌经商。

2014 年 6 月 5 日，习近平主席在中阿合作论坛第六届部长级会议开幕式上的讲话提到，"在阿拉伯商人云集的义乌市，有一位叫穆罕奈德的约旦商人开了一家地道的阿拉伯餐馆。他把原汁原味的阿拉伯餐饮文化带到了义乌，也在义乌的繁荣兴旺中收获了事业成功，最终同中国姑娘喜结连理，把根扎在了中国。一个普通的阿拉伯青年人，把自己的人生梦想融入中国百姓追求幸福的中国梦中，执着奋斗，演绎了出彩人生，也诠释了中国梦和阿拉伯梦的完美结合。"现在，穆罕奈德与中国妻子、两个孩子快乐地生活在义乌，一家人经营着一家叫"花"的餐厅和一家外贸公司。数千年前，中国人沿着古丝绸之路前往中东、欧洲谋求商机，穆罕奈德的祖辈们已见证。如今，数万名像穆罕奈德一样的外籍商人沿着新丝绸之路，前往它的起点义乌并常居于此。他们在这里生活，找到了财富甚至爱情，实现了自己的梦想。

穆罕奈德是常驻义乌市的 4000 多位阿拉伯客商之一。他说："在义乌生活了这么久，最大的收获就是认识了不少中国和阿拉伯国家的朋友，妻子和两个孩子都能在义乌快乐生活。现在，义乌是我的第二故乡。其实，习主席说的中国梦也是我的梦。今后，我要把餐厅经营好，争取到广州、上海、北京开分店。同时，把我的外贸公司办得更好，把中国产品远销到阿拉伯国家，努力成为中国与阿拉伯国家的友好使者。"穆罕奈德还是一名足球爱好者，他组织在义乌的约旦人成立了一支足球队，基本上每周都要与当地球迷踢场比赛。①

现年 55 岁的菲利普出生于印度孟买，他的家族一直在迪拜做转口贸易。20 世纪 90 年代，他到中国香港经商，当时大部分商品都从广东进货，再销往北美和中东等地区。2002 年，菲利普在广交会上听说义乌小商品种类齐全、价格便宜。于是，他来到义乌，从此一发不可收拾，业务重心已转向义乌，一年出口上百个货柜的义乌小商品。2010 年，菲利普得知义乌国际商贸城进口馆正在招商，政策优惠。他毫不犹豫地递交了申请商位的材料，表示要把印度最好的商品带到中国来。2012 年，菲利普入园拿到现在的商位，并把公司总部从香港迁到了义乌，成立了外商独资企业——义乌市皮艾仕梵兄贸易有限公司。他说，义乌政策好、市场繁荣，是非常适合做国际贸易的地方。目前，菲利普的生意非常好。除了给中国带来优质的印度商品，菲利普说，他还有一个梦想，就是在中国推广印度文化，为中国游客去印度做文化指引，传播印度文化。他的成功更是吸引了许多印度商人，义乌成了印度商人创业的福地。②

相关方面管理人员表示，商品买卖中因合同订立、拖欠货款、产品质量等问题难免产生纠纷，每年都有很多外商上门寻求帮助。过去，就是找个翻译，从中调解；由于语言和文化不同，往往使"老纠纷未化，新矛盾又添"。2013 年，义乌市司法局设立了义乌市涉外人民调解委员会，聘请

① 吴献华. 世界商贸之都［J］. 人民画报·2017 义乌特刊，2017：68-71.
② 吴献华. 世界商贸之都［J］. 人民画报·2017 义乌特刊，2017：66-67.

外籍调解员参与涉外纠纷调解，有来自亚非拉等 15 个国家的 16 名外籍调解员组成。他们精通多国语言，熟悉中国国情，深谙调解之道。第一批外调员中，有来自塞内加尔的贸易公司董事长苏拉，他是义乌市人大列席代表，掌握四国语言；有来自新加坡的潘树法；有来自苏丹的欧麦，他是一家贸易公司的总经理，经济学博士，他们都在义乌经商多年。

外籍调解员参加纠纷调解，往往能够换位思考，从人性、法律、情理等方面提供涉外调解建议，制订合议方案，利于打破僵局，提升调解成功率。在义乌经商 10 多年的新加坡商人潘树法，每个月都有两天雷打不动要去义乌市涉外纠纷人民调解委员会值班，参与调解涉外贸易纠纷。许多纠纷在外籍"老娘舅"的调解之下达成和解。苏拉回忆，一次，一位苏丹商人在义乌采购了价值 300 多万元的商品后失联了，义乌方面许多经营户未能拿到货款。他得知后，自掏腰包专程赶往苏丹，通过自己在当地的人脉关系，千方百计找寻当事人下落，最终讨回了这笔欠款。涉外人民调解委员会的外籍调解员实行一年一聘，没有一分钱报酬，但是每个人都将其作为自己的一项光荣使命。迪亚罗表示，"我能参与人民调解工作，还能帮到那么多和我一样在国外做生意的人，这是一件让我感到很自豪的事情。"他希望能在涉外人民调解委员会学到中国的人民调解精髓，带回祖国。

截至 2016 年，义乌涉外人民调解委员会已成功调解涉外纠纷近 300起，调解成功率达 96.7%，涉案金额 4526.17 万元，为中外客商挽回经济损失 2336.98 万元。目前，义乌市还吸纳"一带一路"沿线和中欧班列沿途国家的优秀外商加入调解员队伍，为商贸发展和沟通交流服务。①

中欧班列连接的不仅是商人和商品、城市与市场，还有无数与之相关人的财富、生活、梦想与未来。它让古老的中华文明与世界文明不断碰撞、交汇，彼此尊重并相互汲取营养；随着外商的不断增多，中外人文交流日益加深，一种开放文明的社会形态在义乌逐渐形成，来自世界各地的人在此和谐共生，享受着世界大家庭的美好生活。

---

① 吴献华. 世界商贸之都［J］. 人民画报·2017 义乌特刊，2017：72-79.

四、结论

义乌人勤劳的秉性、经商的传统、包容的心态、创新的精神、闯天下的勇气，充分迎合了"一带一路"倡议的发展理念。义乌的成功给我们很大的启示，通过贸易畅通，促进民心相融，世界大同。

在践行"一带一路"伟大倡议中，小小的义乌发挥着示范作用，为实现人类命运共同体的美好未来不懈努力。

在考察实地、收集相关资料过程中，笔者对义乌有了进一步了解，并深受启发。作为一名中学生，作为一个浙江人为义乌的成就倍感自豪。"一带一路"倡议是国家的构想，也是我们的未来。

"一带一路"背景下的金融创新

——以丝路基金为例

陈思语①

摘要：丝路基金是为服务"一带一路"建设而专门成立的投资机构，在践行"一带一路"倡议过程中，发挥了巨大作用。本文以丝路基金为例，阐述其创立的背景和过程、定位以及特点，分析其在解决基础设施建设融资缺口、加快我国对外开放进程、推动国家间产能合作等方面的作用，探究"一带一路"背景下的金融创新。

关键词："一带一路"　丝路基金　金融创新

一、引言："一带一路"倡议的提出和丝路基金的创立

2008 年金融危机之后，世界经济缓慢复苏。为了摆脱产业空心化，发达经济体逐步开展"再工业化"，以工业发展带动国家经济发展。美国提出"重振制造业"，欧盟制定了总规模达 3150 亿欧元的"容克计划"，德国推出"工业 4.0"。发展中国家也纷纷制定国家中长期经济发展战略，试图通过加快工业化和城镇化进程，促进经济结构多元化，寻找新的经济增长引擎。哈萨克斯坦推出"光明大道"计划，印度尼西亚提出"海洋强国战略"，波兰提出建设"琥珀之路"等。②

从资源禀赋来看，"一带一路"沿线国家资源和劳动力要素丰富，与中国互补性较强；同时，多数国家在基础设施建设等方面仍旧有待加强，市场前景广阔。在自然资源方面，哈萨克斯坦的铬和铀、泰国的锑、印度

---

① 陈思语，女，宁波效实中学高中二年级。
② 蒲佳琪.经济全球化的实践困境与"一带一路"建设的新引擎 [J].现代营销（经营版），2017（5）：111.

尼西亚的锡、土耳其的硼、伊朗以及俄罗斯的石油和天然气等资源储量均居于世界前三位，这些矿产资源正是我们较为短缺的，彼此互补性较强。在劳动力资源方面，"一带一路"沿线国家人口总数超过 40 亿，人口抚养比均值低于 50%，正处于人口红利期[1]；沿线国家劳动力供给充足，社会负担相对较轻，既利于当地经济的快速发展，也利于中国企业属地化开展项目运营，降低相关成本。同时，"一带一路"沿线国家近 5 亿人口还没有用上电，沿线国家电力基础设施建设有较大的发展空间。随着沿线国家与中国互联互通关系进一步加强，"一带一路"沿线国家的市场潜力将得到进一步释放。

从国内经济形势来看，我国正处于经济增长方式转变、发展动能转换的关键阶段。一方面，传统行业需要去杠杆、去产能，转变经济增长方式，开拓国际市场；另一方面，我国需要引入高端制造业和先进技术，来提高经济增长质量，培育核心竞争力，推进供给侧结构性改革和产业链升级。[2]

在此背景下，习近平主席 2013 年秋在哈萨克斯坦和印度尼西亚访问时提出共建"丝绸之路经济带"和"21 世纪海上丝绸之路"，即"一带一路"倡议。该倡议立足于各国经济发展需求，倡导各国以共商、共建、共享为原则共同推进互联互通、产能合作，优势互补，实现互利共赢的发展局面。"一带一路"沿线各国各有所长，资源优势各不相同，互相之间具有较强的经济互补性，因此各国之间合作的潜力和空间非常大。"一带一路"倡议以"五通"为主要内容，即政策沟通、设施联通、贸易畅通、资金融通、民心相通，并以此为重点加强沿线各国的合作。

二、资金融通及其主要内容

资金是经济发展的重要推动力，资金融通是"一带一路"建设的核心内容。"一带一路"倡议涉及基础设施和产业项目跨国投资，融资"瓶颈"

---

① 庞超然.合作逆势升温"一带一路"沿线国家发展潜力需深挖［N］.中国经济时报，2017-04-25.

② 杨捷汉.丝路基金对推进"一带一路"建设的作用［J］.区域金融研究，2017，537（7）：8-10.

是互联互通的重大挑战之一。通过资金融通，为跨国投资构建可持续、稳定的融资体系，深化金融合作、构建稳定的货币体系是落实"一带一路"倡议的重要保障。

资金融通主要包括国际金融机构合作、金融市场开放融合、金融监管合作等方面。国际金融合作方面，资金融通在于推动亚洲货币稳定体系、投融资体系和信用体系建设，扩大沿线国家双边本币互换、结算的范围和规则；共同推进亚洲基础设施投资银行、金砖国家开发银行筹建，深化中国—东盟银行联合体、上合组织银行联合体务实合作，以银团贷款、银行授信等方式开展多边金融合作等。金融市场开放融合方面，资金融通在于推动亚洲债券市场的开放和发展；支持沿线国家政府和信用等级较高的企业及金融机构在中国境内发行人民币债券；符合条件的中国境内金融机构和企业可以在境外发行人民币债券和外币债券，鼓励在沿线国家使用所筹资金。金融监管合作方面，资金融通在于推动签署双边监管合作谅解备忘录，逐步在区域内建立高效监管协调机制；完善风险应对和危机处置制度安排，构建区域性金融风险预警系统，形成应对跨境风险和危机处置的交流合作机制；加强征信管理部门、征信机构和评级机构之间的跨境交流与合作，充分发挥丝路基金以及各国主权基金作用，引导商业性股权投资基金和社会资金共同参与"一带一路"重点项目建设。

"一带一路"倡议提出以来，资金融通快速推进。第一，国家间战略合作不断增强，如中国和埃及两国中央银行在2016年底签署双边货币互换协议，以便利双边贸易和投资。又如2018年10月，中国银行和菲律宾13家银行签署一份协议备忘录，以促进人民币和菲律宾比索的直接外汇交易。菲律宾人民币交易社群（Philippines RMB Trading Community）建立和推广人民币/比索市场，通过该平台，比索可以直接转换为人民币。中国银行预计，菲律宾和中国交易员之间的人民币交易量有望超过100亿元人民币。第二，成立多个多边国际金融机构，如2015年12月成立的亚洲基础设施投资银行，成为资金融通的重要平台。又如，2019年5月10日，亚洲金融合作协会"一带一路"金融合作委员会在北京正式成立，旨在更好地推动"一带一路"区域的各金融行业、领域开展经验、信息共享，搭建业务交流合作的国际平台。第三，金融机构层面的国际合作加速发展。

目前，已有 11 家中资银行设立了 71 家金融机构，与欧洲复兴开发银行、泛美开发银行和非洲开发银行等国际多边金融机构开展联合融资合作。外资银行积极与中资银行合作，共同参与"一带一路"融资项目，如埃及银行与国家开发银行签署了多项贷款协议。

三、丝路基金的定位、特点和投资进展

（一）丝路基金的定位

2014 年 11 月 8 日，习近平主席在北京 APEC 会议期间宣布，中国将出资 400 亿美元成立丝路基金。2014 年 12 月 29 日，丝路基金有限责任公司在北京注册成立并正式运行，高级经济师金琦出任公司首任董事长，丝路基金由中国外汇储备、中国投资有限责任公司、中国进出口银行、国家开发银行共同投资。

丝路基金是为服务"一带一路"建设而专门成立的投资机构，秉持"开放包容，互利共赢"理念，为框架内的经贸合作和双边多边互联互通提供投融资支持。它的成立是中国推进"一带一路"建设的一项重要举措，同时也是中国利用自身资金实力支持"一带一路"建设，参与扩大全球基础设施投融资、促进世界经济可持续增长的一个实际行动。

丝路基金是中长期开发投资基金，投资期限比商业性投资基金更长。其重点围绕"一带一路"建设推进的相关国家和地区的基础设施、资源开发、产业合作和金融合作等项目，以股权投资为主，综合运用股权、债权等多种投融资方式，从而推动国内高端技术和优质产能"走出去"，确保中长期财务可持续和较好的投资回报。

（二）丝路基金的主要特点

从投资方式来看，丝路基金灵活运用股权投资和债权投资方式参与企业海外项目，以企业为主体，以合理的投资回报为投资基础，以市场化运营保障可持续投资。截至 2018 年 8 月底，丝路基金投资总额中（签约承诺额），股权类投资占比约 70%。丝路基金还积极参与 PPP 项目投资，以提高项目建设和运营效率。

从投资领域来看，丝路基金主要投资于铁路、公路、机场、港口、市

政官网等基础设施建设；支持油气、矿产等传统资源能源领域，水电、风电、核电等清洁能源的开发（与沿线各国资源异禀相契合）；提供资金便利，推动沿线各国之间的产业合作及金融合作，并着重考虑各国发展战略和产业规划的对接。到2018年8月底，丝路基金向"一带一路"沿线国家和地区油气开发、能源电力等基础设施项目投资总额约占全部承诺投资额的70%，为沿线国家经济发展和民生改善发挥了重要作用。

从投资理念来看，"一带一路"倡议明确提出"共建绿色丝绸之路"，而"一带一路"沿线国家主要为新兴经济体和发展中国家，多数致力于工业化、城市化发展，高度依赖矿产等能源产业，面临着如何平衡好社会效益、经济效益与生态效益的问题。同时，"一带一路"沿线如我国的中西部地区，中东、中亚等地区，面临较为严重的土地荒漠化问题。我国西部地区三分之一是沙漠，土地沙化等日益加剧；哈萨克斯坦66%的土地在逐步退化，近1.8万公顷土地沙漠化①……土地荒漠化严重威胁"一带一路"沿线各国人民的生存、发展和安全以及"一带一路"倡议的顺利推进。因此，丝路基金遵循国际通行规则和投资所在国的法律政策和文化习俗，倡导绿色环保和可持续发展理念，贯彻绿色发展、绿色金融的理念。

（三）丝路基金的投资进展

丝路基金自成立以来，在推动"一带一路"资金融通中发挥了重要作用，积极参与跨国项目投资并与境外金融机构建立合作伙伴关系，取得了丰硕成果。

丝路基金的首个项目是2015年4月参与投资三峡集团巴基斯坦的卡洛特水电站项目，不仅有力地支持了巴基斯坦清洁能源的开发和基础设施建设，也推动了中国装备和技术标准"走出去"。2015年6月，丝路基金参与中国化工集团收购意大利轮胎生产项目，成为丝路基金首个并购项目，在支持企业从国外引入先进技术和管理经验、开拓海外市场方面发挥了重要作用。

丝路基金充分发挥多元化投融资合作优势，投资了迪拜哈斯彦清洁燃煤电站项目（PPP项目）。迪拜哈斯彦清洁燃煤电站项目是采用PPP模式的绿地开发项目，是迪拜第一个清洁燃煤电站建设项目。该项目采用国际

---

① 邱淑群. 美丽中国壮哉中国生态梦［J］. 华人时刊（上旬刊），2015（4）：1-3.

先进的超临界清洁燃煤技术，开启了阿联酋等海湾石油国家能源合作的进程，逐步改变当地能源结构单一的现状。同时，丝路基金作为财务投资人，与迪拜水电局（DEWA）、中东地区有影响力的电力运营企业沙特国际电力和水务公司（ACWA）以及哈电共同提供股权融资，丝路基金还加入由中国国有银行及中东银行组成的银团解决项目建设和运营资金来源问题。

四、丝路基金的作用

（一）解决基础设施融资缺口问题

基础设施是保持经济可持续增长的重要推动力，是丝路基金投资的重点。"一带一路"倡议覆盖的国家和地区经济规模大，且普遍处于发展期，对交通等基础设施投资需求旺盛。仅就亚洲地区而言，基础设施建设存在巨大的资金缺口。据亚洲开发银行测算，2020年以前，亚洲地区每年基础设施投资需求高达7300亿美元，而世界银行和亚洲开发银行目前每年能够提供给亚洲国家的资金只有约200亿美元，其中用于基础设施建设的资金仅占40%~50%（即80亿~100亿美元）。"一带一路"沿线发展中国家的基础设施建设面临融资"瓶颈"，基础设施项目与市场化融资方式难以有效匹配，基础设施投资面临较大融资缺口。[①]

丝路基金以建设投融资平台为抓手，打破"一带一路"沿线国家和地区互联互通的资金"瓶颈"。通过成立基础设施联合投资平台等，加强沿线国家之间的产业制造合作，促进经贸发展，同时通过发挥各国自身的优势等，共同推进所在区域的经济发展。截至2018年8月底，丝路基金已签约投资项目25个，承诺投资金额超过82亿美元，实际出资金额超过68亿美元。丝路基金以股权投资为主、债权投资为辅的产品设计和搭配，参与基础设施项目。股权投资的优势在于不增加所在国的债务负担，还可以对项目融资起增信作用，带动吸引私人资本和债权类资金共同参与投资，在解决资金缺口的同时避免加重欠发达国家的债务负担。

---

① 曾睿，唐安冰. 首届中新（重庆）战略性互联互通示范项目金融峰会在渝成功举行服务"一带一路"打造中国—东盟金融合作新典范［J］. 重庆与世界，2018，497（21）：20-23.

（二）加快我国对外开放进程

丝路基金通过建立激励约束机制、设计合理的风险缓释和补偿机制以及合理的退出机制等多种方式鼓励企业"走出去"，助力已"走出去"的企业走得更远。资本"走出去"是"一带一路"建设的重要支撑。通过资本"走出去"，带动优质产业和高端技术"走出去"，是更高层次的对外开放。丝路基金以资金"走出去"推动企业"走出去"，通过创新投融资方法，综合运用多种融资方式和货币组合，为各类项目的实现和企业"走出去"提供大力支持。当前，中国装备制造、电子信息、现代农业等方面技术已处于国际领先地位。为此，丝路基金大力支持能够带动中国优势产能"走出去"的项目，包括高铁、电力及高端装备制造业等。

丝路基金参与国际项目投资有利于推动人民币国际化。从国际货币的职能看，目前人民币主要充当跨境贸易结算货币及部分支付货币，但人民币作为计价货币和储备货币尚处于起步阶段。"一带一路"建设以贸易圈和投资圈为基础，在夯实跨境贸易结算货币基础的同时，可通过国际投资助推人民币计价货币和储备货币等国际货币职能的发展。随着中国与"一带一路"沿线国家贸易圈和投资圈的不断扩大，人民币在这一区域的接受程度、使用程度和流通程度将不断提高，国际影响力将不断扩大，从而为人民币国际化开辟重要路径。改革开放以来积累了大规模外汇储备，我国外汇储备资本配置不够合理和多元，导致资本利用效率较低。丝路基金作为运用外汇储备进行国际投资的重要渠道，可为提升外汇储备的资金回报率发挥作用。

（三）推动国家间产能合作

丝路基金不仅投资基础设施建设，还通过投资产业项目，在发挥国家资源优势、推动国家间合作共赢方面发挥重要作用。

自 2013 年"一带一路"倡议提出以来，中国企业对外投资合作快速增长。2014 年，中国对"一带一路"沿线国家和地区的投资流量为 136.6 亿美元，年末存量达到 924.6 亿美元。2015 年，在与"一带一路"相关的

49 个国家中国企业有直接投资，投资额合计 148.2 亿美元，同比增长 18.2%；① 在"一带一路"相关的 60 个国家承揽对外承包工程项目 3987 个，新签合同额 926.4 亿美元，占同期中国对外承包工程新签合同额的 44%。② 截至 2015 年底，中国企业正在推进的合作区共计 75 个，其中一半以上是与产能合作密切相关的加工制造类园区；建区企业累计投资 70.5 亿美元，入区企业 1209 家，合作区累计总产值 420.9 亿美元，上缴东道国税费 14.2 亿美元，③ 带动了纺织、服装、轻工、家电等我国优势传统行业部分产能向境外转移。

丝路基金在产能合作方面做出了巨大贡献。例如，2015 年 12 月 14 日，丝路基金与哈萨克斯坦出口投资署（后改组为哈萨克斯坦投资公司）签署协议，丝路基金单独出资 20 亿美元设立中哈产能合作基金，重点支持中国与哈萨克斯坦两国之间的产能合作及相关领域项目。这是丝路基金设立的首个专项国别基金；同时，丝路基金设立了一期 150 亿美元的中哈产能合作专项贷款。到目前为止，中哈合作的第一批项目已经竣工投产，共34 个项目，如阿克托盖 2500 万吨/年铜选矿厂、巴甫洛达尔 25 万吨/年电解铝厂、里海 100 万吨年产沥青厂、梅纳拉尔日产 3000 吨水泥厂等。还有43 个项目正在实施，包括阿特劳炼油厂石油深加工项目、阿拉木图钢化玻璃厂、10 万吨大口径螺旋焊钢管等项目。这些项目填补了哈萨克斯坦电解铝、铜采选、高端油品、特种水泥等行业的空白，推动了哈萨克斯坦工业化进程；同时提供了许多就业岗位，促进了哈地方发展。2018 年 6 月，丝路基金与哈萨克斯坦阿斯塔纳国际金融中心签署战略合作伙伴备忘录，并通过中哈产能合作基金购买阿斯塔纳国际交易所部分股权。经丝路基金提议，中哈双方又共同建立了联合工作组，与两国相关政府部门、使领馆、大型企业等建立并保持工作联系。在项目开发、政策协调等方面密切配合，共同对中哈产能合作领域兼具社会效益和经济效益的项目重点跟踪，

① 郭朝先，刘芳，皮思明．"一带一路"倡议与中国国际产能合作 [J]．国际展望，2016，8（3）：17-36.

② 马莉，孙美玲．习近平"一带一路"建设思想的哲学思维论析 [J]．聊城大学学报（社会科学版），2018.

③ 刘一贺．"一带一路"倡议与人民币国际化的新思路 [J]．财贸经济，2018（5）：103.

以此来推动中哈产能合作。

五、结论

本文阐述了丝路基金创立的背景、过程及其定位、特点和作用，并以此为例叙述了"一带一路"背景下金融模式和国际合作模式的创新。不难看出，"一带一路"倡议提出至今，中国不断推进与其他国家的合作，为实现人类命运共同体、共建美好的地球而不断努力。身为高中生的我们，虽然离推进"一带一路"发展的要求还非常远，但是作为十几亿中国人的一分子，"地球村"的成员，我们有义务为"一带一路"倡议的实现献出我们的力量。

1953年12月，周恩来总理在会见印度代表团时第一次提出和平共处五项原则，即互相尊重主权和领土完整、互不侵犯、互不干涉内政、平等互利、和平共处。"一带一路"倡议则在此基础上，秉持共商、共建、共享原则，即坚持开放合作、和谐包容、市场原则和互利共赢。60多年前，和平共处五项原则的提出是国际关系史上的重大创举，为推动建立公正合理的新型国际关系做出了历史性贡献。时至今日，"一带一路"倡议的建设目标则是要通过国际合作新平台，增添共同发展新动力，把"一带一路"建设成为和平之路、繁荣之路、开放之路、绿色之路、创新之路、文明之路。该倡议的提出深刻反映了中国的大国担当精神，必将对整个世界做出历史性贡献。我们应刻苦学习，认真实践，努力成为"一带一路"倡议和人类命运共同体的建设者。

基于"一带一路"倡议，面向中国青年的旅游文化教育研究

石绍君①

摘要：改革开放 40 多年以来，随着经济大发展，中国人均可持续收入不断增长，大家的腰包鼓起来了，越来越多的人走出国门。随着时代的变化，旅游不仅是外出观光，还能促进民众文化品位提升和民心相通。在多元化时代，文化作为一种软实力，越来越成为扩展国家影响力的重要因素。可以说，文化实力是一个国家除了传统的政治实力、经济实力、军事实力等硬实力之外综合国力的重要组成部分。随着我国硬实力的逐渐强大，软实力的提升成了当前一个无法回避的话题。笔者以一个青年人的视角，结合"一带一路"旅游与文化之间的关系，"一带一路"的历史由来，对当代旅游文化的传承和交流，旅游文化对沿线国家的经济意义和民心相通的影响，旅游文化对国际形势和青年视野的影响等方面进行探究。笔者认为当代中国青年要有责任、有担当，积极投身于这一伟大实践，推进"一带一路"旅游文化建设，这和共建人类命运共同体相辅相成，广大青年大有可为。

关键词："一带一路"　旅游文化　软实力　硬实力　人类命运共同体

一、引言

2013 年，习近平主席提出共建"一带一路"倡议。短短几年，"一带一路"建设，尤其是旅游文化建设方面，取得了累累硕果。2013 年以来，我国与"一带一路"沿线 17 个国家签署了 24 份设立文化中心的政府文件，创办了 16 家"一带一路"沿线中国文化中心，举办了 1600 余场中国嘉年华文化活动。中国文化中心在世界各地的朋友圈不断扩大，含金量越

---

① 石绍君，男，宁波市兴宁中学高中二年级。

来越高，发展前景越来越好，成为"一带一路"沿线青年了解中华文化和我国社会发展的重要平台。

世界正发生复杂而深刻的变化，金融危机的深层次影响依然严峻，世界经济复苏缓慢，国际投资贸易格局和多边贸易规则深刻调整，各国发展面临各种"瓶颈"，如何顺应经济全球化的时代潮流是摆在各国面前一个无法回避的问题。当前，"一带一路"旅游文化建设正如火如荼地推进，青年肩负着"一带一路"倡议从理念到行动、从愿景到现实的历史重任，青年人要积极探究"一带一路"旅游文化，用心实践，以此来推动沿线各国民心相通、文明互鉴和共同发展。

二、"一带一路"倡议提出的历史背景

"一带一路"倡议启迪于古代丝绸之路。众所周知，早在汉武帝时期，张骞就出使西域各国。游历过程中张骞意识到这是一个推动经贸往来、民心相通和民族融合的新机遇。同样，古代海上丝绸之路也是伴随汉朝的日渐强大而诞生。古代丝绸之路途径西域列国，到中亚、西亚以及欧洲各国，丝绸贸易和各种文化交流为推动当时世界经济贸易发展发挥了重要作用。

古罗马诗人维吉尔和地理学家庞波尼乌斯多次提到"丝绸之国"，一部《马可·波罗游记》更是掀起西方世界第一次"中国热"。"一带一路"倡议是对丝路精神的创新和弘扬，丝绸之路是中西方商贸往来的重要通道，促进了跨文化的相互渗透、商贸活动和文化交流，催生了文化融合、民心相通的多元格局，凝聚了开创新时代的动力。"一带一路"旅游文化建设为各国青年提供了中外文化交流互鉴的机会。

三、当下旅游文化现状分析

"一带一路"倡议秉承"共商、共建、共享"的合作理念，坚持"开放合作、和谐包容、市场运作、互利共赢"的合作原则，凝聚了以习近平同志为核心的党中央的集体智慧。作为新时代青年，我们要积极响应"一带一路"的伟大倡议，继承和发扬丝路精神，与时俱进，抓住契机，与沿线各国人民共同推进旅游文化建设，更好更多地惠及沿线国家民众。这既

符合中国的国情,也彰显了时代的呼唤。

(一)青年要加强对"一带一路"倡议认识的积极性

当代青年了解"一带一路"的渠道有很多,包括报纸、网络等。当代青年要在推进"一带一路"旅游文化的进程中坚定理想信念,要深度探究"一带一路"历史足迹找准目标定位,通过"一带一路"旅游文化建设这个平台,实现自我价值,更好地服务全人类。

(二)青年要提升对"一带一路"认识的深刻性

笔者曾询问身边同学对"一带一路"倡议的看法,多数人认为"不就是丝绸之路嘛"。至于"一带一路"经过哪些国家及意义作用,多数不知所以。时代赋予当代青年历史使命,作为社会发展的重要力量,青年人应当有着强烈的社会责任感和历史使命感。作为最富朝气和活力的群体,青年要深刻理解"一带一路"倡议的内涵,勇于创新和实践,积极参与"一带一路"建设。这一伟大倡议事关沿线各国的未来,其作用之大、影响之深远,不言而喻。

(三)青年要增加对"一带一路"认识的迫切性

旅游文化具有涉及面广、关联性高、带动性强等特点,可以通过创新旅游文化新模式,运用旅游文化这一独特平台,推动"一带一路"沿线国家经济的快速发展和民心相通。每个国家、每个民族都有自己的文化传统。中国文化博大精深,其他文化也有好的东西,我们可以取其精华,把其他民族的优秀文化拿来。各个民族、各个国家的优秀文化相互包容互鉴,就能促进民族融合和民心相通。

(四)青年要深化对"一带一路"重要性的认识

文化是旅游业不可缺少的底蕴和灵魂,是旅游业保持特色、提高国际竞争力的关键。物质方面的需求是较低层次的需求,易于满足;而精神文化方面的需求,是较高层次的需求,不易得到满足。旅游业若不能满足旅游者文化方面的需要,则易失去优势。文化具有地域性、民族性、传承性等特点,往往为一个国家和地区所独有,且少有可比性,易于创新品牌和特色。打造品牌是旅游业发展的法宝,更是促使旅游业可持续发展的一个制胜策略。所以，必须高度重视旅游文化建设，深挖旅游文化的内涵，努力营造旅游文化氛围，建立一套具有中国特色的旅游文化体系。①

四、"一带一路"与旅游文化相结合，兼容并蓄

(一)旅游文化的定义及探究的意义

《中国大百科全书·人文地理卷》是这样定义"旅游文化"的："所谓旅游文化，是指某个民族或某个国家在世世代代的旅游实践中所体现出来的本民族或本国家的文化。它包括只有这个民族、这个国家独有的哲学观念、审美习惯、风俗人情等文化形态。或者说，旅游文化，就是一个民族的共同文化传统在旅游过程中的特殊表现。"

旅游需要文化作为资源，而文化需要旅游来实现其价值，二者是一种相互包容、相互融合、共同繁荣的关系。根据旅游资源的基本属性，可以将旅游资源分为自然旅游资源和人文旅游资源两大类。自然旅游资源包括地文景观、水域风光、大气与太空景观、生物景观；人文旅游资源包括实物形态的文物古迹、古典园林和意识形态的文学艺术、宗教文化。

文化因素渗透于现代旅游活动的方方面面。旅游者的旅游行为是一种文化消费行为，其旅游的动机和目的在于获得精神上的享受和心理上的满足。无论是自然资源还是人文资源，都需要独具特色和魅力无穷的民族文化来吸引和激发旅游者的旅游动机，一旦缺少本民族特有的文化底蕴，便失去了特色，就不能反映本民族独有的精神内涵，也便失去强大的吸引力。实践表明，"举凡旅游业发达之国，无不以旅游文化取胜"。

2018年是改革开放40周年，站在这样一个历史节点上，青年人研学探究"一带一路"旅游文化教育意义重大。要"温故而知新"，包容互鉴，知道过去，未来之路才能走得更好，从古老的丝绸之路到现在的"一带一路"，"共商、共建、共享"合作理念更深入人心。青少年要理性、务实、有责任感和担当精神，积极提升旅游文化品质，努力把旅游文化打造成21世纪的战略产业。

---

① 汪东亮，胡世伟，陆依依，等. 旅游文化［M］. 北京：清华大学出版社，2016.

（二）探究的原则和目的

"各美其美，美人之美，美美与共，天下大同。"这十六字箴言，出自著名社会学家费孝通先生 80 寿辰聚会上的主题演讲，指出了处理不同文化之间关系的原则。以旅游景点为例，结合历史底蕴来发掘景点的文化底蕴已成为基本策略。旅游与文化密不可分，这提示我们要与时俱进，唯有积极发展和创新"一带一路"旅游的文化特色，才能彰显旅游文化的生命力。

随着"一带一路"倡议和旅游文化建设的推进，文化输入输出不平衡的局面将得到改观。俗话说，"金杯银杯不如口碑"，旅游文化品牌作为一种无形资产，能够潜移默化提升旅游消费群体的意识。当代青年肩负着"国家之复兴，民族之复兴"重任，我们探究旅游文化的目的就是要学好用好相关理论知识，多方位、多举措积极推动旅游文化品牌建设，把五千年中华文明推向全世界，促进各国民心相通。

"一带一路"沿线国家要共同发展旅游文化，铁路交通等基础设施建设成为必然，这给中国高铁"走出去"带来了前所未有的发展新机遇，中国高铁在促进亚欧经济交流及亚非经济发展中扮演着极其重要的角色。据中国新闻网报道，2018 年中国铁路共开行中欧班列 6300 列，同比增长 72%。在过去的几年里，雅万高铁、亚吉铁路的开建，以及称为"世纪工程"的蒙内铁路，都将极大地促进当地经济和旅游文化的发展。

（三）旅游文化建设方兴未艾，催生手机支付文化

"移动支付利器"支付宝和微信让国人出国旅游更加方便、快捷。目前支付宝已经在欧美、日韩、东南亚、中国港澳台等 33 个国家和地区上线使用，而且支持美元、英镑等 20 余种货币，涉及包括餐饮、超市、百货店、免税店、主题乐园、海外机场、退税店等几乎所有消费场所。最新腾讯报告显示，微信支付目前已登陆超过 13 个国家和地区，覆盖全球超过 13 万境外商户，支持 12 种以上外币结算。

尤其值得一提的是，整个泰国全面使用微信进行支付，去泰国旅游的朋友不用换汇就可以"说走就走"，再也不用担心兑换的现金不够用了。

五、"一带一路"中外旅游文化交流成果丰硕

文化和旅游部 2017 年文化发展统计公报显示，中国已与 157 个国家签署了文化合作协定，累计签署文化交流执行计划近 800 个，初步形成了覆盖世界主要国家和地区的政府间文化交流与合作网络；大力推进文化交流品牌建设，举办了中国—中东欧、中国—东盟、中国—欧盟等十余个文化年、旅游年。

自 2015 年起，连续 3 年以"美丽中国——丝绸之路旅游年"为主题进行系列宣传推广，成功打造"欢乐春节""丝路之旅""青年汉学研修计划""中华文化讲堂""千年运河""天路之旅""阿拉伯艺术节"等近 30 个中国国际文化和旅游品牌。"欢乐春节"2017 年在全球 140 多个国家和地区的 500 余座城市举办了 2000 多项文化活动。另外，还举办了丝绸之路（敦煌）国际文化博览会、丝绸之路国际艺术节、海上丝绸之路国际艺术节等以"一带一路"为主题的综合性文化节会。

自"一带一路"倡议提出以来，中国携手联合国教科文组织，积极搭建各国青年互动友谊之桥，推动跨文化对话和交流互鉴，尤其是各国青年间的交流，围绕这一主题举办的中外青年文化交流活动精彩纷呈。2017 年 12 月，海上丝绸之路非物质文化遗产展在福建泉州举行，来自世界各国的 117 个项目参展。[①]

六、展望未来，再谱新篇

（一）深化传统友谊，推动人文交流

2019 年 3 月 21 日至 26 日，国家主席习近平对意大利、摩纳哥、法国进行国事访问。人文交流方面有声有色，中国京剧与意大利歌剧《图兰朵》的精彩"碰撞"，故宫文物展和摩纳哥王室文化展的举办，四川自贡彩灯点亮法国南部小城……在东西方文明交相辉映中，民更亲，心更通。发展"一带一路"旅游文化无疑是中国撬动世界的一个支点，对世界的未

---

① 林善传.海上丝绸之路非物质文化遗产展在泉州举行 ［DB/OL］. 新华网，2017-12-12. http：//www. xinhuanet. com//overseas/2017-12/12/c_ 129762662_ 3. htm.

来发展来说，影响深远。①

（二）深耕厚植，前景广阔

2019 年 3 月 21 日，习近平主席在意大利发表题为《东西交往传佳话 中意友谊续新篇》署名文章，指出两国之间的人文交流之路越走越宽广。虽然远隔千山万水，早在两千多年前，古老的丝绸之路就把中国和古罗马联系在一起。3 月 23 日，习近平主席在法国发表题为《在共同发展的道路上继续并肩前行》署名文章，指出：两国文化、旅游、教育、体育、地方、青年等领域合作可以迈出更大步伐，在中西方文化交流中更好地发挥表率和带动作用。

意大利总理孔特则亲自参加了第二届"一带一路"国际合作高峰论坛。在这次论坛筹备和举办期间，与会各方达成了 283 项务实成果。论坛期间举行的企业家大会吸引了众多工商界人士参与，签署了总额 640 多亿美元的项目合作协议。这些成果充分说明，共建"一带一路"应潮流、得民心、惠民生、利天下，推进旅游文化建设前景很广阔。②

（三）旅游搭台，文化相鉴

一个国家的旅游业若是缺少本国民族传统文化底蕴，便失去了特色，不能反映本民族独有的精神内涵，从而失去强大的竞争力和吸引力。实践表明，"举凡旅游业昌盛之国，莫不以旅游文化取胜"。所以，建立具有中国特色的旅游文化体系，打响旅游文化品牌，合作共赢，是未来的发展方向。

随着"一带一路"旅游文化事业的推进，必定会增加对旅游人才的需求。据教育部统计，2017 年共有 48.92 万名外国留学生来中国各高等院校学习，增速连续两年保持在 10% 以上，中国已成为亚洲最大的留学目的国，中国的国际影响力与日俱增。此外，中国在全球 149 个国家（地区）建立 530 所孔子学院和 1113 个孔子课堂，通过推进校际友好合作与文化输出，在各国青年心中播下相互尊重与学习、维护正义与共同进步的思想种

① 习近平. 东西交往传佳话 中意友谊续新篇［N］. 人民日报，2019-03-21：01.
② 习近平. 在共同发展的道路上继续并肩前行［N］. 光明日报，2019-03-24：01.

子，促进了文化交流互鉴和民心相通。①

七、推进旅游文化建设，青年大有可为

（一）正确认识旅游文化与青年之间的关系

青年是未来，青年是希望，中国政府特别重视中外青年的互动交流。青年人充满活力、思维活跃，不愿墨守成规，以自己独特的方式参与社会发展与创新，影响社会和文化的发展进程与方向。正是青年的这些特点，使得青年人同时具有叛逆性、多元性和开放性。为此，在深化改革开放的关键时期，应发展健康有益、充满活力的旅游文化，保持好文化方向的先进性。

当前满足广大人民日益增长的美好生活需要成了当务之急，人们已经从过去单一追求物质需求（吃饱穿暖），转向日益追求精神需求的满足。国内小到奶茶店、创意用品店，大到网购和微商，主流消费群体都是青年人。因此，"一带一路"旅游文化建设重点，要倾向青年，让青年成为推动"一带一路"旅游文化发展的生力军。

（二）共建共享，争做旅游文化传播者

中华传统文化的复兴，要从我们做起，更要从青年做起。我们这一代青年是幸运的，赶上了中华民族伟大复兴的新时代。作为新时代的亲历者和见证人，每个青年当勇立潮头，争做旅游文化使者。文化既要走进每个国人的内心，更要走向世界，与各国文化相通、相融、相亲。②

2018 年 5 月，"一带一路"青年创意与遗产论坛在长沙和南京举办，来自 51 个国家的 70 余名青年代表参加了论坛。来自埃塞俄比亚的汉娜·格塔丘等，向习近平主席写信汇报了参加论坛的感悟，并就"一带一路"建设、中非合作、中非青年交流等提出了建议。习近平主席则于 2018 年 8 月给青年代表回信，强调青年是国家的未来，勉励他们为构建人类命运共

---

① 牛弹琴. 第二届"一带一路"峰会中国取得十大成就 ［DB/OL］. 新浪网，2019－04－28. http：//news. sina. cn/gn/2019－04－28/detail-ihvhiqax5451077. d. html.

② 宋德全. 让文化自知成就文化自信 当代青年大有可为 ［DB/OL］. 中国青年网，2017－12－27. http：//t. m. youth. cn/transfer/index/qnzz. youth. cn/zhuanti/ggyj/sdq/201712/t20171221_ 11210479. htm.

同体而努力奋斗。①

八、结论与思考

1957 年，毛泽东主席在莫斯科对留苏学生演讲时说："世界是你们的，也是我们的，但是归根结底是你们的。你们青年人朝气蓬勃，正在兴旺时期，好像早晨八九点钟的太阳。希望寄托在你们身上。世界是属于你们的。中国的前途是属于你们的。"推进旅游文化建设无疑是一个撬动世界的支点，而青年作为新时代的新生力量和先锋，肩负着"一带一路"建设的使命。文化上的沟通与交流可以让各国互相包容，不断增强互信，同时可以培育青年的价值观，弘扬良好的社会风气。发展"一带一路"旅游文化，符合我国现实国情，是顺应时代潮流的伟大举措，"一带一路"这一伟大倡议，从国家层面为当代青年指明了发展方向和奋斗目标。

文明因交流而多彩，文明因互鉴而丰富。有道是，"河海不择细流，故能就其深"。如果人为地阻断江河的流入，再大的海也终有干涸的一天。文化交流是民心相通的桥梁，在国际交往中具有不可替代的作用。因此，以历史为横轴，以机遇为纵轴，在这样一个交点上，青年应对"一带一路"旅游文化的发展抱有坚定的信念：相信持续推进的"一带一路"旅游文化建设必将为推动世界文明繁荣发展注入新动力，共创人类命运共同体。

---

① 杨俊峰．"一带一路"五年来 中外文化交流成果丰硕［DB/OL］．人民网，2018-11-27. http：//ip. people. com. cn/GB/n/2018/1127/c179663-30423646. html.

从历史角度浅析丝路各国民俗与文化

沙禹舟①

摘要：众所周知，"一带一路"的前生，是丝绸之路。古丝绸之路绵亘万里，延续千年，积淀了以和平合作、开放包容、互学互鉴、互利共赢为核心的丝路精神。早在一千多年前，我们的祖先就已经在丝绸之路上找到了对外交流的方法，因为丝绸之路，中国得以成为天朝上邦，万国来朝。笔者从历史角度出发，通过对古丝绸之路文化交流与经济发展进行分析，以"民心相通"为主题，结合当代国际社会、世界多极化发展形势，分析各国民俗与文化的融合与交流，探讨如何正确处理外来文化，以及如何让中国文化"走出去"。文化建设是我国现代化建设的重要一环，也是"一带一路"建设的重要一环。我们应当批判地引进与融合外国优秀文化，"取其精华，去其糟粕"。既要认同本国的文化，又要尊重其他民族文化，相互借鉴，求同存异，和睦相处。尊重世界文化多样性，促进人类文明繁荣与进步。

关键词："一带一路"　民意相通　文化力量　多元文化　批判继承

一、引言："一带一路"的前生——丝绸之路

丝绸之路是我国古代对外交往的重要通道，要了解"一带一路"，需从历史出发，看看古人是如何同外国交往的。

西汉时期，张骞从长安出发，其真正的目的虽然不是与西方交流，但张骞的这一次西行开拓了丝绸之路，被后人称为"凿空之旅"。东汉时期，班超从洛阳出发，再次出使西域，他到达了西域，他的随从最终到达罗

---

① 沙禹舟，男，宁波效实中学高中一年级。

马，带去了众多丝绸产品，"丝绸之路"因此得名。这是东西方文明的第一次对话。除此之外，东汉时期印度僧人沿着丝绸之路到达洛阳，佛教因此传播到中国，丰富了丝绸之路的内容。到了唐代，玄奘沿着丝绸之路去往印度求取真经，促进了中华文明与印度文明的交流。他取经归来，著有《大唐西域记》。宋代，我国的瓷器沿着丝绸之路传到西方诸国，丝绸之路一度被称为"瓷路"。

总而言之，丝绸之路始于中国，连接亚、非、欧三大洲，促进了各国之间的经济与文化交流。由此可见，丝绸之路不仅把中国物品带到世界，也将西方的许多东西带回了中国。这与我们所提倡的"走出去、引进来"理念不谋而合。"一带一路"作为古代丝绸之路的发展与延伸，秉承相同的理念，自然需要我们加强与各国交流，共同合作。

二、目的与意义——从历史出发

历史上我们就很重视对外交流。可以说，正是因为丝绸之路的发展，才奠定了大汉盛世、大唐盛世。遥想大唐盛世，天朝上邦，万国来朝，长安城汇集了来自世界各地的能人异士。在长安城的大街上，外国人随处可见，老百姓也是见怪不怪，而且还能与他们友好交往，更不会驱逐外国人。为什么会这样呢？原因在于唐王朝思想比较开放，善于接受新鲜事物，唐朝统治者不仅不排斥百姓与外国人交流，还鼓励百姓与外来者多交往。正是唐朝与各国进行密切的文化交流，各国人民"民心相通"，唐朝才成为当时世界上最繁荣的国家。

随着世界多极化趋势的进一步加强及我国综合国力的不断增强，我们应汲取历史经验，努力践行"一带一路"倡议。这不仅会对我国经济发展起到良好的促进作用，还会促进世界经济共同繁荣发展，强化世界各国间深层次联系。

要做好"一带一路"建设，则要优先实现"五通"，即政策沟通、设施联通、贸易畅通、资本融通和民心相通。本文着重对"民心相通"做详细研究。

三、语言与文化

（一）语言与文化的关系

世界上有很多国家，各国的语言也不尽相同。语言无疑是一个国家最易认人感受到的文化。早在 20 世纪 20 年代，美国语言学家萨丕尔（E. Sapir）在他的《语言论》一书中就指出："语言的背后是有东西的，而且语言不能离开文化而存在。"[①] 语言学家帕尔默也曾在《现代语言学导论》一书中提道："语言的历史和文化的历史是相辅而行的，他们可以互相协助和启发。"[②] 由此可见，语言是文化的一个重要组成部分。

当我们要同一个国家进行深度交往，抑或是了解一国的文化时，自然少不了沟通工具，语言是"民心相通"的第一步。

（二）古人对外来语言的态度

秦汉时期，西域（今新疆、青海，西藏、甘肃等地）的语言与中原语言尚不相通，中原各地的方言也不尽相同，翻译官因此成为一个重要的角色。据《周礼》记载，古时的翻译官被称为"舌人"，不过当时舌人的地位不是很高。后来，随着各民族的不断融合，那些难以理解的语言，或很少人说的语言渐渐消失。据记载，先秦文献中只有几十个外来词，汉朝与匈奴时战时和，汉语竟引进了 100 多个匈奴词汇，如"单于""祁连"就是那时传入的，还有我们熟悉的"阿爷无大儿"中的"爷"字，最初是鲜卑语，"挺好"的"挺"字，原是满语。[③]

汉唐之后，随着佛教的盛行，梵语逐渐传入我国。相传在东晋时期，和元帝司马睿"共天下"的王导，经常和胡僧周旋，还会说几句梵语，同一时期著名文学家谢灵运，梵语比王导还要好。由此可见，古人对外来语言，是非常重视的。

对其他民族语言的学习，使得汉族与其他民族迅速融合。北魏孝文帝进行改革，让鲜卑人学习汉语，改汉姓，并鼓励鲜卑贵族与汉人士族联

---

① ［美］萨丕尔. 语言论［M］. 北京：商务印书馆，2019.
② ［英］帕尔默. 现代语言学导论［M］. 北京：商务印书馆，2019.
③ 王北静. 古人怎样学外语？［DB/OL］. 梨视频，2019-01-24.

姻，少数民族与汉族民心相通，其乐融融。佛教也随着梵语在中国的盛行而广泛传播。在唐朝，小到黎民百姓，上到皇亲国戚，都会说几句梵语，且大多信奉佛教。①

（三）外国学习中国

一则新闻这样写道：

俄媒称，俄罗斯的首套汉语教材将向学生介绍现代中国，俄罗斯的中学生将学习汉语书法和成语。

据俄罗斯卫星通讯社 3 月 7 日报道，制订俄罗斯首套汉语教材的编者亚历山德拉·西佐娃透露，中学生所用的汉语教材将加入关于现代中国的相关信息。

她表示："这套教科书是根据 21 世纪的需要改编的。简单地说，这些书不仅用于今天，也可以用于明天。利用它们，俄罗斯学生将在学习汉语的同时了解世界。"她指出，文化差异是俄罗斯学生学习汉语的一个重大困难。俄罗斯学生很难掌握汉字和汉语发音。

报道称，2018—2019 学年 11 年级学生将首次参加国家统考汉语科目考试。据悉，汉语成为继英语、德语、法语和西班牙语之后第五种全国统考外语科目。

俄罗斯联邦教育科学监督局副局长安佐尔·穆扎耶夫表示，俄罗斯 43 个地区共计 289 人登记参加全国统考汉语科目考试。另据俄罗斯卫星通讯社 3 月 7 日报道，亚历山德拉·西佐娃表示，俄罗斯中学汉语教学大纲将包含书法和成语基础。

西佐娃称："书法是中国文化不可分割的组成部分。课本、学习笔记、教师用书的材料和习题，当然也包括象形文字专用参考资料，用于同时发展和巩固词汇与象形文字技能，学习优美的书法，理解汉语象形文字的构造、哲学和伦理。俄罗斯 11 年级的毕业生需要知道 1000 个以上汉语词汇，教学大纲中将包括现代词汇以及成语。汉语成语、谚语、俗语、谜语、成

---

① 佚名. 大唐时大街上随处可见外国人？唐朝时期经济实力怎么样？[DB/OL]. 百家号.

语故事等必须在教材中得到体现，在语言学习的最初几个阶段就必须涉及。"①

诚然，俄罗斯的做法虽然仅是个例，但汉语的重要性在不断上升，影响力在扩大。而且，随着孔子学院的兴办，也将汉语推向了世界，据统计，"一带一路"沿线国家中有 50 多个国家建立了 100 多个中小学孔子课堂，激发了外国人竞相学习汉语的热潮。在全球经济普遍疲软的背景下，中国经济和对外贸易的稳定快速发展引人注目。在经济一体化趋势下，世界各国对通晓汉语的技术人才需求有了明显增加。伴随着中国经济走向世界，中国文化的影响力越来越大，汉学成为"显学"。世界范围内的"汉语热"已成为全球语言交流的一种普遍现象。

2018 年，南开大学将孔子学院作为加强与泰国国家关系的桥梁，除了开设中文课程外，还通过表演重庆名歌《幺妹乖》以及著名川剧《变脸》等剧目，以传播民俗文化的形式，促进两国关系的发展，不失为典范。②

(四)中国学习外国

众所周知，我们对待外来语言一向秉承包容开放的原则，像大家常用的词"沙发""可乐""咖啡"等，都是由外来词加以衍生而来。国内有很多人在学习外国语言，一些中学开设了德语、法语、日语等选修课程，许多大学都开设了研究外国语言的专业。

从"一带一路"的角度来看，学习一门外语可以让我们更方便地与外界交流，只有通过交流与学习，才能使"民心相通"，才可以理解彼此共同的利益，促进合作。通过语言学习，还可以了解别国的风俗。因此，从国家层面来看，应该支持民众学习外国语言，对"翻译"这个职业加以重视，提供支持，让更多人看到希望。

在全球化浪潮之下，国际交流越来越密切，而语言是各国人民沟通的桥梁。掌握一门外语，不仅可以打开我们的视野，还可以让我们了解世界

---

① 佚名. 看外国人这么学中文……极度舒适［DB/OL］. 参考消息网，2019-08-19. http：//www.xiangyizc.com/xuexijiaocai/1326.html.

② 史欣. 从孔子学院到孔子课堂，西南大学搭建中泰友谊桥梁［DB/OL］. 百家号西南大学，2018，279（900）.

文化的多样性，从而尊重不同民族文化，遵循各民族文化一律平等原则。在文化交流中，要尊重差异，和睦相处，促进世界文化的共同发展与繁荣。

四、饮食文化切入——以马来西亚和意大利、中国为例

（1）马来西亚：马来西亚餐食普遍使用冬炎、阿三、参拜、咖喱四大香料调味烹制，以口味酸辣、颜色鲜丽见长。由于当地盛产椰树，因此菜品普遍采用椰汁，是其食品的主料。有名的菜品有冬炎花枝、阿三鱼头等。[①] 马来西亚作为一个多元社会，食物同样多元化。马来西亚食物汇集马来西亚本土民族、中国、印度、西方的食物，美食琳琅满目。与中国类似，马来西亚人的主食是米饭，面类也相当普遍。

（2）意大利：意大利菜系十分丰富，菜品众多。意大利饮食文化源远流长，对欧美国家产生了深远影响，并发展出法国菜、美国菜等多种派系，享有"西餐之母"美誉。意大利菜多以海鲜为主料，辅以牛、羊、鱼、番茄、黄瓜、萝卜、青椒、香葱等。制法不外乎煎、炒、炸、煮、红烩或红焖，喜加蒜茸和干辣椒，稍辣，十分重视口感，以略硬而有弹性为美。有名的菜品有佛罗伦萨牛排、罗马魔鬼鸡、那不勒斯烤龙虾、巴里甲鱼、奥斯勃克牛肘肉、扎马格龙沙拉，米列斯特通心粉、鸡蛋肉末沙司、板肉白豆沙拉子、青椒焖鸡、烩大虾、烤鱼、火腿切面条等，[②] 令四方游客垂涎欲滴。

（3）中国：中国菜肴品类、品种繁多，因地区和民俗差别，衍生出多种菜品，每种菜品的加工制作方法也存在差异。中国是一个多民族国家，由于地理、文化、信仰、气候等差异，菜品的种类和风味差别很大，因而流派众多，民间自古有四大菜系、八大菜系之说。中国菜肴讲究美感，注重色、香、味、形的协调一致。对美感的表现是多方面的，无论是红萝卜，还是白菜心，都可以雕刻出各种造型，独树一帜，色、香、味、形和

---

　　① 李丽．马来西亚的三大菜系 ［DB/OL］．新浪博客，2017－02－08. http：//blog. sina. cn/dpool/blog/s/blog_ 13812b3250102zxjwm. html.

　　② 高小秋．欧洲美食巡游记：意大利篇 ［DB/OL］．2018－10－22. http：//m. jieju. cn/News/20181022/Detail 8070b/. shtml.

谐统一，给食客以视觉和味觉上的美好享受。

马来西亚菜、意大利菜与中国菜之间存在很大差异，除地区不同外，更多的原因还是文化差异。马来西亚地处低纬度地区，为热带雨林气候，全年高温多雨，十分适合种植业和养殖业的发展，椰树是当地随处可见的植物；当地人多信奉伊斯兰教，Nasi Kandar 是广受欢迎的一种伊斯兰教美食，食用时拌以香浓的咖喱汁煮的鸡、鱼、肉等菜肴，口感甚佳。

意大利地处地中海沿岸，海鲜种类丰富。此外，意大利属于地中海气候，适合发展地中海式农业，以种植水果、花卉、蔬菜等经济作物为主。另外，意大利的小麦和大麦，除了远销他国，还用来喂养牲畜。因而，意大利畜牧业十分发达，牛肉、羊肉、猪肉等肉类食品十分丰富。众所周知，意大利首都罗马曾是西方文明的中心，来自不同国家的文化，充分体现在其菜肴品种及特色上。意大利的"西餐"菜式与马来西亚和中国完全不同，体现了意大利文化的丰富多彩和独具特色。

中国幅员辽阔，气候多样，各地环境不同，风俗也不同，菜肴难免有差异，中国菜肴注重色、香、味、形、器和谐统一。

三个国家的饮食文化都具有多样性。不同的是，马来西亚和意大利菜品的多样性是因为其与周边国家交流密切，吸收了各国文化而融进其饮食文化中，呈现出多样性；中国则是因为地域辽阔，国内菜系丰富。

马来西亚国土面积虽然不大，但民众包容开放，汇集了世界各地的美食。通过吸收他国文化，奠定了古罗马及意大利的国际地位。中国改革开放以来，对外开放程度不断提高。

俗话说："要想抓住一个人的心，必须得先留住他的胃。"当我们在饮食方面求同存异、相互融合，我们离"民心相通"也就近了一步。首先，饮食文化可促进人们的归属感，在异国他乡，突然见到家乡的美食，自是特别激动；其次，当一国饮食走向世界，并被异国民众接受，可促进各国人民之间的认同感，如当我们喜欢上意大利菜时，必定会对意大利怀有好感，自然愿意更深入了解意大利这个国家；最后，对饮食的研究利于我们对当地文化的研究。

五、总结：民俗与文化的力量

经济全球化，促进了各国民俗、文化的融合与交流。文化表现形式多种多样，不同地域的文化各有特色，这就需要我们正确对待外来文化，思考中国文化"走出去"的方式。

文化由经济、政治所决定，又反作用于政治、经济，并对政治、经济产生重大影响。先进的、健康的文化会促进社会的发展。当今世界，国与国之间综合国力的竞争日趋激烈，文化成为民族凝聚力和创造力的重要源泉，成为经济社会发展的重要支撑，成为综合国力竞争的重要因素。因此，文化建设是我国新时代社会建设的重要一环，也是"一带一路"建设的重要一环。我们应当批判地引进与融合外国优秀文化，"取其精华，去其糟粕"。既要认同本国的文化，又要尊重其他民族文化，相互借鉴，求同存异，相互理解，和睦相处，尊重文化多样性，促进人类文明共同繁荣与进步。

"一带一路"背景下宁波文化旅游产业发展再思考

胡义阳①

摘要：2013 年习近平主席提出了"一带一路"倡议，即"丝绸之路经济带"和"21 世纪海上丝绸之路"。作为开放性、综合性产业，旅游业在"一带一路"建设中具有先联先通的独特优势。"一带一路"倡议成为我国旅游业发展的新引擎，为我国旅游产业转型升级注入了新的活力。宁波是海上丝绸之路的始发港之一，在这样的背景下，探索宁波文化旅游产业发展的战略思路，应在了解和分析宁波文化发展的现状及存在的问题前提下，围绕"一带一路"倡议的影响，明确完善宁波文化旅游产业"走出去"的平台，把握好"请进来"的重点，才能实现宁波文化旅游产业发展的目标和效益。

关键词："一带一路"　宁波　旅游业　文化旅游

一、引言

"一带一路"建设是我国在新的历史条件下，培育国家竞争新优势、打造对外开放新格局、寻找区域经济发展新动力的重大举措。通过"一带一路"建设，未来将出现一条横贯东西、连接南北的欧亚海陆立体交通大通道。这必定会促进我国的对外贸易发展，也将加深与沿线各国的文化、旅游交流。宁波地处"一带一路"建设的黄金地段，是古代"海上丝绸之路"的东方始发港，享有"古丝绸之路活化石"的美誉，拥有开展文化旅游的优势。在"一带一路"深度发展的大背景下，如何借助自身优势，发展文化旅游产业，以文化旅游产业的发展带动和促进宁波社会经济全面提升？笔者通过实地考察和走访了解，就宁波文化旅游产业发展的现状和特

---

① 胡义阳，男，宁波市鄞州高级中学高中一年级。

色、存在的问题及对策，提出自己的一些想法。

二、宁波文化旅游产业发展的现状和特色

（一）宁波文化旅游产业发展现状

2017 年，全市接待入境游客 186.91 万人次，实现外汇收入 9.9 亿美元。

2017 年，宁波市共有景区 100 多个，包括 52 个 A 级旅游区，其中 5A级旅游区 1 个，4A 级旅游区 32 个，3A 级旅游区 19 个，2A 级旅游区3 个。

重点旅游项目投资建设进展加快，2017 年，宁波市在库建设旅游项目191 个，计划总投资 2116.69 亿元，实际完成投资 164.32 亿元，旅游项目占全市固定资产投资的 3.28%。

海港旅游发展迅速，2017 年海港旅游人数 1200 多万人次，总收入达250 多亿元，其中象山县年接待游客 730 万人次，旅游收入 76 亿元。

2018 年，宁波全年接待旅游总人次 1.25 亿，同比增长 13.76%，实现旅游总收入 2005.71 亿元，同比增长 19.7%。

（二）宁波文化旅游产业的特色

"书藏古今，港通天下"是宁波的城市形象，也是对宁波城市特色最形象的描述。悠久的历史文化、优越的地理位置赋予了宁波旅游文化鲜明特色。

1. 古建筑，彰显了宁波历史名城的魅力

建于清朝咸丰年间的鼓楼，是宁波历史上正式置州治、立城市的标志，是全国文物保护单位之一。老外滩坐落于宁波三江口北岸，比上海外滩还要早 20 年，是目前国内仅存的几个具有百年历史的外滩之一，沿着甬江边，外国领事馆、天主教堂、银行、轮船码头一字排开，记录了宁波开埠的整段历史。天一阁是中国现存最早的私家藏书楼，也是亚洲现存最古老的图书馆和世界最早三大家族图书馆之一，其藏书文化闻名全国，内有秦氏祠堂，具有江南园林风貌，是宁波居民建筑集大成之作。创于东汉、建于唐代、兴于北宋的保国寺大雄宝殿，"鸟不栖、虫不入、蜘蛛不结网、

梁上无灰尘",历经千年风雨沧桑,巍然如初。在多雨潮湿、台风频多的江南,这确实是个奇迹。始建于公元 1233 年,地处宁海县西南,面积 68 平方公里的前童镇,是一个历史悠久、文化积淀深厚、地理位置独特的江南古镇,历经了 760 余年的风雨沧桑,仍完好保留一片清明时期的古建筑群。还有宁波周边的慈城古建筑群、蒋氏故居等,这些古迹珍宝,在风雨的打磨中,更加耀焰生辉。

2. 洋洋东方大港,彰显了宁波海洋文化亮点

作为世界级深水良港,北仑港因历史上经此向海外源源不断输出丝绸瓷器而闻名中外,如今作为"新海上丝绸之路"的起点,宁波更是被赋予了发展海洋文化的新机遇,成为宁波旅游文化的新亮点。宁波海洋文化历史悠久,源远流长,内涵丰富。海洋民俗文化、海洋生物文化、海洋渔业文化、海洋名人文化、海洋商业文化、海洋影视文化、海防文化、航海文化、港口文化,一并构成了富有宁波特色的海洋文化旅游资源。

3. 独特的地方特色饮食,彰显了宁波饮食文化别样风情

民以食为天,旅以食为先。在"食、住、行、游、购、娱"旅游六要素中,饮食居于首位。这不仅因为饮食是不可或缺的,还因为饮食文化对旅游业有着潜在的多重促进作用。海鲜产品、宁波菜和宁式糕点、小吃,饮食文化成为宁波良好的旅游资源。宁波菜又叫"甬帮菜",是中国八大菜系之一浙菜的一个重要支脉,可谓源远流长。以东海大黄鱼、梭子蟹而著名,宋代诗词大家苏东坡有对宁波梭子蟹给予诗赞:"半壳含黄宜点酒,两螯研雪劝加餐。"宁波传统工艺制作的宁波汤圆、酒酿圆子、龙凤金团、慈城年糕、水晶油包、溪口千层饼、豆沙八宝饭、猪油汤团、宁波油赞子、豆酥糖十大小吃深受游客喜爱。宁波南塘老街、城隍庙、宁波老外滩等特色街景,更是反映了独具风情的宁波饮食文化。

4. 文化与旅游相融合,彰显了宁波旅游文化特色

宁波历史文化旅游主题有:以天一阁藏书楼为主题的书香文化之旅;以河姆渡为主题的历史文化之旅;以东方大港为主题的港口文化之旅;以慈城古镇为主题的历史建筑之旅;以天童寺、阿育王寺为主题的修心养生

之旅；以蒋氏古居为主题的民国风情之旅；以四明山根据地为主题的红色文化之旅；以石浦渔港为主题的海洋文化之旅；以十里红妆文化为主题的十里红妆之旅；以"宁波帮"为主题的商帮文化之旅。这些旅游文化主题反映了宁波旅游与文化的深度融合，若能对其进行充分利用和深度开发，定能为宁波旅游经济带来勃勃生机。

三、宁波文化旅游产业的优势

宁波区位优势突出，旅游发展动力强劲。宁波是长江三角洲地区南翼的经济中心，也是该地区新兴的旅游目的地。宁波已建或在建的高速公路骨架呈明显的"十"字形，一条从舟山向西经宁波、杭州到达安徽的黄山，另一条是分别从上海和苏州越过跨海大桥的沿海大通道，宁波正处于两条高速公路的交点，南北向江，通华东和华南两个国内最大客源地，东西向连接江西和安徽，深入旅游腹地。另外，杭州湾大桥的建成联通了沪杭和沪甬高速公路，变以前长三角旅游交通"一条道走到头"为"三角形回路"，宁波正式跻身以上海为核心的长三角2小时交通圈，铁路、公路、航空等都非常便利。这种区位条件对于宁波旅游业发展具有重要意义。

宁波重视城市品牌形象建设，旅游品牌提升有支撑。从早期确立市树、市花到十年前全球征集城市形象主题口号，从"爱心城市""文明城市""智慧城市"再到现阶段的"名城名都"国际城市形象定位，宁波一直重视城市形象建设。城市品牌与旅游品牌之间是共生关系，健康、良好的城市形象势必给旅游品牌的塑造和传播带来正面影响。

宁波市政府把文化作为开发旅游产业和培养旅游业新的增长点的重要抓手。在《宁波市国民经济和社会发展第十一个五年规划纲要》中，市政府提出要高起点、高品位开发旅游资源，挖掘和提升奉化溪口、余姚河姆渡、天一阁藏书、月湖文化等旅游资源的文化内涵，完善提升一批文化品位高、影响力大的风景名胜区和旅游度假区，这些为文化旅游产业的发展提供了有力的政策支持。

四、宁波文化旅游产业存在的问题

1. 宁波的旅游业与宁波特色文化融合不深

宁波是文化荟萃的历史名城，旅游文化资源丰富，历史文化遗迹数量多、层次高，各年代文化在这里都可以寻找到印迹。然而，在保留或开发建设各种旅游资源过程中，缺乏基于文化内涵的深度挖掘，旅游景点与历史文化融合度不高，造成宁波旅游形象的历史厚度明显不足。老外滩、城隍庙、鼓楼、蒋氏故居等历史古迹，已被浓厚的商业气息所侵染，缺乏历史的厚重感和文化感，历史传承不同程度地受到破坏，文化旅游价值没能体现。

2. 宁波古文化遗迹的开发建设在价值取向上存在偏差

宁波古文化遗迹在旅游资源中占据较大的份额。距今已有7000多年的河姆渡遗址、梁祝古迹遗址、上林湖青鉴窑址、天封塔等，还有保国寺等古老寺庙，都是宁波悠久历史、文化名城的真实写照。但是，在文化旅游开发和管理宣传上存在价值取向偏差，如河姆渡遗址与梁祝古迹遗址。河姆渡遗址的发现，证明了长江流域和黄河流域一样是中华民族古老文化的发祥地，然而旅游旺季这里却游客稀少，淡季更是冷冷清清。相反，在梁祝古迹遗址，每年都举行"梁祝文化节""相亲会"等大型活动，深受游客青睐。举行这些活动无可厚非，但对古老的文化发祥地开发有待提高，这是需要认真思考和探索的问题。

3. 宁波海洋文化没有发挥应有优势和效应

宁波主城区距海域较远，滨海旅游的环境氛围明显不足，用于工业发展的港口和区域较多，用于旅游开发的不多。除了海滨浴场景点和少量的海防遗址，以海洋文化为主题的旅游景区很少，与"东方大港"、海滨城市的定位不相符。注重港口经济的发展，忽视文化旅游的开发建设，这是"以港兴市"战略的一个缺陷。

4. 缺少明晰的形象定位和核心理念

宁波虽然坐拥丰富的旅游文化资源，却缺少明晰的形象定位和核心理念。宁波至今没有一个明确的定位和公认的城市形象。从"四张名片"到"信用宁波""智慧城市""美丽宁波""文明城市"，再到"国际港口名城""东方文明之都"，城市定位和形象理念不清晰，旅游品牌自然受影响。

5. 品牌构建缺乏系统性和连续性

旅游品牌包括旅游宣传口号、旅游形象标识、旅游主题品牌等，是一个系统工程。这些年，宁波旅游宣传口号变换多次，配套始终未跟上。

6. 缺乏高水准的专业策划团队和有效宣传

文化旅游品牌的塑造和传播要达到理想的效果，必须借助高水准的专业策划团队或机构。目前，负责宁波文化旅游品牌塑造和推广的机构没有高水准的专业策划团队。缺少有效整合和规划，未能达到期望的宣传效果。

五、"一带一路"倡议对宁波文化旅游事业发展的意义

"一带一路"是"丝绸之路经济带"和"21世纪海上丝绸之路"的简称，2013年9月和10月，习近平提出建设"新丝绸之路经济带"和"21世纪海上丝绸之路"。"一带一路"是合作发展的理念和倡议，是依靠中国与有关国家既有的双多边机制，借助既有的、行之有效的区域合作平台，旨在借用古代"丝绸之路"的历史符号，高举和平发展旗帜，主动地发展与沿线国家的经济合作伙伴关系，共同打造政治互信、经济融合、文化包容的利益共同体、命运共同体和责任共同体。

2015年3月28日，经国务院授权，国家发改委、外交部、商务部联合发布《推动共建丝绸之路经济带和21世纪海上丝绸之路的愿景与行动》。文件明确提出："加强旅游合作，扩大旅游规模，互办旅游推广周、宣传月等活动。联合打造具有丝绸之路特色的国际精品旅游线路和旅游产品，提高沿线各国游客签证便利化水平。推动21世纪海上丝绸之路邮轮旅游合作"；同时，文件指出，"抓住交通基础设施的关键通道、关键节点和重点工程，优先打通缺失路段，畅通瓶颈路段，配套完善道路安全防护设施和交通管理设施设备，提升道路通达水平。"

2017 年 5 月 14 日，习近平在"一带一路"国际合作高峰论坛开幕式上指出，宁波等地的古港是记载古丝绸之路历史的"活化石"。讲话高度评价了宁波的历史地位，这是宁波提升文化旅游形象的良好机遇。

古丝绸之路"活化石"这一评价为挖掘宁波文化旅游提供了新思路。在"一带一路"建设大背景下，通过深入挖掘、系统整理古丝绸之路"活化石"评价内涵，将底蕴深厚的海丝文化与现代都市文化融合，丰富宁波旅游文化内涵，明晰旅游文化形象，为提升宁波文化旅游形象提供有利契机和丰厚内涵。

"一带一路"枢纽城市的建设为宁波文化旅游形象提升提供了新动力。目前，宁波正在积极谋划发挥"一带一路"与长江经济带的区位优势，加快建设现代化国际港口名城，努力在新一轮国际竞争中占据有利位置，为提升宁波文化旅游形象提供强大动力。

全域旅游的推进为提升宁波文化旅游形象提供了新支撑。2017 年12 月宁波市委、市政府印发的《关于推进全域旅游促进旅游业改革发展的若干意见》，指出要坚持将旅游业改革发展融入全市大局，逐步形成全域旅游发展格局，努力把旅游业培育成宁波市现代服务业发展的引擎产业。文件提出的相关举措为宁波文化旅游形象的提升提供了有力支撑。

六、"一带一路"背景下宁波文化旅游产业发展建议

"一带一路"倡议是全方位的，为新时期宁波的文化旅游产业发展提供了全新的创新思路。通过对宁波文化旅游产业相融合的实际情况进行分析，我们可以得出宁波文化旅游产业的发展应该把重点放在发展模式的创新方面。

（一）政府层面

1. 加强监管，把握政策的助推作用

首先，招聘高素质旅游人才，大力培养高素质从业人员；其次，国家旅游管理部门严格相关执业资格考试，提高景区从业人员及管理人员的素质，提升景区运营能力及管理能力，以此提高景区综合吸引力；最后，应

加大监管力度，严厉查处无证导游等扰乱旅游市场秩序的行为。

2. 整合资源，实施多元战略，开发特色文化旅游品牌项目

要对宁波的旅游资源进行系统整合，重点开发和保护现有的旅游景点，打造全新的旅游线路及产品，充分发挥宁波旅游资源特色。深度发掘海洋文化、宗教文化、梁祝爱情文化、商帮文化、民间文化等优秀地域文化，通过对特色文化的产品化、市场化重组，最大限度地发掘、提升并实现宁波旅游资源所蕴含的文化附加值，进一步打造特色文化旅游品牌项目。

（1）海洋旅游文化产品以海洋渔业资源、渔产品等为核心，开辟游客在观光娱乐的同时体验海洋文化的旅游空间，规划设计一批相关主题活动，例如建设象山、大榭岛等景点的海洋休闲渔业文化和美食文化旅游项目。

（2）都市文化旅游产品以历史文化名城和国际港口城市为依托，形成都市观光旅游圈，将其打造为宁波都市文化旅游品牌。例如，东钱湖可利用自然山水打造一流的旅游度假区，延长三江文化长廊，形成百里景观带，集中塑造宁波都市游憩商务区和游憩文化带。

（3）佛教文化旅游产品要以天童寺、保国寺、阿育王寺、雪窦寺等佛教旅游资源为基础，除了针对佛教信徒开辟佛教朝圣游之类的文化旅游专线，还可以针对普通旅游者举办各种佛教文化活动，增强佛教旅游产品的趣味性和知识性，从而使佛教旅游产品的文化内涵得到进一步挖掘。

（4）古镇名村文化旅游产品可以发掘那些历史文化底蕴深厚又各具特色的古镇名村资源，在古镇名村文化旅游产品的开发上应该注重可参与性，强化旅游者的文化体验，使旅游者从旁观者转变为积极的参与者。例如，把古镇名村的渔文化和农耕文化有机地融合于现代休闲旅游产品中，让旅游者亲身参与古镇的渔事或农事活动；充分挖掘古镇名村民俗文化，加深旅游者对他们的了解，塑造古镇的独特形象。

3. 打造生态旅游和丝路文化产业基地

发展生态旅游是发展旅游经济的有力抓手，打造生态旅游就要加强对宁波生态旅游区的环境保护，政府不可缺位。政府和相关部门需要制定相

应的法规制度加强对生态旅游区的环境保护，并做好宣传与教育工作，确保发展旅游产业的同时尽力减少对生态环境的破坏。同时，以"一带一路"建设为契机，建设丝绸之路新起点文化旅游中心。凭借得天独厚的旅游资源，挖掘传统与历史文化，推进旅游产业由人文型向山水型、观光型向休闲型转型，打造生态旅游和经济文化产业基地。

4. 加强与丝路沿线国家地区交流，创新区域合作形式

一方面，加强与丝路沿线城市的旅游合作力度，成立丝绸之路旅游合作机构或组织。例如，宁波可以与相邻的杭州、苏州共同打造横向区域旅游圈，使区域联动带动发展，打造丝绸之路文化遗产旅游走廊，开拓旅游市场。另一方面，加强与东南亚各国旅游合作，促进出入境旅游的健康发展，积极推进"走出去，请进来"，通过设立驻外办事机构、简化出入境旅游签证手续等措施，加快国际旅游市场的开发。

（二）旅游企业层面

1. 充分利用资源，打造国际旅游精品

首先，旅游企业应充分利用好现有的旅游资源，因地制宜地开发旅游产品，突出宁波旅游资源的优越性和独特性；其次，加强同行之间的信息、经验及资源的交流与整合，形成良好的竞争环境，促进旅游业向生态化发展；最后，打造国际旅游精品需要对游客需求进行研究，如品牌餐厅、主题酒店等，把握游客的消费心理和购买需求，调整旅游品牌下各项产品和服务的水准，面向潜在的国际旅游市场进行发掘和推广。

2. 优化旅游产业集群，增强企业社会责任感

旅游企业要自觉履行社会责任，优化旅游产业集群体系，树立良好的品牌形象。对于企业来说，应将社会责任意识融入企业日常管理中，细化责任到个人；将宁波旅游景区的线路加入丝绸之路规划，重新加以开发。同时，企业内部应建立与绩效挂钩的考评体系，让每位员工都认识到履行社会责任的重要性，从而形成有效的企业社会责任管理体系，提高旅游企业的社会责任感。另外，优质的旅游产业集群有利于旅游业整体质量的提升，旅游企业之间形成良性竞争，从而开发出更多创新性旅游线路、产品

等，最终带动宁波旅游业质的飞跃。

3. 强化丝路旅游营销宣传，加强旅游产品开发

首先，旅游企业可以参加国内外各种旅游交易会或博览会来加强丝路旅游产品的宣传，组织特价优惠旅游产品到国内外的一些主要客源地进行有针对性、主体式宣传促销；其次，与周边旅游热点城市、口岸城市加强沟通合作，构建开发旅游精品线路、新型旅游专题项目等；再次，充分借助媒体宣传宁波丝路文化旅游品牌形象和旅游产品，对丝路旅游进行大力宣传；最后，针对不同客源市场制作不同类型的旅游主题促销活动，如历史文化游、宗教文化游、丝路文化游等，使不同受众群都能了解感受宁波文化旅游的特色。

（三）媒体层面

1. 有效传递信息，提升宁波旅游品牌形象

媒体宣传是影响游客出行决策的重要因素，文案措辞、新闻元素的运用及把握直接影响大众的认知。因此，媒体宣传要确保旅游景点介绍、旅游信息的真实性和可靠性。宁波的旅游景点多，景点秩序和环境维护需要投入更多的精力。首先，媒体不能为追求经济效益、吸引受众眼球而主观歪曲事实；其次，媒体应避免过度报道，宣传要公正、客观，摆脱宁波旅游业在大众眼中的"刻板印象"；最后，选择正确、适宜的方法和途径积极引导大众对宁波的认知，发挥媒介的导向作用，树立正面公正的媒介形象。

2. 积极构建文化话语权，促进国际文化交流

现代信息与通信技术突飞猛进，电子媒介飞速发展，跨国传播更为快捷。在"一带一路"倡议下，要提升中国文化话语权、促进国际文化交流，媒体传播必不可少。然而，要提升中国文化话语权，在文化全球化的今天却面临很大挑战。一方面，媒介传播需要摒弃生硬刻板的叙述方式，要站在大众的视角下看问题，增强传播效果和吸引力；另一方面，媒介的传播方式要有效恰当，这样才能正确引导公众的价值观念和行为方式。目前，传播形态过于概念化、说教化，易使受众群体产生审美疲劳。

七、结论

宁波文化旅游产业前景广阔，发展潜力巨大。加快发展文化旅游产业，对于拉动第三产业发展、促进经济结构调整、推动发展方式转变、推进新型城镇化进程、扩大对外开放、打造宜居宜业人居环境，提升城市形象和竞争力，具有重要意义。在全域旅游理念指导下，全社会应该为提升宁波文化旅游形象做出努力。在“一带一路”背景下，宁波要牢牢抓住新时代提供的历史机遇，多条线路齐头并进。城市公共空间的规划，要充分考虑城市文化旅游形象的塑造，利用老外滩、庆安会馆、高丽使馆、永丰库遗址等，搭建鲜明又丰富的旅游空间格局。例如，“海丝活化石”旅游路线的开发，一方面要把海上丝绸之路遗迹与其他旅游资源串联推出主题路线；另一方面，要整合媒体资源进行市场推广。例如，建立“海丝”专家智库，为“海丝活化石”提供宣传资料等。为此，我们一定要统一思想、厘清思路、抢抓机遇、乘势而为，不断加强宁波文化旅游活动的体验感与参与性，让宁波文化旅游产业走出中国、走向世界。

"一带一路"倡议下基层丝路文化建设的途径研究

张艺萌①

摘要："一带一路"蕴含着深厚的中国思想和智慧。推动"一带一路"建设行稳致远，要有广泛、深厚、坚实的群众基础。笔者站在"民心相通"这一角度，从政府、传媒、群众三个不同层面，阐释了开展基层丝路文化建设的原因、存在问题及途径。

关键词："一带一路" 文化建设 民心相通 原因 问题 对策

一、引言

2017 年 5 月，环境保护部、外交部、国家发改委、商务部联合发布《关于推进绿色"一带一路"建设的指导意见》，系统阐述了建设绿色"一带一路"的重要意义，开始全面推进"政策沟通""设施联通""贸易畅通""资金融通"和"民心相通"的绿色化进程。要推进"一带一路"建设，"民心相通"可谓举足轻重；要实现民心相通，基层文化建设是首要任务。只有让丝路文化推进到社会生活的方方面面，潜移默化地影响基层民众的社会实践与生活，才能为"一带一路"建设奠定坚实的群众基础。

作为青少年，我们应该把目光放到身边人身上，也就是基层群众身上。"一带一路"是国家级倡议，每个人，无论是干部还是普通群众，无论身处城市还是乡村，每个人都应了解它，贡献自己的一份绵薄之力。本文着重论述"一带一路"基层丝路文化建设的途径。

---

① 张艺萌，女，驻马店遂平县第一高级中学高中二年级。

二、基层丝路文化建设的必要性

若论基层丝路文化建设在"一带一路"倡议中的必要性，我们可类比基层干部在国家发展中的重要性。清代郑板桥在《墨竹图题诗》中写道："些小吾曹州县吏，一枝一叶总关情。"基层干部虽身处基层，却责任重大。尤其是当下，从农业补贴到专项扶贫，再到征地拆迁、工程建设，基层干部与群众联系甚为密切。基层干部的工作态度如何，直接影响基层工作的开展、群众权益的保障。正是因为村支书黄大发的坚持与付出，贵州遵义草王坝村才能历时 30 余年凿通绝壁上的"生命渠"，结束当地长期缺水的历史。基层干部与广大群众相向而行，才能不断拉近彼此距离，凝聚创业的力量。习近平总书记说："干部要深入基层、深入实际、深入群众，在改革发展的主战场、维护稳定的第一线、服务群众的最前沿砥砺品质、提高本领。"基层是一方取之不尽用之不竭的资源，为我们提供了创业的广阔舞台，广大基层干部可以大有作为，必将大有作为。百舸争流，奋楫者先。广大基层干部要解放思想，奋勇争先，见贤思齐，履职尽责，为做好新时期的基层工作增加新动力、注入正能量。基层干部如此，基层丝路文化建设亦是如此，不仅可满足人民群众日益增长的精神文化需求，而且在推进"一带一路"建设中具有举足轻重的地位。

三、基层丝路文化建设成就及不足

自"一带一路"倡议提出以来，在经贸合作方面取得了以下成就。

（1）截至 2018 年 6 月，我国与"一带一路"沿线国家货物贸易累计超过 5.5 万亿美元，年均增长 1.1%，中国已经成为 25 个沿线国家最大的贸易伙伴。

（2）对外直接投资超过 700 亿美元，年均增长 7.2%，与沿线国家新签对外承包工程合同额超过 5000 亿美元，年均增长 19.2%。

（3）中国企业在沿线国家建设境外经贸合作区共 82 个，累计投资 289 亿美元，入区企业 3995 家，上缴东道国税费累计 20.1 亿美元，为当地创造 24.4 万个就业岗位。目前，中国企业正在探索开展"一带一路"建设领域的第三方市场合作。中国还不断放宽外资准入领域，营造高标准的营商环境，吸引沿线国家来华投资。

（4）中国加快与沿线国家建设自贸区，已与 13 个沿线国家签署或升级了 5 个自贸协定，立足周边、覆盖"一带一路"、面向全球的高标准自由贸易网络正在加快形成。我国还与欧亚经济联盟签署经贸合作协定，与俄罗斯签署了欧亚经济伙伴关系协定。

（5）2018 年 11 月，中国举办首届中国国际进口博览会，有 172 个国家、地区和国际组织参会，3600 多家企业参展，超过 40 万境内外采购商到会洽谈采购。据统计，通过百度百科搜索出的"一带一路"数百万条相关资讯，有七成与经济有关。由此可见，"一带一路"更多时候是被作为经济策略来实行的。

从国内来看，各省区关于"一带一路"建设的有关举措过于独立化，缺乏分工与合作，缺乏地方性特色。盲目跟风、随波逐流的现象比较普遍，许多省未能找准自身发展定位与目标取向。

四、基层丝路文化建设的途径

（一）政府层面

其一是加大与沿线各国文化交流与合作的力度。"一带一路"倡议并不仅是单纯的经济安排，而且是以文化交流推动政治、经济、军事、外交等合作的倡议。其二是实行"一省一国一侧重"战略，即"1+1+1"战略。"一省一国"是指着重发展毗邻丝路沿线国的省区经济，如内蒙古、新疆、黑龙江等。黑龙江省于 2015 年 4 月发布《中蒙俄经济走廊黑龙江陆海丝绸之路经济带规划建设》实施意见。黑龙江毗邻蒙古国与俄罗斯，地理位置优越，可借力"一带一路"推进经济发展步伐，弥补其相对于东部沿海省区的地理劣势，化劣为优，紧随"一带一路"大潮，推进发展。西藏自治区 2017 年发布的《西藏面向南亚开放重要通道建设规划》；内蒙古自治区于 2014 年先后发布《内蒙古自治区创新同俄罗斯、蒙古国合作机制实施方案》《内蒙古自治区深化与蒙古国全面合作规划纲要》。这些战略的推进需要具备一定的条件，而"一带一路"

经过的省区，如陆路所经的山西、陕西、内蒙古、宁夏、新疆、西藏等，海上丝绸之路途经江苏、浙江、山东、福建、广东等可利用其地理位置优势，积极融入"一带一路"建设。"一侧重"是指侧重河南等省份的发展。河南省地处中原，省会郑州地处我国交通大十字架的中心位置，京广、陇海两条铁路在这里相交，新建成的京珠、连霍高速公路和 107 国道、310 国道穿城而过，4E 级新郑国际机场与国内外 30 多个城市通航。此外，郑州拥有亚洲最大的列车编组站和全国最大的零担货物联运站，已建成设备完善、机制健全、管理先进、吞吐量大的航空口岸、铁路口岸和公路口岸，货物在郑州可以联检封关直通国外。可以说，河南省的交通优势为其融入"一带一路"建设提供了强大助推力。因此，河南省于 2017 年 9 月发布《推进郑州—卢森堡空中丝绸之路建设方案》。因此，"1+1+1"战略可充分发挥各省区优势，促进各省分工合作，增强内部凝聚力，推进"一带一路"建设行稳致远。

（二）传媒层面

大众传媒要走出"一带一路"倡议宣传"瓶颈"，方法有三。

一是设置"一带一路节点代言人"。明星代言作为市场化的产物，是必然之势。世界卫生组织在 2017 年就邀请中国三名青年艺人担当中国区控烟倡导者，2019 年又诚邀中国青年艺人易烊千玺作为中国健康特使出席联合国青年论坛。因此，明星艺人的"带货能力"，不仅可应用到商业宣传之中，也可以应用到"一带一路"宣传之中，用人民群众喜闻乐见的方式宣传推广"一带一路"倡议。"节点代言人"就是在"丝绸之路"沿线各重要节点设置"丝路节点代言人"，利用明星效应提高民众对于"一带一路"的关注度，从而增强参与度。在选用节点代言人时，可采用"双代模式"，即针对受众群体的年龄分别设置针对青少年和中老年群体的代言人，以期达到更好的宣传效果。

二是制作大型电视剧。电视剧的感染力及受众群体之大是毋庸置疑的；电视剧艺术化的展现手法更容易深入人心，比起高端路线的纪录片更要亲民。"一带一路"体裁电视剧制作要摆脱传统纪录片模式，不能生硬地介绍"一带一路"，应用艺术化的表现手法真实再现丝绸之路各国风俗人情，通俗化、生活化。电视剧具体内容可依照地域性，深入挖掘演绎丝绸之路的历史渊源。让情节代入感更强，观众的感触更深，从而于潜移默化中加深人们对"一带一路"的认同。

三是开发"一带一路"文化交流软件。分不同国家、不同领域、不同板块，及时发布官方资讯；设置"意见征收平台"，通过互联网收集民众对于"一带一路"的观点看法及建议，拓展民意征收渠道，确保公平公正，激发民众参与热情。可与手机产销商协作，将软件设置为出厂自带模式。

（三）群众层面

笔者认为，"一带一路"的宣传推进要以青少年为主。原因有三：

一是"娱乐至死"问题在青少年中较为普遍。

二是青少年正处于世界观、人生观、价值观形成的关键时期，正向宣传教育对他们影响大。

三是青少年是未来国之栋梁，是"一带一路"建设的积极引领者与践行者。如何将"一带一路"倡议深深植根于青少年心中，激励其为"一带一路"建设努力？一是在中小学设置"一带一路"研究社团，定期举行知识竞赛，竞赛得分计入学分。社团作为学生在校娱乐的重要场所，设置"一带一路"研究社团可满足学生们的娱乐需求，使其在娱乐中获得知识，受到影响。短期内学生们或许只是抱着"来看看"的心态，但随着研究的推进与深入，学生们必然会逐渐转变心态，端正态度，从单纯的娱乐蜕变为有目的、有侧重的研究。知识竞赛和学分制无疑更能激发学生的热情，吸引更多人参与。二是开展"'一带一路'进校园"活动。"戏曲进校园"的大范围开展就是最好范例，形式包括戏曲演出、戏曲知识、戏曲人物服饰等学习和认识，并组织师生进行演出。这类方式无疑更接地气，更具感染力，参与度更高。"一带一路进校园"，可通过巡演模式，为中小学生展示数字化丝路，传导"一带一路"成果，定期组织优秀学生参观"古丝绸之路"遗址，访问丝绸之路沿线国家，了解其风土人情，激发凝聚力与向心力。

五、结束语

基层丝路文化建设者作为"一带一路"的执行者和代言人,直接与社情民意挂钩,与丝路文化交流挂钩,影响"一带一路"建设成效。丝路文化是实施"一带一路"倡议的精神保障,是增进"一带一路"沿线国家和民众思想认同的基础。而人民群众是社会历史的主体、社会实践的主体,基层文化建设在丝路文化建设中占据不可代替的地位。文化从人民中来,到人民中去,为人民造福,为人民服务。作为新一代青少年,我们所要做的,就是努力学习,积极宣传"一带一路"建设成就,增进共识,推动丝路文化传播,为推进"一带一路"伟大进程贡献自己的绵薄之力。

后　记

　　时光飞逝，2018 年 12 月 31 日在中国人民大学附属中学做开题报告的画面仿佛就在昨天。"我们立志做大事"。在习近平主席的号召下，我们 8 人一边忙于繁忙的高中阶段学习，一边争分夺秒地进行《"一带一路"与我们的未来（二）》课题研学。历时将近一年，总算圆满地告一段落了。我们利用"刷题"的间隙忙里偷闲、见缝插针，完成了各自的任务。对于课题组所有成员来说，这都是一件大事。应该说，研学是我们一生的事业，相信参与这次课题研究的同学都会大有收获。大家在完成各自独立研究的同时，参与了整个研究过程，掌握了方法，认识了社会，也了解了世界。

　　在这里，我们感谢学校的教育与培养，感谢社会各界的关注和支持；感谢中国人民大学附属中学、中国传媒大学国家传播创新研究中心、北京青年领袖文化发展中心宁波分中心为我们的课题联合立项；感谢中国教育学会的学术支持；感谢全国人大教科文卫委员会、国家发改委社会发展司、国务院教育督导委员会、教育部学位中心、教育部社会科学委员会、北京大学全球治理研究中心、清华大学公益慈善研究院、中国铁建、中国银河证券股份有限公司、全球能源互联网发展合作组织、航天科工集团有限公司等单位的大力支持；感谢来自中国人民大学附属中学、中国人民解放军军事科学院、清华大学、浙江大学、中国人民大学、清华大学、首都师范大学、中国政法大学、浙江万里学院、中国农业大学、郑州大学、韩国仁荷大学、北京大学、北京邮电大学等高校和中国铁建等央企的领导和专家：何雷、欧晓理、翟小宁、王立生、郑保卫、范德尚、邓国胜、苗宝今、李春霞、张磊、苏尚锋、高秋明、闫国庆、陈晓飞、崔俊健、宁叶、王维伟、苏米尔、陈刚、杜咏梅、刘炜等，感谢他们的讲解和指导；特别感谢课题策划李春霞教授的全程指导和协调；同时，也要感谢各位家长的大力支持，感谢新华网、人民网、中新网、光明网、法制日报、中国教育报、中国教育电视台、英国侨报等媒体和社会各界的关注和支持。更要感谢我们的课题发起人——浙江大学竺可桢学院学生，师从罗卫东教授（浙江大学副校长）的李绩双同学。该同学在中国人民大学附属中学读书期间出版两部专著，其中由她主持的课题《"一带一路"与我们的未来（一）》（中英文对照版）成果由商务印书馆出版发行，受到全国人大相关领导和国家发改委主要领导以及教育部、中宣部主要领导的肯定和认可，人民日报在重要版面进行了宣传报道。大学期间，该同学积极参与社会实践活动，并在全国核心期刊发表论文；曾为新西兰国家党主席、前移民部长等访华时翻译；担任学校寒假期间剑桥大学访问团团长，取得了较好成绩。我们将更加努力，以前辈为榜样，争取以最好的成绩回报家庭、学校和社会，为"一带一路"的未来贡献青春和智慧。

因"家国天下"情怀，我们有为梦想而努力的壮志，有为"社会更美好，世界更和平"而奋发的豪情。"少年心事当拿云"，我们是有担当的新一代，尽管梦想尚在远方，但前行的步伐必须如于当下。我们已经踏上"一带一路"的建设征程，希望有更多力量的注入，继续前行。

值此论文集出版之际，我们愿与天下青少年携手共进，砥砺前行，以"一带一路"为契机，以"拿云"之志为引领，以身践志，走得更远，飞得更高。

课题组组长：董叙含　张思齐　宋政翰

2019 年 8 月 1 日

The Melody on "the Belt and Road" Initiative:

A Comparative Study on Music Talent Cultivation between China and Hungary

Dong Xuhan[①]

Abstract: Music is an indispensable part of every country's culture. This paper selected Hungary and China along "the Belt and Road" for detailed comparative analysis. Starting from the current situation of music talent cultivation in China and Hungary, by comparing the differences of music talent cultivation systems in China and Hungary, this paper probes into the different influences on music culture in the two countries and puts forward suggestions on the development of music education in China.

Key words: music education   the Kodály method   Kodály   higher music institutions   music education

I. Introduction

Liszt once said: "Music expresses both the content of emotions and the intensity of emotions. It is the essence of our mind that can be felt." [②] Music education is one of the ways of cultural inheritance, and is the successor, transmitter and innovator of music culture. As a model country in the world of music education, Hungary ranks among the top in the world in terms of cultivation mode of music talents, curriculum theory and practical application level, and it has cultivated many outstanding music talents such as Liszt. Therefore, learning from the success-

---

① Dong Xuhan, female, a student of Grade 2 in Ningbo Science Middle School.
② 邹力宏. 让道德素质在欣赏中提升——论戏曲艺术与德育的关联 [J]. 江西财经大学学报, 2005 (6).

ful experience of training music talents in Hungary and exploring the development law of music education in China has become a new epochal topic under the current educational innovation framework.

Based on the above purposes, this paper compares the Hungarian cultivation system of music talents to that of the China, and provides countermeasures and suggestions for the cultivation of music talents.

II. Analysis of music talent cultivation in China and Hungary

1. Analysis of music talent cultivation in China

The education and cultivation objectives of Chinese music academies are constantly adjusted with the changes of social and economic systems in different periods. China's professional music education system and mode basically follow the higher professional music teaching mode of the Soviet Union, learn from the advanced teaching ideas of Europe and America at the same time, and continue to develop on the basis of the original teaching methods and system reform. [①] Taking Central Conservatory of Music as an example, we can explore the development track and vein of professional talent cultivation in higher music institutes and universities in China from its constantly adjusted goal of music education talent cultivation.

(1) From 1955 to 1958, the cultivation goal of the second teaching reform clearly stipulated that music teachers should be trained to cultivate music professionals with higher music education level. Therefore, pedagogy, teaching methods and teaching practice courses are offered in each major.

(2) In March 1964, the cultivation objectives of teaching reform were: to develop traditional European music schools, styles and technologies, combine with Chinese characteristics, cultivate professional creative and performing talents, and provide professional music education training target training for

---

① 杨洋. 中波高等专业音乐教育人才培养模式比较研究——以帕德莱夫斯基音乐学院与天津音乐学院为例 [J]. 肇庆学院学报, 2018, 39 (3).

ordinary middle schools and teachers for the first time. It put forward that teacher training in ordinary middle schools and normal schools should be included into the training goal of professional music education for the first time.

(3) In 1977, in the early stage of reform and opening up, Central Conservatory of Music set up a new training goal: to cultivate music professional talents to develop morality, intelligence and physique in an all-round way.

(4) In the *Work Plan of Central Conservatory of Music from* 1988 *to* 1992, it mentioned that "to cultivate specialized talents at a higher level, that is, 'the goal of training is not one-sided talents pursuing the abnormal development of technology, but more comprehensive talents with a solid foundation of skills, a broader music quality and a greater potential'." At present, the training target of Central Conservatory of Music is high-level music talents with international vision. [1]

As of 2016, there are 11 public music institutes in China, including Shanghai Conservatory of Music (1927), Shenyang Conservatory of Music (1938), Sichuan Conservatory of Music (1939), Xi'an Conservatory of Music (1949), and Central Conservatory of Music (1950). Wuhan Conservatory of Music (1953), Xinghai Conservatory of Music (1957), Tianjin Conservatory of Music (1958), China Conservatory of Music (1964), Harbin Conservatory of Music (2013) and Zhejiang Conservatory of Music (2016). Among them, Central Conservatory of Music is the only art college listed in the national "Project 211" key construction. The 11 conservatories continue to optimize and adjust disciplines and major settings, teaching system structure, teaching staff, organization and management, and jointly undertake the task of cultivating high-level music talents in China.

2. Analysis of music talent cultivation in Hungary

People in Hungary believe that good music education will benefit people

---

① 李鸣镝. 高等艺术教育体系中有关问题的借鉴与反思 [J]. 河南师范大学学报（哲学社会科学版），2004（6）：142-144.

throughout their lives. Music education corresponds to the non-secular spiritual requirements of human nature. Therefore, children music education will keep people pleasant, make people pure, and beyond the thought. Music education in Hungary is based on the educational concept of music educator Kodály.

The Kodály method is based on the "natural development of the child", that is, the sequence of lessons is arranged according to the physical and psychological abilities of a normal child at various stages of natural development. Music teaching changes from the previous way to the logical and orderly music theoretical system, arranging the theme sequence of the traditional teaching mode, so that children and young people can participate at each stage of the course. [1]

Based on the advantages of music education in the world, the Kodály Method advocates to learn reasonably from the excellent results of music teaching methods in various countries in the world, and to transform and combine them according to the actual situation of Hungary, so as to make it a teaching framework with Hungarian characteristics. Symbols in rhythm letters are good examples. They are successfully modified and combined according to the British tonic sol-fa system, Curwen Hand-Sign, the French rhythm time reading method and the Italian lyrics name, making it a new music teaching tool. It reflects Kodály's emotional focus and teaching focus. In the process of training difficult teaching concepts, it leaves a straight and flat road to the concert hall for children, which reflects Kodály's difficulty dispersion teaching methods.

Kodály's course thought and practice process can be summarized into six characteristics:

(1) Back to the origin of music. The origin of music is the sound form of music. Therefore, Kodály emphasized that music education should start with auditory training and experience. This idea is emphasized throughout his music course. He liberated the children from the accepted music, that is, from music to feel music directly, instead of recognizing music from dull concepts and lan-

---

① 马磊. 柯达伊音乐教学法的启示 [J]. 甘肃科技, 2003 (12): 166–167.

guage interpretation. [1] Therefore, Kodály believed that the purpose of music theory is not to spread special terms and concepts. Music reading and writing should not be abstract theoretical learning, but first practical, auditory development, and the ability to use music to think and develop creative abilities.

(2) Music in native language emphasizes the use of Hungarian folk music. Music education in Hungary is based on music of Hungarian folk, which is indispensable to its music curriculum. Kodály said that music is his second native language, he said: "In terms of music, as far as language is concerned, it is only in the beginning that Hungary is the center that we can conduct a reasonable education. Music learning will be confused if it is not based on a simple and rigorous system. A simple and rigorous system will lay the foundation for other aspects and higher levels of development." [2]

(3) Emphasis on basic training. This is another feature of Kodály music. Fundamental training of Kodály music emphasizes three kinds of training: somatosensory training, auditory perception training and psychological perception (singing) training. Therefore, music experience, auditory training, strong music reading and writing training as well as singing training mainly based on Hungarian folk music appear in Kodály's music course.

(4) Develop students' musical ability. In 1945, under the leadership of Kodály, the music curriculum and teaching tasks were defined as follows: consciously enable students to master the native language of music; stimulate students' singing interests; develop and guide students' musical interests; develop students' musical ability; develop music literacy based on folk songs. The core is: cultivate students' musical ability by taking music of Hungarian folk as the starting point, stimulate and cultivate students' interest in music.

(5) Cultivate listeners and musicians. Another prominent feature of

① 马磊. 柯达伊音乐教学法在农村幼儿音乐教育中的应用研究 [D]. 兰州: 西北师范大学, 2004.

② 李方元, 吴祖英. 论柯达伊音乐课程思想与实践 [J]. 中国音乐, 2002 (3): 25-31.

Kodály music is its goal and evaluation, which is to cultivate musicians and listeners. In people's mind, music education is far from professional music education, but the brilliance and success of Kodály's music lies in its success in putting the two on a common footing, and it turns out that his curriculum not only
gave Hungary's music education a common music foundation, but also gave
them a common cultural foundation.

(6) Save the people of mechanization. In the middle of the 20th century,
the wave of industrialization in Hungary just emerged, but the culture with
mechanization naturally affected people's spiritual life. It is valuable that Kodály
had been acutely aware of the negative effects of the industrial age on the human
spirit and realized the positive role that music education can play in eliminating
this effect. In 1966, he wrote in the foreword to the book Hungarian Music Education written by Sandel Vorkesh："The book now published confirms that music
education is operating in the right track in Hungary. The purpose is not only to
cultivate musicians, but also to cultivate listeners. If someone tries to express the
essence of this education in one word, it can only be 'singing'. In our mecha-
nized age, we will eventually go along the road of making people become machines, thus only the spirit of singing can save us from this fate." [1]

III. The Comparison of music talent training between the two countries

1. Similarities in the Chinese and Hungarian music talents cultivation

China and Hungary have similar goals in music talent cultivation, that is
to say, teachers are specially trained in music education of ordinary middle and
high schools. Therefore, there are many similarities between the two countries
in music talent cultivation for undergraduate education. On this basis, the two
countries have the following similarities in music talent cultivation：

---

① 王丹琴. "回归人的本性"——柯达伊合唱教育思想对我国音乐教育的启示 [J]. 中国科
教创新导刊, 2009 (2)：99-100.

(1) All students must pass the professional quality examination, the training period is four years, and students must have certain basic quality and professional quality. After four years of learning and training, students must reach the professional level of middle school and high school music education.

(2) The training courses are basically the same, and they pay attention to improve the comprehensive quality of music education talents. The course categories basically include vocal music, musical instruments, musicology, music theory, music education, rehearsal and practice, etc. and focus on students music theory, practice and quality cultivation, training and edification, and the cultivation of students' comprehensive ability. ①

(3) The two countries pay attention to "one major and multiple capabilities" in personnel training, so that students can have a variety of qualities and abilities and have professional music skills when facing teaching work after graduation.

2. Differences in Chinese and Hungarian music talents cultivation

"There are indeed differences between Chinese and western culture, but music has no national boundaries, it can make the combination of Chinese and western culture, connect the contemporary with the ancient, and direct to the holy land of heart," according to Chinese Pianist Lang Lang. There are still some differences in teaching curriculum design and examination between China and Hungary:

(1) Differences in specialization of talent cultivation

For example, the difficulty of entrance selection examination is different; requirements for the entrance selection examination music theoretical knowledge threshold are different; the training programs and compulsory and optional course is different; teaching intensity of compulsory and optional course is different.

(2) The difference between the flexibility of textbook selection and the

---

① 王贞贞. 中德音乐教育学专业（本科）人才培养比较研究——以曼海姆音乐学院和泉州师范学院对比为例 [J]. 黑河学院学报，2017（12）：32-35.

openness of course content

For example, selection of teaching materials, auxiliary teaching materials and diversity of teaching forms are different.

(3) Different enrichment of course

The rehearsals and vocal music courses of domestic universities are not as rich as Hungary's music institute curriculum. For example, rehearsal courses, band arrangement, band director, chamber music ensemble and jazz ensemble greatly improve students' multiple abilities and exercise their different professional skills. The course of vocal music and voice protection can help students to master the correct use of sound more clearly, scientifically and objectively. The establishment of language courses (German, Italian and French) greatly improved the standard level of the language and the interpretation of foreign songs, operas, and other art works.

(4) Differences in flexible and rigorous test

In Hungary, students in music institutes are not required to take exams for all their courses. Students are only required to attend the lectures of some teachers. The assessment system can provide students with more flexibility and more time to focus on the courses they are interested in without spending any other energy. Especially vocal music, piano, musical instrument music major, only mid-term examination and graduation examination are required. In contrast, music institute students in China usually have exams at the end of each semester. In order to get good grades, Chinese students spend the whole semester on one or two songs and neglect the solid basic skills training. At the same time, the limited number of tracks involved in training results in a narrow field of vision for music.

It is understood that music institute in Hungary has very strict requirements in the graduation examination, which is reflected in three aspects: firstly, prospective undergraduates must give a 60-minute solo or solo concert to measure whether a student can enter the thesis defense; secondly, the topic of the paper is designated through conversation between the examination committee and students, and it must be completed within 6 months of the topic being de-termined; thirdly, a large number of practical courses with different directions and forms are provided to cultivate students' musical ability and promote their learning enthusiasm.

(5) Selection of time for course learning

In Hungary, students can choose the study time of certain courses according to their own conditions, or apply for exemption from certain courses and graduate in advance. For example, students can be excused from entrance examination if they meet standards after being tested by an assessment group of professors. Students can also apply for a graduation concert in advance, as long as the professor confirms in writing that the students have finished the graduation concert in advance. These measures are aimed at each student's own professional curriculum, rather than strict teaching arrangements. As for the re-quirements of optional course, although the school also provides students with enough space to choose the courses they like, they need to complete the courses within the semester stipulated in the syllabus and limit them to a certain extent.

Ⅳ. Suggestions on countermeasures of music dducation development in China

Through comparison, it can be seen that Music institute in Hungary has many advantages in cultivating music educational talents, which has good ref-erence significance for music education reform in China.

In fact, since the 1950s, the music industry in China has started Kodály teaching method. Since the beginning of the 21st century, a large number of in-troductory works and foreign textbooks have been published to introduce this teaching method. The works mainly introduce the concept of the Kodály Method and its implementation in Hungary, and they have not put forward constructive suggestions according to the actual situation in China. Textbooks translated into

Chinese are farraginous and lack of practical value. For example, Lois Choksy, a Canadian scholar who did not know Hungarian, and in his second book "*From Folk Songs to Classics*", he even used the name of the music textbook of Hungarian primary school "Singing and Instrumental Music" (Enek Zene) as the title of the textbook editor. And he believed that all textbooks were compiled by this so-called Enek Zene. In addition, there is a huge deviation in overemphasizing the contents of classical music in western Europe. This book was quoted as a joke in the Hungarian music circle, but it was published in China as an excellent textbook translation. Some teaching materials are very good, such as *Music Reading and Writing* written by Hungarian experts, introduced Colvin gesture, first tone singing method, rhythm reading method and other teaching methods. Good textbooks are of great reference value to us. However, we must apply Kodály teaching methods in a Chinese way, in order to make its greater impact and play a greater role in our country. Here are some strategies and suggestions.

1. Give full play to the advantages of talents and cultivate professional music educational talents

Attach great importance to the cultivation of teaching talents and give full play to their abilities and advantages. As future music teachers, we need strong music quality as our major. For example, students with excellent piano skills can concentrate their teaching resources and energy to train their piano performance, explore their own potential, and truly teach different students in accordance with their aptitude. some students with excellent music talents lose their own advantages due to insufficient training, and this is not conducive to the development of music education and teaching. It is suggested that music institutes in China learn from the educational policy of "one subject with many abilities" in Hungary, and run "one major" throughout the school for four years, paying attention to the cultivation of students' professional skills, so as to make the talent cultivation more accurate and professional.

2. Enrich and improve the major setting

The richness of music courses broadens the students' horizontal music knowledge. The wider the music field, the more beneficial it is to improve learning interest and expand thinking ability.

Music education is a subject with strong practicality. Its theoretical system comes from the practice of music education and in turn guides the practice of music education. It is suggested that some music universities in China can provide a large number of practical courses in different majors. For example, different forms of music schools in Hungary develop music abilities defined by students and promote students' independent learning.

3. Carry out discussion-based teaching and enrich teaching modes

In the form of special research, the development of teaching curriculum is proposed to make the teaching modes more diversified. It not only avoids the phenomenon of single teaching modes and low teaching efficiency, but also promotes the common progress of teaching and scientific research, and cultivates music talents in the spirit of independent exploration.

4. Improve the utilization rate of teaching materials and avoid the single choice of teaching materials

It is suggested that music institutes in China learn from the teaching materials set by music institutes in Hungary, introduce new teaching contents constantly, and avoid the outdated teaching materials and teaching cases many years ago. The development of library collections and the increase of foreign music books, audio and video resources are of great benefit to learning and teaching.

5. Reform the examination system with considering the flexibility and strictness

Music institute of Hungary adheres to the teaching concept of "strict entry and strict exit", pays attention to the flexibility of examination, and emphasizes the flexible grasp and application of students' knowledge rather than the learning ability of rote memorization. This examination system ensures that graduates are of high quality and can quickly adapt to new jobs. It is suggested that domestic universities can also learn from this examination system and give consideration to flexibility and strictness, so as to raise the overall level of graduates to a new level.

6. Attach great importance to the cultivation of music quality and the artistic atmosphere of the school

The artistic atmosphere is directly related to students' enthusiasm for learning. In schools with strong artistic atmosphere, students have a high level of aesthetic appreciation and art appreciation. Most conservatory of music in Hungary provide free music exchange courses for students, and invite famous musicians to participate in master classes, music week performances and other activities every year. These activities with great international influence will play an immeasurable role in improving students' artistic quality and vision. In the past decade, music communication in China has been increasing. For example, the Central Conservatory of Music holds music week, instrumental music exhibition, master class and other free exchange classes every year to broaden students' horizons and promote art quality. It is suggested that conservatory of music in China carry out beneficial exploration in this aspect and build up music artistic atmosphere of the college.

V. Conclusion

In the research and exploration of this topic, the author has some thoughts and experiences on music talent cultivation in China and Hungary.

Nowadays, more and more emphasis are put on cultural diversity, so it is necessary for other countries to learn culture, and the same is true for music education. Under the communication teaching of Chinese scholars and foreign scholars, China has been exposed to the four major music teaching systems abroad. The new system starts with prospective teachers, college students majoring in music, through the training of future teachers, these new teaching methods are applied to the future teaching practice. However, many graduates blindly copy foreign modes in practice, but the result is below expectations.

After reading and looking up various materials, the author had some ideas, including reflection and fantasy, learning and perception. What to re-think? What can we imagine current music education in China? What can be learnt from future music education in China? What can we learn from Kodály educational thought and Hungarian teaching system? The word " perception" has the deepest meaning. It has both feeling and understanding. It seems that China's music education lags behind the world level too much.

The reason for taking Hungary as an example is that the author thinks that music education in China is very similar to music education in Hungary in the past. China is a country with a long history and rich folk music culture, but most people like the western music, greatly ignoring the study of Chinese native music culture. From the examples mentioned in this paper, many children start learning English when they are very young, it can be said to learn another language when they are not proficient in mother language. Many children learn to play piano and violin at an early age, and they are influenced by music abroad. They have ignored the importance of their own national culture in consciousness, so that a lot of Chinese parents now pay more attention to western countries than choosing Chinese folk musical instruments for their children. Our national music culture is also the crystallization of the wisdom of the Chinese people, as Chinese people have the obligation to learn and pass on the Chinese folk culture from generation to generation.

At the same time, the author believes that it is necessary to strengthen the cooperation of music talent cultivation between China and Hungary. Since 2015, Shanghai Conservatory of Music has formed a joint school-running mode with four top conservatories of music in the world: " SHCM-RCM Joint Institute" SHCM-Berklee Contemporary Music Institute" " SHCM- Liszt-Chopin Music

Institute Alliance". ① These high-end international cooperation platforms have brought more possibilities for promoting music performance discipline development and cultivating top music performance talents.

Take SHCM-RCM Joint Institute as an example, with the philosophy of "tutor management, master guidance, learning through performance and practice through competition", the institute adopts the personalized teaching method of "short-, medium- and long-term", with intensive teaching on weekends. In the teaching team, the chief professor includes 8 members of the SHCM team and 10 members of the RCM team, all of which are top professors.

In SHCM-Berklee Contemporary Music Institute, students who are recruited by both parties can be graded together upon graduation, this is equivalent to establish the same quality system, and graduates can get diplomas issued by both institutes. Professor Chen Qiangbin, the project leader and dean of Shanghai Conservatory of Music, said that current curriculum of Shanghai Conservatory of Music has been fully recognized by Berkeley and achieved mutual recognition of credits.

In 2017, Shanghai Conservatory of Music has also established an alliance with Franz Liszt Academy of Music and Chopin University of Music in Warsaw. The alliance will take the series of music festivals and international touring performances as a leverage to push the classical music creation and performance to the world-class level and carry out all-round international exchanges and cooperation.

"Top music talents need tailor-made, personalized training. If you can get a hand-in-hand instruction from a master musician, it likes giving wings to a tiger." Liu Yan, Deputy Secretary of the Shanghai Conservatory of Music, said. Yes, only through cooperation can China continue to base itself on an international perspective, learn from other culture, reform the cultural exchange mode between China and Hungary, carry out a series of art exchange activities between China and Hungary, and build a bigger and broader

---

① 阙政. 中国好声音：上音奏响时代音符 [J]. 新民周刊, 2017 (46): 18-23.

exhibition platform for children who love arts. Only by working hand in hand can we promote a win-win situation in education. We must open our doors to good foreign art works. No matter what country they belong to, they will only enrich our culture.

Innovative Research on Financial Globalization Brought by "the Belt and Road" Initiative

Zhang Siqi[1]

Abstract: The current nature of the globalization dominated by developed countries such as the United States is capital globalization. The manifestation of financial globalization is featured with the nature of financial inequality. The essence of "the Belt and Road" is to promote a new type of globalization, with the aim of achieving a balanced development of the global economy and building a more equitable globalization system. In 2013, since President Xi Jinping proposed "the Belt and Road" Initiative, "the Belt and Road" Initiative has become the world's most popular global public product and the international cooperation platform with the best prospect. Within the framework of "the Belt and Road" international cooperation, all parties adhere to the principles of extensive consultation, joint contribution and shared benefits, work together to meet the challenges facing the world economy, create new opportunities for development, seek new development momentum, expand new development space and achieve complementary advantages, strive for mutual benefit and win-win situation, and thereby continue to move toward the community of human destiny. Different from the globalization system of the capitalist world, "the Belt and Road" adheres to the spirit of internationalism, advocates the sharing of results, peaceful development and mutual benefit, and promotes political mutual trust, economic integration and cultural tolerance in countries along the route.[2] As a high school student

---

① Zhang Siqi, male, a student of Yuyao Middle School, Zhejiang Province.
② 引自《吕氏春秋·慎大览·察今》。

in the new era, the author has a limited knowledge but from his own point of view, based on his innovative spirit, he analyzes the tremendous innovation brought by "The Belt and Road" Initiative in the field of financial globalization.

Key words: "The Belt and Road"   financial globalization   capitalism   innovation

Ⅰ. Introduction

In 2013, President Xi Jinping proposed "the Belt and Road" Initiative. In December 2014, the central government identified "the Belt and Road" Initiative as a national construction project and established a 40 billion USD Silk Road Fund as the support. "The Belt and Road" Initiative has promoted the facilitation of trade and investment in countries along the route, enriched international public goods services, improved the level of infrastructure in various countries, and helped people from countries along the route get rid of poverty and become rich. "The Belt and Road" Initiative has also developed an open financial platform through the development of Internet finance, realized communion and commonality, improved the international division of labor of developing countries under the new financial globalization system, and enabled the countries along "the Belt and Road" to achieve self-reliance and self-improvement. In addition, "the Belt and Road" explores effective ways to solve the current global dilemma, build a mutual benefit and long-term sharing mechanism as well as build a community of human destiny.

However, it must be seen that there are many countries along "the Belt and Road" ①, which have intertwined in many fields, complex cultural background, unbalanced economic development, and great differences in beliefs and customs. With the traditional industrial globalization model, "the Belt and Road" construction cycle is promoted step by step with many difficulties. It is

---

① The countries along "the Belt and Road" Initiative involve 65 countries in East Asia, South Asia, Central Asia, West Asia and Central and Eastern Europe.

necessary to overcome the difficulties in the implementation. However, the adoption of financial globalization innovation means is an effective innovation and entry point, which can accelerate the implementation of "the Belt and Road" Initiative. On the other hand, financial development is a necessary condition for promoting "The Belt and Road" initiative. As long as the financing channels are smooth enough, the smooth implementation of the project can be guaranteed. Only with sufficient funds can construction be guaranteed and the grand blueprint be realized.

This research topic is innovative in its research methods, attempting to analyze the issues of "the Belt and Road" Initiative and financial globalization within the framework of political economy. Different from the model discussion model based on the econometric model advocated by western economics, the author believes that economic issues should not only focus on the field of economic research, but also should deeply grasp the cultural, moral and philosophical issues at a deeper level in the region, so as to explore the root of the problem from a broader perspective. Therefore, the research of this topic will be more innovative thinking in the light of political economics combined with the law of economic development.

The financial globalization led by the traditional capitalist countries not only continues to plunder wealth from developing countries, but also transfers its domestic contradictions to developing countries, resulting in the continuous expansion of global income. Today's Sino-US trade friction is a typical case. The United States is afraid that China will grow and develop, so it will block in trade and technology. "The Belt and Road" has built a new financial globalization order. Through infrastructure construction and other urgently needed financial support of developing countries, "the Belt and Road" Initiative has really helped developing countries solve their own problems and enabled the developing countries to achieve self-reliance and self-development and get rid of the dependence on developed countries and thereby realize a series of major innovations in the field of financial globalization.

II. Question presentation

1. Capitalist countries have established a new exploitation system through financial globalization

Firstly, the globalization of capitalist finance has brought the economies of developing countries into a vicious circle. The capitalist global financial crisis and the sovereign debt crisis are essentially resulted from the disparity between the rich and the poor in the world, and capitalist countries transferred the risks and contradictions to developing countries through globalization. Under the financial globalization led by capitalism, neither population nor wealth can be accumulated indefinitely. Only the new financial globalization under "The Belt and Road" Initiative can solve this problem.

Figure 1   Vicious Circle of Capitalist Financial Globalization

Globalization was predicted by karl Marx. As the capital continues to accumulate, interests are monopolized by a few capitalists,[1] and the growing social problems in Europe and the United States has shifted to developing countries. The reason why the capitalist countries seem to circumvent the results of the deduction of Marxist theory and escape from systematic collapse is that their domestic contradictions are transferred to developing countries through global expansion. Through international economic and trade cooperation, developed countries transfer highly-polluting industries, excess capacity and inflation to developing countries, or pluck resource products from developing countries and meanwhile curbing their industrial chain moving to the upstream, presently US imports rare earth resources at low cost from China while levying tariffs on

---

① 叶险明. 世界历史理论的当代构建 [M]. 北京: 中国社会科学出版社, 2014.

high-tech products so as to take chips as a breakthrough to curb the development of China's science and technology industry. In recent years, the economic climate of developed countries dominated by the United States has shown a downward trend, and employment pressure has become more prominent. In order to create enough job opportunities, the United States has narrowed trade deficit by increasing tariffs on Chinese export commodities, and even gossiped that China's surplus with the United States has deprived the job opportunities of the Americans. However, in contrast, the China Silk Road Fund has created a large number of jobs for the working people including the majority of women in the countries along "the Belt and Road".

Secondly, the dissatisfaction of the various circles of capitalist countries with traditional financial globalization has been long-standing. In the development history of capitalism for hundreds of years, there are endless criticisms over capitalists. In the philosophical world, Kant pointed out that history begins with evil, because it is human creation, essentially exposing the greed of the rentier.①In the literary world, for the criticism over rentiers, many characters in Balzac's works have distinctive features, the most famous is Eugenie Grandet, who depicts the face of the rentier. Even in the most financially developed United States, the debate over capital has never stopped. At the beginning of the U.S.A independence, Jefferson and other founders denied capitalism. Franklin criticized personal capital accumulation throughout his life. In *Declaration of Independence*, they did not mention that the U.K. government cracked down on the U.S. manufacturing industry. In the capitalist countries, the vast working masses and the grassroots people have been holding extremely hatred towards financial capital, and their dissatisfaction with the capitalists has accumulated in the heart for quite a long time.

Thirdly, financial globalization has inherited the system of the colonial era. In a sense, from the development of financial globalization in contemporary

---

① ［德］康德. 历史理性批判文集［M］. 何兆武，译. 天津：天津人民出版社，2014：66-67.

capitalist countries, the shadow of the colonial era can still be seen. *Capital* says that the first globalization began in the period of colonial expansion. Marx proposed that European powers used war and colonial methods to plunder the resources of the American and the African labor force to achieve bloody capital accumulation. Without industrial development, there is no modern financial power. In other words, today's financial globalization inherits the capitalist colonial era in which global trade began in the great discoveries in geography. the author realizes this is the beginning of the global expansion of capitalism. Capital-dominated globalization has never got rid of colonial consciousness and exploitative thinking. Jefferson, who had longed for the political ideal of small farm owner, possessed more than 600 slaves. His ideal country of democratic agriculture is based on slavery. Jefferson forbad the importation of slaves because the descendants of slaves were slaves for life and much cheaper than purchased slaves. Thomas Piketty[①] pointed out in the *Capital in the Twenty-First Century* that the number of slaves in the South increased from 400,000 to 4 million from 1770 to 1860. Before the Civil War, the market price of slaves was more than 10 times that of free labor force. In 1860, a slave owner could spend MYM2,000 to buy a young adult slave. The wage level was MYM200 a year. In fact, slave owners paid almost nothing to slaves, and it is enough to support their minimum living needs.

2. Systematic defects of capitalist financial globalization

Firstly, the core contradiction of capitalism is that capital gains are greater than labor returns. Capital owners do not need labor, just sitting and collecting rents, and the value accumulation in a worker's lifetimes is not as much as the one-day gains of a big capital. This is most evident in resource-based industries such as real estate and mining, where capitalists can claim ownership of these resources. In the colonial era, capital traveled around the world. When the colonists arrived in the America, they took the gold mines in Mexico as their

---

① ［法］托马斯·皮凯蒂. 21 世纪资本论 ［M］. 北京：中信出版社，2014.

own. They arrested slaves in Africa and engaged in criminal triangle trade. Only by claiming ownership of these resources, they could legally plunder in an imposing manner, forced the slaves work under the whip in the Mexican gold mines and North American plantations. Today, while capital is walking around the world in the form of financial instruments, most of the grassroots in the society have to bear debt for a lifetime. They have to pay high interest rates. Their monthly income has to be used for repayment of expensive loans. Subprime mortgage crisis happened because of the collapse of the capital bubble. Once the financial crisis occurs, it will endanger the global economic system. This has been proved by the Great Depression of 1929 and the subprime mortgage crisis of 2008.

Secondly, workers have been struggling with machines, but few people realized that workers are essentially fighting with the capital behind the machine. According to the statistical data in 2014, a robot can replace 12.24 to 14.37 human labor force, which has a significant impact on mining industry, manufacturing industry, water and electricity supply as well as construction industry. New machines constantly diminish the importance of human labor. The excessive financial capital of the capitalist countries flow around the world, and advanced machinery and equipment are used to deprive the work positions of developing countries, resulting in industrial poverty in these countries.

Thirdly, financial capital cannot be accumulated indefinitely. The larger the capital, the lower the rate of return on capital. In order to maintain its own income, capitalists must further lower wages or conduct malicious competition. Capitalists set up factories around the world, utilized surplus capital to squeeze workers in developing countries and thus formed a scissors gap in financial capital.

3. Capitalist financial globalization is conservative and closed

Realities such as trade friction show that developed countries have always tried to use capital and technology to limit developing countries, resulting in global economic and social inequalities. For example, in the early days of the industrial revolution, it was identified as illegal to export textile technology even in U. K. performing the most moderate globalization system. The proliferation of knowledge and technologies has weakened the inequality brought about by capital accumulation. However, in the process of globalization, knowledge sharing is the key to break the seclusion of science and technology. Substantially speaking, the United States maintains its global supremacy by relying on its capital monopoly over technology but not innovation and technology. The rise of China has made the US technology constantly challenged. *The New York Times* pointed out that in the past 10 years, the patent share has fallen to 52%, and the Nobel Prize share has fallen to 51%. In the works *They Made America: From the Steam Engine to the Search Engine: Two Centuries of Innovators*, Harold Evans et al. pointed out that American history was really created by ordinary people from all walks of life. Although these inventors and innovators had a moral consciousness of redemption and nearly crazy creation drive, they had devoted their lives to giving the general public the goods that the upper class could enjoy in the past, but the capitalists had used these inventions to seek for monopolistic interests for themselves. Capitalist financial capital had a repressive effect on innovation. Even Thomas Edison, who owned 1,093 patents, warned his assistants: "We have to bring out research outcomes, and we must not behave like some German professors who devoted their lives to studying the fluff on a bee. "① The great inventors and innovators of the United States often spent their lives in poverty. For example, John Fitch desperately committed suicide because he did not have the funds to promote the steamship. Before he died, he predicted that the capitalists would get fame and wealth from his invention and he would be forgotten by history.②Just like Whitney's cotton ginning machine strengthened the slavery system of the South, the de-globalization dominated by the US today is

---

① ［美］哈罗德·埃文斯, 等. 他们创造了美国 ［M］. 北京: 中信出版社, 2013.
② ［美］哈罗德·埃文斯, 等. 他们创造了美国 ［M］. 北京: 中信出版社, 2013.

essentially to establish technical barriers and thereby achieve its monopoly.

4. Summary

capitalism-dominated financialization serves capitalists but not serves the toiling masses. Capitalists plunder the masses' wealth by means of financial globalization. This is essentially shifting domestic contradictions to developing countries. For example, the debt crises in Pakistan were essentially results of financial plunder by the United States and other developed countries over the years, and China's "the Belt and Road" financial support is gradually helping Pakistan recover from economic difficulties, so Pakistan began its fight against the United States and deepening cooperation with China.

Ⅲ. "The Belt and Road" Initiative has constructed a new financial globalization system

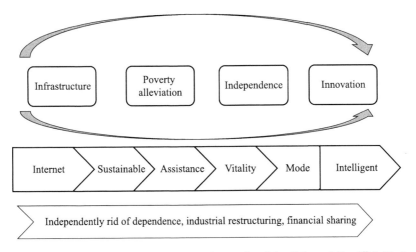

Figure 2   Features of Financial Globalization under "the Belt and Road" Initiative

As shown in Figure 2, "the Belt and Road" Initiative truly supports these countries by supporting the infrastructure construction, poverty alleviation, industrial independence and technological innovation of developing countries in Europe, Asia and Africa. By building Internet information facilities, improving transportation, financial model innovation, establishment of sharing mechanisms as well as precision assistance, countries along the route will be energized and enabled to achieve industrial restructuring and financial sharing.

Therefore, "the Belt and Road" Intiative is an effective prescription for the shackles of capitalist financial globalization. This part has also demonstrated "the Belt and Road" approach to build a new type of financial globalization system while prescribing for the problems of the globalization of capitalism. This parer aims to analyze the advantages of the new financial globalization system over traditional financialization.

1. China's high-speed economic development promotes the construction of "the Belt and Road".

The rapid development of China's economy has laid the foundation for "the Belt and Road" Initiative. In 1978, China's per capita GDP was only 385 yuan, while this figure was nearly 60,000 yuan in 2018. In 1978, hundreds of millions of peasants in our country earned only 10 cents or more a day. In 2020, China will achieve comprehensive poverty alleviation. In some areas, the income of farmers has increased by 10,000 times compared to that of 1978. In the past ten years, China has surpassed Japan to become the world's second largest economy, surpassing Germany to become the world's first exporter, surpassing the United States to become the largest trading country, and surpassing the United States as the world's number one in patent technology applications. The total number of Chinese enterprises ranks the first in the world. Among Fortune 500 Companies, there are 120 Chinese companies, and there are 3 Chinese companies among the top 10, and 4 among the 10 most profitable companies in the world are Chinese companies. In terms of the supply of public goods, China's electrical power supply capacity has continued to increase, and the level of electrical power marketization has continued to increase. With the largest number of mobile phones in the world, China's information communication capability has been continuously enhanced, the railways, highways and other transportation facilities have been constantly improved, the number of private vehicle holdings is steadily on the increase, and the supply capacity of rural public goods including science, education, culture and health continues to strengthen. In the past few decades, China has not only led the Chinese people to achieve poverty alleviation, but also actively assisted poor countries. In the construction of "The Belt and Road", China has also increased the supply of international public goods and improved its global service capabilities through financial globalization. In the past four decades, China's economic development has achieved miracles that could be realized in the capitalist world in hundreds of years. This is an unprecedented accomplishment. In the context of the fatigue development of global economy, "the Belt and Road" Initiative are essentially sharing of development achievements with developing countries through financial means. This is essentially different from the financial globalization promoted by capitalist countries and aimed at the exploitation of resources of developing countries.

2. "The Belt and Road" is the effective prescription for the capitalist financial globalization.

Paul Baran and Paul Sweezy have long argued in their works that financing expansion is the result of stagnancy of capitalist production. In other words, in the new era, capitalist accumulation reflects the characteristics of financial globalization. The focus of economic activities has shifted from industrial sector (even the service sector) to financial sector. " [1] In the era of Internet finance, financial capital accumulation has more advantages than industrial capital accumulation. Financial capital can be accumulated instantaneously on a global scale. Hundreds of millions of dollars of capital can flow freely between international financial centers such as London, New York, Tokyo and Hong Kong. It doesn't have to be constrained by time and space. The author personally understands that through Western Union remittances, MYM can be remitted to countries along "The Belt and Road" to support the cause there. The post-Keynesian

---

① 约翰-贝拉米·福斯特. 资本主义的金融化 [J]. 国外理论动态, 2007 (7): 9.

school analyzed the money borrowers as rentiers and believed that the rentier class was the main force driving financial development. Developed countries are currently playing this role, putting developing countries get lost in a debt trap. Despite this, the trend of economic financialization has become prominent. [1] As François Shanai pointed out, "The most profound changes in capitalism today occur in the financial sector, while economic globalization and economic financialization have led to a new phase of capitalist development. " [2] In this circumstances, China has led the investment of countries and regions along "the Belt and Road" to promote the development of related industries, comprehensively promote various economic and cultural activities, and facilitate emerging economies to develop their own economic development systems in order to achieve global economic rebalancing.

In the fluctuating waves of de-globalization, the Sino-US trade friction has resurfaced, the United States built border walls to cause harm to the benefit of neighboring countries, and the United Kingdom has withdrawn from the EU to maintain its own benefit, and the global political and economic environment tends to be turbulent. Voters in developed countries began to use voting rights to express their dissatisfaction with the government. In the process of financial globalization, developed countries face three problems: Firstly, Occupy Wall Street and other events show that financial oligarchy is profiting from globalization, while 99% of the people have not benefited from financial globalization, and even their lives have been damaged by financial capital. Secondly, in the process of financial globalization, physical economy has been damaged; the shadow banking and bubble economy continue to push the economy to a false high. However, the areas that really need financial support, such as infrastructure, scientific and technological innovation and industrial incubation, are not

---

① 戈拉德·A. 爱泼斯坦. 金融化与世界经济 [J]. 温爱莲, 译. 国外理论动态, 2007 (7): 14.

② 弗朗索瓦·沙奈. 金融全球化 [M]. 齐建华, 胡振良, 译. 北京: 中央编译出版社, 2001: 4-6

developed as they should be. Thirdly, in the process of globalization, developing countries do not receive financial support at all and have to bear relatively high financial costs, and the economic gap between places like sub-Saharan Africa and the developed world continues to grow. This is due to the profit-seeking nature of capital, which tends to flow to the area where returns can be made in the shortest time, while the least developed countries have investment risks, low profits and slow returns. From the events that have taken place internationally, we can see that the financial globalization led by capitalism is encountering various difficulties and is resisted on a global scale. Therefore, the current global finance driven by "the Belt and Road" Initiative essentially supports developing countries and helps them to be freed from poverty. At the same time, it resists the tide of de-globalization and allows the people of the world to share their development interests and effectively solve their development problems rather than giving a few financial capitalists the opportunity to get rich.

3. "The Belt and Road" Initiative brought innovation to financial globalization.

First of all, the huge infrastructure construction of countries and regions along "The Belt and Road" has created financial demand. In some Asian and African countries, imperfect infrastructure construction is the fundamental reason for hindering the country's economic development. Extremely backward traffic and severely depleted electrical power have deprived the momentum of economic growth. For example, in Tanzania, Africa, only 10% of households among the population of 50 million can have access to electricity, which not only brings great inconvenience to people's daily life, study and work, not to mention the development of modern technology. The countries and regions along "the Belt and Road" have a huge gap in funding. Zheng Zhijie, President of China Development Bank, proposed that infrastructure construction demand will reach 94 trillion US dollars in 2030, 20% of which cannot be effectively supported. As we all know, infrastructure construction is a project with huge investment and slow return. The governments of many underdeveloped

countries in Asia and Africa cannot afford the funds of infrastructure. Many people in Africa still live in simple primitive wooden houses. Roads, water conser-
vancy, electricity, communication, and sanitation are very imperfect, not to
mention air traffic. Ethiopia is one of the most developed countries in East Africa, but many cities in the country are still using such simple houses made of
clay and stone. Tailors can be seen everywhere in the street, and many areas
have to rely on Chinese tourists for food. The support of "the Belt and Road"
Initiative has played an important role in improving their lives, especially in
terms of road transportation, with the financial support and technical assistance
from China, local residents can take light rail in Ethiopia and no longer have to
worry about traffic problems. Coupled with the low return on investment and
long investment period, it is very difficult to introduce market capital and social
capital. If it is not operated properly, many unpredictable risks may be resulted. Public expenditure on infrastructure construction in sub-Saharan Africa is
only 2% of GDP per year, which is only 3% of the world's lowest standard. The new financial globalization system built by "the Belt and Road" can
provide trillions of dollars of financial support to various countries'
infrastructure construction, and help countries to get rid of the vicious circle of
backward infrastructure—educational and cultural depletion—economic development stagnancy, and fundamentally realize self-reliance and self-development. Education backwardness is a serious problem in Africa. In the past, long-
term pro-Americans have put Liberia in poverty and war. Unlike China where
children can enjoy compulsory education, there is still 60% illiteracy rate in Liberia where the best university was funded and built by China, "the Belt and
Road" has greatly improved the education level of African countries.

Secondly, financial support is tilted towards the underdeveloped
countries. In traditional international division of labor, underdeveloped countries
are at the low end of the industrial chain. The balance of international financial
and trade rules formulated by developed countries has always tilted toward itself,
causing the gap between the rich and the poor in the world to be sharply wid-

ened. "The Belt and Road" Initiative is committed to building a community of human destiny, allowing the people of the world to share the fruits of financial globalization, opening up a new stage of world development, reforming capitalist finance into inclusive finance and restructuring the international division of labor system. Unlike the traditional financial globalization, "the Belt and Road" focuses on those least developed countries, and will connect the countries that have not participated in globalization through infrastructure construction and create a new global system. China has helped African countries such as Angola and Ethiopia to carry out infrastructure construction, promote the development of science, education, culture and health, improve health care and education environment, build hospitals and schools for free, help the poor to see a doctor and reduce the illiteracy rate. These countries have been freed from the heavy debt burden of the past, and no longer tolerate western countries monopolize their industrial resources. With the financial support of China, they gradually move toward self-reliance and self-improvement, and gradually develop national industries and get rid of the control of capitalist financial capitalists, and thereby make industries and resources truly serve the workers and the masses. By drawing a comparison between the new financial globalization under "the Belt and Road" Initiative and the financial globalization of capitalist countries, we can find the biggest difference as follows: the former offers help with goodwill and selflessness, while the latter's support is based on the insatiable greed of the old capitalist countries; the former's financial support of "The Belt and Road" Fund aims to promote the economy of the countries along the route. With the financial support, these countries can be enabled to gradually realize the goal of independence and autonomy, reduce debt ratios and achieve sustainable development. While the latter capitalist countries, while extracting interest, also force these countries fall into the trap of circular debts.

Thirdly, it is conducive to improve the international labor division status of developing countries. In the past, developing countries traded resources for developed countries' technology. Extremely precious natural resources flow into

Europe and the United States at a very low price. Europe and the United States use the low-cost labor market of developing countries to make further plundering. At the same time, the international financial dominance of the United States comes from the monopoly of international currencies. The global countries purchase large amounts of US treasury bonds and return capital to the United States, which objectively constitutes a model of low-cost financing in the United States, forming high consumption and low savings in the United States. The hegemony status quo of the U. S. dollar is inseparable from the status of its financial power. Since the Bretton Woods system, the United States has exported trillions of US dollar bills in exchange for goods of the same value. This kind of financial means is called shearing wool in the process of financial globalization. Through currency issuance, the US dollar becomes the settlement currency of global circulation and realizes the purpose of plundering wealth from other countries.

The existing international financial order uses the global circulation of capital to plunder the resources of developing countries. Under this distribution system, developing countries and developed countries are like tricycles chasing cars. The gap is getting bigger and bigger, as we can see today, the phenomenon of the polarization between the rich and the poor in the world has tended to be more sharply. "The Belt and Road" construction has changed this phenomenon, and has substantially built a new financial system and order, and effectively helped and supported poor countries to obtain financial support.

Under "the Belt and Road" system, developing countries gradually become independent and self-improvement. They no longer relied on the capital and technology from European and American countries, and have gained the capacity of independently carrying out technological research and development. Through inter-industry complementary cooperation, relying on their comparative advantages, various developing countries have achieved high-end orientation and industrial upgrading in the value chain. Especially in the context of the current rise of international trade protectionism, "the Belt and Road" Initiative has created a large market for developing countries, so that products and technologies no longer depend on developed countries' markets, and thereby realized internal circulation of developing countries, and change the vertical division of labor of industries in the past and the way to undertake industrial transfer. Through financial support, "The Belt and Road" provides developing countries with a set of supporting systems for independent scientific research and production, and promotes the escalation of regional division of labor status. With the financial support of "the Belt and Road", developing countries no longer rely on low-end value-added exports to earn foreign exchange, breaking their long-term status at the bottom of the "smile curve".

IV. Challenges and recommendations faced by "the Belt and Road" in the innovation in the field of financial globalization

1. The challenges faced by "the Belt and Road" in the innovation in the field of financial globalization

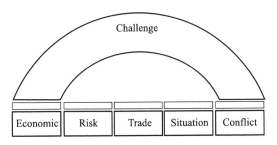

Figure 3   The Challenges Faced by "the Belt and Road" in the Innovation in the Field of Financial Globalization

As shown in figure 3, "The Belt and Road" is also facing enormous challenges in the innovation in the field of financial globalization. The developing countries still has a big gap with the western developed countries in economic development, so it is difficult to shake the leading position of capitalist countries in the short term. At the same time, the global economy is also facing certain downside risks. The economic difficulties of developed countries are shifting to developing countries, and financial risks tend to be prominent. The Sino-US trade friction has intensified, and the United States has stepped up its blockade against Chinese companies such as Huawei in an attempt to curb the rise of China. The sudden changes in the international situation and the intensification of conflicts in major powers have created challenges for China to promote financial globalization.

Firstly, the financial crisis has brought the economies of Europe and the United States into a continuing downturn. The down side pressure on global economy tends to be intensified. The United States has increased its containment against China to improve the domestic economic difficulties.

Secondly, developed countries have spread their inequality to the world, not only turning developing countries into their low-end manufacturing plants, but also causing political instability and polarization within developing countries. In essence, developed countries have transferred domestic environmental pollution, economic exploitation, and ecological destruction to underdeveloped countries.

Thirdly, the United States and other developed countries practice racism under the name of nationalism, which is in essence to maintain the maximized interests of interest groups, regain unilateralism and trade protectionism, which is in a serious confliction with humanistic care thought advocated by "the Belt and Road" Initiative.

Fourthly, the international situation has changed dramatically, the European debt crisis, the Brexit, the rise of the right-wing forces, and the right-wing parties hold hostile attitude to immigrants, refugees and the poor population, and oppose the sharing of refugee costs and offering relief assistance.

Trump's "US First" Strategy implemented after his taking office has accused developing countries of depriving Americans of jobs. The US government has created the longest lock-up record in history for the construction of the border wall. The United States has withdrawn from many international organizations and de-globalization is tending to rise as a result.

Fifthly, the historic achievements of the Chinese economy have made the United States feel more threats than opportunities. In order to maintain its status in international division of labor, the United States is afraid that its exports of goods will be impacted after China's technological progress, and consequently launches the historically largest trade friction with China to impose technical blockade. Trump administration has announced an increase in tariffs on China's MYM200 billion list of goods from 10% to 25%, and threatens to impose tariffs on the remaining MYM300 billion in product listings, all indications prove that the U. S. has serious unilateralism in curbing China's development, and international trade conflicts have caused a negative impact on "the Belt and Road" Initiative.

2. The principle of "the Belt and Road" in the field of financial globalization innovation

First of all, we must change the traditional exploitation thinking based on the principle of shared development. The relationship between financial capital and industrial development is mutually beneficial, not predatory. In the process of financial support, we must achieve complementary advantages and solve the problem of local shortage of funds. Therefore, China should promote the excessive domestic financial capital to support the infrastructure construction of countries along the route of "the Belt and Road", and drive the local people to share the fruits of development with the interflow of infrastructure construction. For example, the construction of hospitals, schools, highways and other facilities make local people enjoy better education, medical and living services. Another example, Huawei Corporation has launched extensive assistance to Pakistan and raise a development fund in the local area to train technical talents and improve local people's living standards in Pakistan.

Secondly, use socialist ideology to guide the development of financial globalization, improve the poverty situation in countries along the route of "the Belt and Road", and promote the implementation of targeted poverty alleviation. In Marx's high school graduation thesis *Consideration of Youth in Choosing a Career*, he pointed out that careers in the capitalist world were in conflict with each other because of people's competition for job opportunities. He proposed that one kind of interest should not eliminate another, and human beings should work for others' happiness and perfection. The financial globalization promoted by "the Belt and Road" is based on the ideology that financial capital must work for the happiness of mankind but not to absorb labor. Therefore, it is necessary to give financial capital vitality and practically apply financial support to life improvement and poverty alleviation, science and technology innovation and education and culture and other fields. The reason why China provides financial support to developing countries is to narrow the gap between the rich and the poor, not for financial plunder and international exploitation. This is based on the spirit of sharing. For example, China has launched extensive assistance to Nepal. The Foundation for Poverty Alleviation has sent schoolbags to local students to improve their studying conditions, provide students with feeding programs and offer scholarships. The local poverty alleviation campaign launched and implemented by Chinese government set the students free from hunger and no longer get fainting in the classroom.

Thirdly, help the countries along the route of "the Belt and Road" to achieve independence, change the situation of capital expansion in the past, support local financial capital to freely participate in competition, let funds flow into the enterprises that need development most in the local area and support their technological innovation and industrial expansion. For example, Chinese companies in Pakistan have not only opened up markets, but also established localized enterprises in the local area to support their technology research and development. At the same time, they also set up research and development institutions such as laboratories and science parks to accelerate the construction of science and technology cooperation bases, support technology transfer and foster innovation and entrepreneurship platform, strive to support rather than crack down local industries.

Fourthly, innovative ways of financial globalization, such as changing the way of financial capital expansion, financial globalization in developed countries is especially to plunder industrial workers with financial capital, deprive workers' job opportunities through the use of new machines, and the benefits of machine innovation is owned by the capitalists. The financial globalization promoted by "the Belt and Road" Initiative makes that labor and management side share the ownership in the process of technological innovation, and workers can also enjoy rights and interests after updating the machinery and equipment. Innovate financial sharing methods and break the monopoly of capital, such as establishing a credit development system, increasing the credit sharing quota, enabling the poor to obtain development capital at the start-up period, and changing the shortcomings of financial capital only flowing to large enterprises.

3. Recommendations for the innovation in the field of financial globalization of "the Belt and Road"

Firstly, in the process of "the Belt and Road" construction, we will vigorously spread and share knowledge and technology. Promote China's advanced culture and technology to countries along the route to promote industrial upgrading and technological progress in these countries and regions. Under the traditional financial globalization, the capital of developed countries has mastered the most advanced technology, while technological progress has continuously increased the capital intensity, consequently the more developed technology, the more rapid increase in accumulation. Due to the confidentiality of patented technologies, very few technologies can be transferred and introduced into developing countries, resulting in the slow industrial upgrading in developing countries. To promote the innovative financial globalization on "the Belt and Road", we should break the inequality of capital monopoly technology by accelerating the spread of science, knowledge and technology, to help various developing countries realize the development of independent intellectual property rights and technology, and enhance the competitiveness of enterprises, thereby contributing to enterprises obtain funds at lower financing costs and further expand their scale to achieve leapfrog development. To improve the economic development level and the people's happiness index of countries along the route of "the Belt and Road", it is necessary to increase cultural exchanges and knowledge sharing in order to promote openness. It is required to popularize knowledge and technology through the transfer of intellectual property rights, the establishment of skills training institutions, the establishment of schools and other means. Meanwhile we should cultivate innovative talents to achieve innovative driving.

Secondly, "the Belt and Road" construction is combined with financial innovation. Make innovation in the application of big data and blockchain and other technologies, build a new financial platform, decentralize in structure, governance and logic, break the monopoly of capitalist developed countries on the global market, and form a consensus mechanism in rulemaking. The US-led financial globalization is in fact the financial power and oligarchy manipulating the global financial market. The most wonderful performance of Michael Douglas in Wall Street reveals the greedness of capital. Gege straightly put forwards the suggestion that the United States should maintain its top power status. Today, developed countries in Europe and the United States use their financial power to take advantage of rulemaking rights, monopoly rights, and information priorities in international capital markets to grab the wealth of developing countries. Therefore, it is necessary to construct a decentralized new financial system to achieve equality of financial power and promote financial freedom.

With RMB as the support, WeChat and Alipay financial platforms as carriers, China has realized quick settlement of small amount. On the one hand, China has solved the problem of RMB exchange and constructed a network for foreign currency exchange. The US dollar as the Asian trading currency has a dominant position in "the Belt and Road". China should increase the free exchange of RMB and build a RMB payment system in countries along the route of "the Belt and Road". On the other hand, in the principle of safe and convenient, easy to use, instant transfer and low cost, China has provided fast cross-border payment and exchange support for countries along the route of "the Belt and Road". Currently, traditional financial settlement methods such as wire transfer, mail transfer and draft remittance can no longer satisfy the requirement of the increasing frequency of cross-border SMEs' capital exchanges and the increasingly frequent exchanges in the context of the construction of "the Belt and Road". Therefore, it is necessary to develop Internet-based cross-border payments and reduce barriers to capital flow. We should promote Internet financial innovation with reference to successful experiences such as WeChat and Alipay, develop convenient financial support services in countries along the route of "The Belt and Road", provide microfinance and credit support, promote financial sharing, and use the long-tail effect of the Internet to create accurate services in finance, tilting towards the popularization in consumption, payment, cloud sharing and many other fields.

Thirdly, guarantee measures of "the Belt and Road" innovation in the field of financial globalization. We will never follow the practice of old capitalist developed countries to transfer high-energy, high-pollution, and ecologically-destructive industries to developing countries. China is the world's largest industrial manufacturing country and a world factory, but overcapacity has become a core issue that constrains economic development in recent years. At the same time, countries along the route of "the Belt and Road" are seriously insufficient in the industrial production capacity, which has resulted in effective demand incapable of being satisfied at all. Therefore, China must actively provide products and services to these countries and use financial support to help these countries build their own industries. Use big data and artificial intelligence to combat with financial crimes, avoid negative effects in the development of financial globalization, and create a friendly environment for financial globalization. At the same time, it is also able to establish a comprehensive credit evaluation system through big data and artificial intelligence, increase financial support for the poor group and promote the development of microfinance. Innovative financial globalization is an effective means to resolve the current problem in the capitalist social structure. Therefore, it is necessary to promote shared finance and other means to change the monopoly of capitalists on global financial capital, so that small capital and distributed finance can play a greater role in financial globalization. Through the construction of "the Belt and Road", financial capital is enabled to flow into the economically disadvantaged areas and substantial economy, changing the traditional situation in which financial flows deviate from the poor group. For example, in African countries, the local residents urgently need financial support to improve their current education, living and working conditions. The financial support promoted by "the Belt and Road" should give full play to the role of small capital, and establish student loans and small business start-up fund in these countries. Services such as funds and sickness insurance allow surplus capital to help African people, rather than staying in banks or swallowing short-term profits in the capital market.

V. Conclusions and prospects

We should pursue a just cause for common good. Significant innovations brought about by "the Belt and Road" to the field of financial globalization have changed the situation that the capitalists monopolized the financial market in the past, and truly allowed financial innovation to serve developing countries with undeveloped infrastructure, backward education and weak capabilities in science and technology and are conducive to the creation of a long-term shared financial order and system. Financial globalization is an ambitious subject. The reason why the author chose this subject is to follow President Xi Jinping's instruction "only by setting great goals can we achieve great success. " In the spirit of motherland and global view, the author carried out the research on the innovations brought by "the Belt and Road" in the field of financial globalization. Due to the limitation of the author's knowledge reserve and basic economy knowledge, the expression may be somewhat inappropriate, but the author still firmly believe that under the grand blueprint of "the Belt and Road" Initiative, a new global financial system will be established.

On the Important Role of Yiwu Small Commodities Wholesale Market in the Construction of "the Belt and Road"

Song Zhenghan[①]

Abstract: Yiwu is a county-level city in China's south Zhejiang Province. As a county-level city that opened the road to getting rich from peddling "rattle-drum" and explored a big market with the original mode "chicken-feather-for-sugar", Yiwu Small Commodity Market has been recognized by the world as "the ocean of small commodities, the paradise of shoppers". As one of the important bases participating in the construction of "the Belt and Road", Yiwu is an important platform for Chinese goods to enter the world and world goods to enter China. The successful case of Yiwu explains the great concept of promoting "congeniality of people's aspirations" through "smooth trade cooperation".

Key words: "The Belt and Road"　Yiwu Small Commodities Wholesale Market　Sino-Euro Railway Passenger Transportation　international trade

Ⅰ. Introduction

In September and October 2013, Chinese President Xi Jinping made an initiative to jointly build "the Silk Road Economic Belt" and "the 21st Century Maritime Silk Road" during his visits to Kazakhstan and Indonesia. For more than five years, "the Belt and Road" Initiative, which is based on policy communication, facility connection, smooth trade, financial communication and congeniality of people's aspirations, is interpreting and deducting the script for

---

[①]　Song Zhenghan, male, a student in Grade 3 at Huizhen Academy in Ningbo, Zhejiang Province.

Chinese-style peace construction and development around the world. "The Belt and Road" construction involves about 4. 4 billion people in the countries along the route, accounting for 63% of the global population. The total economic output of the countries along the route is about 21 trillion US dollars, accounting for 29% of the global economy.

Zhejiang Province has been boasting of well-developed economy, especially the private economy has been developing rapidly. The Yiwu Small Commodity Wholesale Market has become the world's largest commodity market. "Creating something out of nothing, pooling all sorts of conceivable fantasies, touching a stone and turning it into gold", this is the evaluation of Yiwu given by the then secretary of the CPC Zhejiang Provincial Committee. Yiwu has trade relations with many countries and regions in the world, which reflects the smooth flow of trade along "the Belt and Road" and promotes the congeniality of people's aspirations. This paper analyzes the case of Yiwu Small Commodities Wholesale Market participating in the construction of "the Belt and Road" and explores how Chinese enterprises can play a better role in the construction of "the Belt and Road".

II . Overview and characteristics of Yiwu Small Commodity Wholesale Market

40 years ago, Yiwu launched an ice-breaking assault into market economy, starting from the small commodities market to applying for commercial license with the government official seal for permission and recognition, and then officially opening up to meet the needs of the people. One of the world's largest small commodity wholesale markets has been leading the industry up to now. With the implementation of international trade comprehensive reform pilot and the proposal and accelerated construction of national "the Belt and Road" Initiative, Yiwu Small Commodity Wholesale Market is even more strenuous and stands proud of the global small commodity trade.

Today, Yiwu Small Commodity Wholesale Market has a large-scale business area of 5. 5 million square meters which is equivalent 12 times of the territorial area of Vatican State of Europe. It has already surpassed the Rotterdam market in the Netherlands, which is recorded by the Guinness World Record and is called the world's first market by westerners. Yiwu Small Commodity Wholesale Market employs 238, 000 licensed employees and sells 1. 8 million tons of small commodities produced by more than 200, 000 companies. It is called "the ocean of small commodities, the paradise of shoppers" . "If you stay in front of each business booth in Yiwu Small Commodity Wholesale Market for 3 minutes, it takes you one and a half years to completely stroll around the market by 8 hours per day. " Shi Zhangyue, the person in charge of *Local Records of Yiwu*, said.

Deserving its reputation in the past, ascending to a higher level at present, Yiwu Small Commodity Wholesale Market is totally different from the internationally renowned small commodities wholesale market confirmed in the report titled *China Figures Shocking the World* jointly issued by the world's authoritative institutions such as the United Nations, the World Bank and Morgan Stanley in 2005. It is also no longer confined to the judgement and description given by a world renowned economist, "Yiwu is the ideal place for businessmen. In this vast wholesale empire, you can find almost any daily consumer goods you can name" . In addition, you can also find any consumer goods that cannot be named. It not only becomes the hub of global consumer goods trade owing to its business scale surpassing any consumer goods market in New York, Dubai, Paris, London, Hong Kong, Milan, Tokyo and Los Angeles which are known as the world's top 8 largest shopping paradise cities, but also unveil itself before the world by carrying out the new path of "mass entrepreneurship and innovation" assuming the new responsibility for helping the underdeveloped regions to get rid of poverty, and adopting new strategies for breaking through trade barriers and implementing more open and free market rules, employing the new measures to promote congeniality of people's aspirations and expand economic ties among various countries, and fulfilling the new mission of sharing wealth and pressing forward to the road to affluence and civilization.

1. Development history of Yiwu Small Commodity Wholesale Market

When President Xi Jinping served as the secretary of the CPC Zhejiang Provincial Committee, he made investigation in Yiwu for ten times. He once said: "Yiwu City is getting flourishing relying on commerce development… Yiwu is a typical example of county economic development in Zhejiang Province since the reform and opening up, and it is also a microcosm of the current economic and social development of Zhejiange Province."

In history, Yiwu was originally a place with a large population with relatively little arable land. The areas only relying on grain production only have poorly harvested crops due to excessive acidity in the soil. Therefore, local farmers had to use chicken feathers as fertilizer to improve soil quality. However, due to the limited amount of chicken feathers in local area, the farmers used the local brown sugar to make sugar cakes so as to peddle and exchange sugar cakes with chicken feathers in surrounding villages and townships. This group engaged in the barter business is called "knocking-sugar pedlar". This history can be traced back to the late Ming and early Qing Dynasties. As time went on, the sugar-carrying pole of the "knocking-sugar pedlar" gradually increased the daily necessities such as needlework, hairpins, handkerchiefs and headscarves.

Feng Aiqian, one of the first batch operators of the Yiwu Small Commodity Wholesale Market, described the situation when the market was established, "my family was very poor, my mother and I, and my five children lived together. My mother washed clothes for others to earn money. I could only earn 2 work points a day which is equal to 4 cents. Life at that time had no guarantee available. I could not support my family and had to appeal to the leader's mercy at the time for running business. In 1978, running business was regarded as engaging in capitalism. It was speculative. Business operators and pedlars will be arrested to be imprisoned. We could only fight with market managers and run away once seeing them. " Later, the leaders at that time were also under tremendous pressure to acquiesce in her stall business. In the end, she became a veteran of the Yiwu Small Commodity Wholesale Market.

In 1980, the local government began to reinstate the registration permit for "feather-for-sugar" and issued more than 7, 000 business licenses. Some sugar-changers specialized in purchasing small commodities and trafficking on a long distance, while some people spontaneously explore small commodities producing and trade at the market. As a result, the small commodity market has gradually taken into being.

In September 1982, the Yiwu County Government officially opened the small store market in Choucheng Town and invested 9, 000 yuan in setting up 700 stalls with cement pavement for the open-air market. The turnover of the small commodity market reached 3. 92 million yuan in this year.

In 1984, the CPC Yiwu County Committee and the County Government put forward the policy of "flourishing the county by promoting commerce", relaxing the enterprise approval policy, and simplifying the registration procedures. As a result, Yiwu County set off a boom in running business and factories. At the end of the year, the number of self-employed households exceeded 10, 000, and the turnover of the small commodity market reached 23. 21 million yuan.

However, the rising number of booths also brings problems such as poor city appearance and traffic congestion. In order to solve these problems, in 1984, the Yiwu County Government decided to build a dedicated small commodity market, further improve the infrastructure and nurture the small commodity market on the original basis. In 1986, the turnover of Yiwu Small Commodity Wholesale Market exceeded 100 million yuan, not only benefiting the surrounding counties and cities arround Zhejiang Province, but also outside the province. In 1986, the third-generation Yiwu Small Commodity Wholesale Market was completed and the number of fixed booth was expanded to 4, 096. The new market is deployed with management and service buildings covering commercial services, industry and commerce registration, taxation, post and telecommunications and finance services. Later, after several times of expansion and reconstruction, by the end of 1990, the third-generation small commodity market had become the national largest wholesale market for small commodities with 8, 503 fixed booths and more than 1, 500 temporary booths.

In 1991, the turnover of Yiwu Small Commodity Wholesale Market exceeded 1 billion yuan for the first time. In 1993, Yiwu Small Commodity Wholesale Market embarked on the development path of the shareholding system and established Zhejiang China Commodities City Group Co. , Ltd. The booth of the fourth generation market of China Commodity City has also increased to more than 23, 000. In the 21st century, Yiwu Small Commodity Wholesale Market embarked on the road of international development and completed the fifth-generation professional market—China Yiwu International Trade City.

The market in Yiwu, after five times of frog-leaping development, has thoroughly remolded itself. Yiwu commerce and trade industry has been gradually stabilized and expanded, and has already embarked on a new path—Yiwu Mode. This mode is spreading outward: Yiwu has established more than 30 markets in more than 20 provinces and cities nationwide, and established five sub-markets in countries such as South Africa and Ukraine; has owned 120, 000 Yiwu traders, 50, 000 of them are distributed throughout the country. ①

2. Enterprise structure and talent policy of Yiwu Small Commodity Wholesale Market

For many merchants and manufacturers in Yiwu market, the one who has more innovative ability can attract more customers and take the lead in occupying the market. In the current Yiwu market, new products are launched almost every week and every day, and the speed of new products upgrading is the fastest in the small commodities field in the world.

The reason for the rapid updating of Yiwu market products lies in the continuous efforts of the CPC Yiwu Municipal Party Committee and Municipal Gov-

---

① 吴献华 . 世界商贸之都[J] . 人民画报 · 2017 义乌特刊, 2017: 10-14.

ernment on strengthening policy, talent introduction, platform and excellent service, thus creating a large number of flexible enterprises, R&D teams and various types that are close to the market demand. In recent years, Yiwu Municipal Government has launched "Yiwu Talents" program, providing up to 50 million yuan as incentives for entrepreneurial and innovative talents of the "Yiwu Talents" program; a grant of up to 1 million yuan may be granted for holding entrepreneurial competitions, entrepreneurial salons, forums and other activities; personal discounted loan up to 300,000 yuan can be granted for the entrepreneur lack of start-up funds. At the same time, this program also set up 2 million yuan as talent housing subsidies and offers the priority enrollment policy for children of the talents. So far, the city has attracted 259,000 talents including 46 experts from national and provincial "Thousand Talents" and 14 academicians of flexible introduction. A large number of professional design and development teams and excellent technological and innovative industrial enterprises have emerged in Yiwu. At present, Yiwu has 98 provincial-level science and technology enterprises, 31 provincial-level R&D centers and 49 state-level high-tech enterprises. Yiwu Municipal Government has invested nearly 300 million yuan in scientific and technological innovation every year, which is at the forefront of all counties and cities in Zhejiang Province. Zhejiang Yingtelai Optoelectronics Technology Co. , Ltd. , located in Yiwu Industrial Park, is an enterprise integrating R&D, production and sales of LED products. The company invests nearly 10 million yuan in innovation every year and has applied for 97 patents of various types. It is rated as a scientific and technological enterprise in Zhejiang Province and a national high-tech enterprise. It is one of the few companies in China that has independent research and development and manufacturing of lighting and display.[1]At the same time, through docking with emerging industries, creating new business models, implementing brand diversification and other means, Yiwu Municipal Government established industrial design, creative culture, e-commerce training and other car-

---

① 施章岳. 义乌市场的新名片——义乌国际商贸城现状调查[J].中国房地产, 2009.

riers around the market so as to build more employment platforms for entrepreneurs.

3. Development status of Yiwu Small Wholesale Commodity Market

In recent years, when the Internet brings huge information flow, business opportunities and so on, Yiwu Small Commodity Wholesale Market does not reject or exclude, but actively cater to the development trend of the times, on the basis of high quality and a full range of market infrastructure, to build e-commerce all-domain development pattern, making the online commodity market and tangible entity small commodity market coexist peacefully, achieving integration development, providing new employment opportunities for business innovators. Their main practice is as follows: build a complete e-commerce industry platform. Yiwu now has 113 Taobao Villages, 9 Taobao Towns and 30 e-commerce parks. The number of Taobao Villages ranks the first in the country, the number of Taobao Town accounts for 11. 5% of the province, and the e-commerce park has a construction area of over 2 million square meters. Yiwu has formed a platform system integrating e-commerce park-professional market-professional buildings-demonstration village. There are more than 200 online shops in the city, nearly 1, 000 photographers and nearly 10 photography institutes with an area of more than 500 square meters. Qingyanliu Village under the jurisdiction of Jiangdong Street is only 6 kilometers from Yiwu Small Commodity Wholesale Market and originally owns less than 2, 000 people, but this small place gathered entrepreneurs from all over the country. They opened online stores, set up companies, and established a public e-commerce platform represented by Taobao. In 2015, the number of new villagers exceeded 15, 000, and more than 3, 200 online stores were opened with sales of 4. 5 billion yuan. In 2016, the number of online stores increased to 3, 500, with the sales amount of 5 billion yuan. In 2017, the number of new villagers reached more than 25, 000, and there were more than 4, 000 online stores. The sales amount exceeded 6 billion yuan and were called "China's First Village of Taobao" by

Premier Li Keqiang. Since 2014, Yiwu has been ranked the first in the "China E-commerce Top 100 Counties" for four consecutive years. In order to allow more self-employed entrepreneurs and e-commerce companies to settle down, Yiwu City plans to set up 50 million yuan each year to set up e-commerce special funds, set up e-commerce industry guidance funds with financial funds of not less than 100 million yuan, and establish e-commerce loan risks compensation mechanisms, and give policy priorities in land, finance, taxation, housing, and schooling for children. Now, in Yiwu, you can achieve non-breakpoint e-commerce and zero cost entrepreneurship. Even a college student who just graduated can start a business in Yiwu with just one mobile phone.

Yiwu took the lead to set up a large platform of Yiwu E-commerce Market with Zhejiang Yiwu E-Commerce Co., Ltd. ("Yiwu Purchase") under the China(Yiwu) Mall Group as the core, which made the traditional small commodity professional market become the main supplier of goods for national online stores, successfully helping the nationwide online business to realize entrepreneurship and innovation. Today, 75,000 shops in Yiwu Market have settled in the "Yiwu Purchase" platform. At the same time, through active initiative and multi-party launch, they have docked with Alibaba, Amazon, Jingdong Mall, Dunhuang Network and other well-known domestic third-party platforms to make Yiwu E-commerce accounts reach as many as 278,000 households, with the density of domestic trade network ranking the highest in the country, and the density of foreign trade network holding the nationwide place only second to Shenzhen. The e-commerce transaction volume of Yiwu Small Commodity Wholesale Market has thereby jumped sharply every year. From 2015 to 2017, it reached 151.1 billion yuan, 177 billion yuan and 222 billion yuan respectively. ①

---

① 施章岳. 义乌市场的新名片——义乌国际商贸城现状调查[J].中国房地产, 2009.

III. The role of Yiwu Small Commodities Wholesale Market in "the Belt and Road"

1. Yiwu small commodities sold all over the world, fully embodying "trade smoothness"

Yiwu launched ice-breaking assault to market economy 40 years ago, and thus was able to lead the economic tide for 40 years. In 2011, appointed as the national strategy—international trade comprehensive reform pilot, Yiwu once again shouldered the banner of reform. Now, because of the country's "the Belt and Road" Initiative, Yiwu once again stood at a new starting point.

As a county-level city that opened the road to getting rich from peddling "rattle-drum" and explored a big market with the original mode "chicken-feather-for-sugar", Yiwu is also called the starting point of the new Silk Road because Yiwu has an unparalleled advantage in the participation in the construction of "the Belt and Road". Yiwu is an important platform for Chinese goods to enter the world and world goods to enter China. It has more than 70, 000 shops and more than 1. 8 million kinds of goods. The daily customer flow has reached more than 210, 000 person-times, and the products are exported to more than 210 countries and regions. The annual exported standard container is more than 770, 000. Among them, Yiwu is the world's largest distribution center for Christmas supplies, and two-thirds of the world's Christmas items are produced in Yiwu. According to statistical data from Yiwu Customs, Yiwu exports Christmas supplies to nearly 200 countries and regions around the world. Christmas has almost become the Christmas of the Chinese.

(1) The China-Europe Railway opened, and goods circulation much easier

In history, the ancient commercial road across the Eurasian is known as the "Silk Road" because of the long-term dominant possession of silk from China, camel squad is the main means of transportation active on the Silk Road. Today, the roar of the train galloping has replaced the sound of camel bells that have been ringing for millennia.

On November 18, 2014, the longest freight train in the world, YTO Express, "Yiwu-Xinjiang-Europe" cargo train was opened: One end is connected to Yiwu, Zhejiang, the world's largest distribution center for small commodities; the other end is connected to Madrid, Spain, the largest distribution center for small commodities in Europe. The first train of "YTO Express", which is loaded with 82 Yiwu small commodity containers, departed from Yiwu and traveled for 13,052 kilometers over 21 days and finally reached the Spanish capital Madrid.

A young man in his thirties from a private enterprise took the initiative to participate in "the Belt and Road" construction through an international railway line, and took the footsteps of global economic integration. Let us see how he accomplished that.

Feng Xubin was born in 1979. His discourse reveals his stability and wisdom that a "successful 40-year-old man" should have. Although young, Feng Xubin has a wealth of experience in business and has long been aiming at the investment on international logistics industry. In 2010, Feng Xubin was preparing to set up Sino-European Freight Train Company, which was officially approved in 2012. However, it is not a business that ordinary people dare to think to operate railway freight train by linking Yiwu with Europe. Moreover, the railway freight train has to pass through so many countries and customs and even have to change their rails in the halfway. The difficulty in the coordination work can be imagined. Feng Xubin had the idea of giving up after touching the wall for several times. In 2013, when President Xi Jinping gave a speech at the Nazarbayev University in Kazakhstan, he proposed the initiative to build the "Silk Road Economic Belt". Feng Xubin's fighting spirit was once again ignited. He took a step-by-step approach, first striving to open the freight train to five Central Asian countries, and then to open the Sino-European freight train.

On January 20, 2014, the train "Yiwu-five-Central-Asian-countries" which started from Yiwu and headed for Kazakhstan, Uzbekistan, Kyrgyzstan, Turkmenistan and Tajikistan was officially launched. The news quickly spread to the Chinese merchant community in Madrid, Spain, they called Feng Xubin, hoping to extend the terminal to Madrid, Spain. However, it is difficult for ordinary people to imagine opening the Sino-European freight train under the operation of private enterprise.

Sino-European freight train covers the total distance of 13, 052 kilometers, entering Kazakhstan through Xinjiang, and then passing Russia, Belarus, Poland, Germany, France, and finally running to the destination Madrid, Spain. It crosses 7 countries and almost runs through the whole Europe.

Sino-European freight train is required to not only run across the cold zone in Russia, but also pass through 6 times of customs clearances and 3 times of rail change. It is not only time-consuming but also costs a great deal of labor forces, and as long as the coordination of a certain link is not in place, the train will not be able to operate normally. To this end, Feng Xubin organized a team of more than 30 people handling public relations and coordination with government, railways, customs and other related departments of involved countries. In 2014, excluding international flights, he flew for 106 times for this business covering more than 130, 000 kilometers.

In order to operate smoothly, Sino-European freight train must have strong assembly capabilities and partners, otherwise transportation costs and normal operations will be affected. For the same distance, the traditional marine shipping needs 30−50 days, the railway freight needs 12−14 days but the price is 2−3 times that of the marine shipping. In addition, there are some losses in the rail changing and custom clearance on the halfway, some owners prefer to the slow marine shipping but not to take the railway freight. Feng Xubin specifically selected two young men as their partners. One is Zhou Xufeng, chairman of Zhejiang Mengde Import Co. , Ltd. , and the other is Lin Huihuan, chairman of COSCO International Freight Forwarding Co. , Ltd. , who has been in Yiwu for many years. Three young people are like-minded, with division of labor and cooperation, Feng Xubin was responsible for operations, Zhou Xufeng for cargo arranging for the train returning from Span and arranging Yiwu small commodities to Spain.

As the only private freight line in China, at the beginning of the freight line operation, the customers refused to offer reasonable price but propose very demanding conditions, and any risks and responsibilities that occur on the way must be borne by the operator. The small commodities that were sent from Yiwu to Spain are resistant to freezing, but the olive oil and wine on the return train were all packaged in glass bottles, which might freeze at low temperature. Therefore, the return train was configured with two thermostatic large cabinets and four standard containers. Although the cost increased, the safety of the goods could be guaranteed; thereby such integrity business attitude gradually won the trust and reasonable price from customers.

After the opening of "YTO Express", the Spanish overseas Chinese cheered and more than 40 traders negotiated cooperation with them and took the freight train. [1]

The opening and successful operation of "YTO Express" Sino-European freight train has endowed Yiwu with more connotations different from the past. Yiwu has thus become the starting point of the "Silk Road Economic Belt" and the bridgehead for goods of countries and regions along "the New Silk Road" entering China, as well as the main passage of onshore cargo of the Yangtze River Delta Economic Circle and the countries and regions along "the New Silk Road". At the same time, it is an important platform for China to achieve policy communication, road connectivity, smooth trade, currency circulation and congeniality of people's aspirations among countries along the Silk Road Economic Belt.

In 2011, Yiwu was approved as a pilot city for international trade comprehensive reform, and has become an important platform for Chinese goods to enter the world and world commodities to enter China. At present, Yiwu Small Commodity Wholesale Market has overseas sub-markets or distribution centers in 10 countries and regions such as Thailand, United Arab Emirates, Russia and

---

① 施章岳, 朱庆平. 义乌商帮[M] .杭州: 浙江大学出版社, 2018: 267-269.

Romania.

Compared with other Sino-European freight trains, "YTO Express" that runs through "the Silk Road Economic Belt" has created a few firsts: It covers a total length of 13,052 kilometers, which is 1,850 kilometers longer than the "SMO Express". It is the longest transportation route among all the train lines in Sino-European freight train. "YTO Express" passes through the largest number of countries, a total of seven, almost running across the whole Europe. It is also the overseas railway line that has the most frequent rail changes. Other Sino-European freight trains need to change rail for twice respectively in Kazakhstan and Poland. In addition, "YTO Express" train still need to change the rail for the third time at the border of France and Spain. This is an important measure for China to accelerate the construction of the "Silk Road Economic Belt" and to open up the "Golden Passage" to the west.

On September 26, 2014, at the meeting between the leaders of China and Spain, President Xi Jinping said that the Sino-European freight trains have a good momentum of development. "YTO Express" railway plan starts from Yiwu, Zhejiang, and arrives at the end of Madrid via Xinjiang. China welcomes the Spanish businessmen to actively participate in construction and operation and jointly improve the level of economic and trade cooperation between the two countries.

On June 28, 2015, Sino-European freight train departed from Yiwu and first stopped in Warsaw, Germany, Duisburg and Paris, France and other important cities along the route, and realized multi-site loading and unloading. This means that Sino-European freight train can serve more and more customers and sources of supply. With the realization of multi-site docking, the goods transported by "YTO Express" are also transformed from Yiwu small commodities into electronic products, brand clothing, high-grade fabrics and other products with higher value of supply sources. It has attracted some new merchants from Shanghai, Hangzhou, Jiaxing, Huzhou and Shaoxing to choose "YTO Express" trains as an important way of freight transportation.

As of August 2016, by bringing daily necessities, hardware, textiles, mobile phone accessories and other goods from small commodity market, returning Spain's wine, wood floor, juice, olive oil and other goods, "YTO Express" train has been traveling for 72 times, with a total of transportation of 5, 176 standard containers, having achieved the normal operation every week. [①]

Yiwu-Central Asia-Europe International Intermodal Railway Transportation Logistics Channel has improved the convenience of Central Asia and European countries purchasing goods from Yiwu, attracting more customers from Central Asia and Europe, and providing a safe, convenient, all-weather, high-traffic green channel for Yiwu import and export commodities. The foreign bussinesmen, looking for business opportunities in China, gave high praise to the diversity of commodities in Yiwu small commodity market and the global trade. They paid this special visit to Yiwu to investigate the market, look for business opportunities and also give a high evaluation of the diversity of Yiwu commodity market and the globalization of trade.

(2)Expand overseas markets and engage global business

Yiwu has a mantra: "Revolutionary people, conquering the world; intellectual, cognizing the world; businessman, winning the world. " This vividly shows the mind of Yiwu businessmen "concerning the world". In the eyes of Yiwu businessmen, where is the market, where is the "world" they are exploring. Business has neither national boundaries nor ethnic differences. As long as there are people, there will be business opportunities. When they have achieved little success in the country, they will resolutely cross the ocean and explore the world.

The Yiwu market model is a pioneering work of Yiwu people. Yiwu merchants not only promoted the market concept and model brand to all parts of China by virtue of the brand advantage of the market, but also established the market in some countries and regions overseas. South Africa, South Korea, Russia, Sweden, Vietnam, the United States, Chile, Colombia, the United Arab

---

① 吴献华. 世界商贸之都[J].人民画报· 2017 义乌特刊, 2017: 10~14.

Emirates, Poland and other places have left the mark of Yiwu businessmen establishing market.

Yiwu businessman Zhao Xianwen has been in business for many years. In 1991, he began to explore the international market and send his products to Kuala Lumpur International Expo in Malaysia. In 1992, he went to Ho Chi Minh City, Vietnam to do business. In 1998, he turned his attention to Africa. He has visited many countries in Africa for several times. During his visit to Nigeria, he happened to encountered power outage for several times. He immediately found the business opportunity and decided to launch a power generation equipment factory in the country. Later, he found that Nigeria is the most populous country in Africa. There are very scarce products of daily use. He set up Yifa Nigeria Co. , Ltd. At the same time, drawing on the successful experience of the development of Yiwu market, he established Nigerian China Mall and other projects, and thereby won the praise and acceptance of Nigerian President Obasanjo. Later, Zhao Xianwen participated in the World Expo held by the Republic of South Africa. He found that South Africa has relatively developed economy. The largest city, Johannesburg, is known as "South Africa's Shanghai". Johannesburg has convenient transportation but is restricted by extremely weak industrial base, and the daily-use products are basically imported. Goods that sold 1 yuan in China can be generally sold for 1 US dollar in Johannesburg. China's home appliances, textiles, footwear and other products are cheap and fine and have unlimited business opportunities in this region. Therefore, Zhao Xianwen decided to establish the "Gate of China" China Commodity Wholesale & Retail Center in Johannesburg. With the strong support of the South African government and the Chinese government, in April 1999, Zhao Xianwen received the approval document from the State Economic and Trade Commission and became the first person running large-scale overseas market. [1]

Born in 1970, Wang Fangmao once ran a market stall, invested in a color

---

[1]　施章岳, 朱庆平. 义乌商帮[M]. 杭州: 浙江大学出版社, 2018: 267-269.

printing factory in Shanghai, and contracted a number of media agency rights, operated audio and video products, and also founded logistics companies, co-hosted markets and cross-border e-commerce companies. He is chairman of Yilei Company. He pointed out that "the role of overseas warehouses should not be underestimated in overseas cargo collection and control of goods. If a cross-border e-commerce enterprise has no overseas warehouse, the goods supply and business operation cannot be accomplished. He maintained that overseas warehouses is a new trend in the development of cross-border e-commerce, and has gradually become more and more important in the cross-border e-commerce industry competition in China.

In 2012, Wang Fangmao integrated a number of logistics companies, co-founded Yilian Logistics Co., Ltd., and integrated the containers scattered in various freight forwarding logistics enterprises to form a large quantity, so as to realize the maximum preferential freight prices for Yiwu enterprises. He also co-operated with many well-known international companies and obtained primary agent power.

Initially, cross-border e-commerce sellers were dealing small commodities with low prices and low gross profit under the fierce market competition. Wang Fangmao found that if an overseas warehouse was built, it could not only hedge the high logistics costs, but also engage bilateral trade. With overseas warehouses, the seller's product categories can be expanded indefinitely. Some products have a long service life and are not classified as "fast consuming goods". However, these products have large market demand and are very suitable for overseas warehouse sales. Overseas warehouses have no special restrictions on products. Merchants could place orders in China and ship them from foreign warehouses. After removing multiple layers of intermediaries, profit margin can be greatly increased.

After the overseas warehouse is established, businessmen can exchange goods with the other party and thereby mutual trust can be strengthened. This way of barter is the copy of Yiwu "chicken-feather-for-sugar" and can avoid the risks from exchange rate. After painstaking exploration and setbacks, Wang Fangmao has established overseas warehouses in Australia, South Korea, the United Kingdom, the United States and other countries, enriching foreign products into the Yiwu market, and introducing Yiwu products abroad, so that foreigners can buy genuine Chinese products without leaving home. Through mutual benefit, the purpose of resource sharing is achieved. ①

At present, Yiwu cross-border e-commerce enterprises have initially formed overseas warehouse outlets all over the world, covering 22 regions in 13 countries including the United States, Australia, Germany, Spain and Russia. The service covers all parts of the world, especially and countries along "the Belt and Road" and "YTO Express". Yiwu has become the starting point of the new Silk Road. Yiwu merchants have also made vivid interpretations for the implementation of China's "the Belt and Road" Initiative .

(3) Yiwu small commodities promote the "congeniality of people's aspirations"

With the expansion of Yiwu International Trade City, the continuous improvement of foreign-related services as well as the deepening of international exchanges, Yiwu enjoyed higher and higher international reputation, and its "internationalization" business card has become more and more beautiful and charming. Yiwu's friends have been all over the world, and its "friend circle" has rapidly expanded. By the end of 2015, Yiwu City has successfully established "sister city" relationship with 24 cities from 18 countries.

Shi Zhangyue, person in charge of local records of Yiwu City, said: At present, Yiwu Small Commodity Whotesale Market not only attracts more than 1. 3 million entrepreneurs of 56 ethnic groups from 31 provinces and cities and including China Hong Kong, Macao and Taiwan, but also attracts businessmen and friends from all over the world. It has trade ties with more than 210 countries and regions in the world, and the number of overseas merchants who

---

① 施章岳, 朱庆平 . 义乌商帮[M] .杭州: 浙江大学出版社, 2018: 251−254.

have purchased from Yiwu every year has reached 550, 000 person times. By the end of 2017, the total number of foreign-funded entities in Yiwu reached 6, 068, including 2, 577 foreign-invested partnerships, the foreign-funded enterprises have 2, 355 representative offices in Yiwu, and 1, 874 foreign-funded companies. There are more than 15, 000 people in the world who often live in Yiwu. The Jimingshan Community in Jiangdong Street around the Commodity Market is home to more than 1, 100 foreign businessmen from 58 countries. There are only 500 native residents in Xitang Village in Futian Street, but there are more than 400 foreign businessmen from 28 countries and regions in the Middle East and West Asia, these communities and villages are known as the "United Nations Community" in Yiwu.

The business owners of Yiwu market know that they are not only dealing with small commodities but also cultural exchanges with foreigners. When a foreign businessman went to see the doctor and was asked to show the "birth certificate", or when he has experienced that some people jump the queue without seriously following "one meter red line" rule when handling business in bank, making him uneasy and unhappy. They understand the desire of foreign businessmen to have their own booths, their own housing and their children's schooling. They hope that the contradictions in trade transactions can be resolved through reasonable channels… and with the government's attention and assistance, Yiwu market operators from the perspective of humanization, can properly grasp the different ethnical psychology, different ways of thinking and different service needs of foreign businessmen. The open and inclusive broad mind of Yiwu Municipal CPC Committee, Yiwu Municipal Government and market managers not only has handled the first business license of individual industrial and commercial household for residents in Hong Kong, Macao and Taiwan of China, but also permits foreigners to apply for business licenses. Residents in Hong Kong, Macao and Taiwan and foreigners are permitted to buy a house with a mortgage loan, and their children can first enter language transition class. For difficulties in language communication in the neighborhood, there are many language translators in the community available for service. It is provided with freedom of religion, rich and colorful food and entertainment. There are more than 30 exotic streets around the market, bringing together food from all over the world. Even if there is a trade dispute, it can be solved through Yiwu Foreign-related Dispute Resolution Committee composed of businessmen from 15 countries from Asia, Africa and Latin America. Yiwu Municipal Government also stipulates that foreign businessmen can participate in the evaluation of advanced workers at the municipal level and can listen to the reports of the Municipal People's Congress and the Municipal Congress of CP-PCC. It is this kind of courtesy for foreign businessmen that Yiwu Small Commodity Wholesale Market has become a hot spot for entrepreneurial innovation chased by businessmen from all over the world. A businessman Sura from Senegal, has introduced more than 200 friends to Yiwu to do business in a year.

On June 5, 2014, President Xi Jinping said in his speech at the opening ceremony of the Sixth Ministerial Conference of the China-Arab Cooperation Forum, "In Yiwu, where Arab merchants gathered, there was a Jordanian businessman named Muhamnide who opened an authentic Arab restaurant. He brought the original Arabian dining culture to Yiwu, and also succeeded in the prosperity of Yiwu. He eventually married a Chinese girl and set his roots in China. An ordinary Arab young man integrates his dream of life into the Chinese dream of Chinese people pursuing happiness, persists in struggle, and interprets his brilliant life and also interprets the perfect combination of Chinese dream and Arab dream." Now, Muhammad lives happily in Yiwu with his Chinese wife and two children. The family runs a restaurant called "Flower" and a foreign trade company. Thousands of years ago, the Chinese traveled along the ancient Silk Road to the Middle East and Europe to seek business opportunities. Muhammad's ancestors witnessed it all. Today, there are tens of thousands of foreign businessmen like Muhammadd travel along the new Silk Road to its starting point Yiwu and settle down here. They live here, find wealth, even love, and realize their dreams.

Muhammad is one of the more than 4,000 Arab merchants residing in Yiwu. He said: "Having lived in Yiwu for so long, the biggest achievement is that I have met many friends from China and the Arab countries. My wife and two children can live happily in Yiwu. Now, Yiwu is my second hometown. In fact, the Chinese dream that President Xi proposed is also my dream. In the future, I will manage the restaurant and strive to establish branches in Guangzhou, Shanghai and Beijing. At the same time, my foreign trade company is in better operation, by which I exported Chinese products to Arab countries, striving to become a friendship ambassador between China and the Arab countries. " Muhammad is also a football fan. He organized Jordanese in Yiwu to set up a football team, holding football games with the local fans almost every week. [1]

Philip, 55 years old, was born in Mumbai, India, and his family has been doing entrepot trade in Dubai. In the 1990s, he went to Hong Kong to do business. At that time, most of the goods were purchased from Guangdong and sold to North America and the Middle East. In 2002, Philip heard at the Canton Fair that Yiwu has a complete range of small commodities and low prices. So he came to Yiwu to take a chance, and from then on, he turned his business focus to Yiwu, where he exported hundreds of containers of Yiwu small commodities every year. In 2010, Philip learned that the Import Pavilion of Yiwu International Trade City is inviting investment and has preferential policies. He did not hesitate to submit the application materials, saying that he would bring the best goods from India to China. In 2012, Philip successfully got his current business stall, so he moved his company headquarters from Hong Kong to Yiwu and established a wholly foreign-owned enterprise: Yiwu Piaishi Sanskrit Brother Trade Co. , Ltd. He said that Yiwu's policy is good and the market is prosperous, which is a very suitable place for international trade. At present, Philip's business is prosperous. In addition to bringing high quality Indian goods to China, Philip said that he still has a dream to promote Indian culture in

---

[1] 吴献华. 世界商贸之都[J].人民画报· 2017 义乌特刊, 2017: 10–14.

China, to provide cultural guides for tourists to India, to spread Indian culture, and to attract many Indian businessmen. Yiwu market has become a blessed land for Indian businessmen to start a business. [1]

Local city administrators said that there will be a large number of disputes arising from contract formation, delayed payment, product quality and other issues, many foreign businessmen come to seek help every year. In the past, we always appointed an interpreter to mediate between them. Due to the different language and culture, there were always "old disputes unresolved and new contradictions added". In 2013, Yiwu Municipal Judicial Bureau established Yiwu Foreign-related People's Mediation Committee and hired foreign mediators to participate in mediation of foreign-related disputes. There were 16 foreign mediators from 15 countries including Asia, Africa and Latin America. They are good at multi-language, familiar with China's national conditions, and understand the way of mediation. The first team of foreign mediators including Sura from Senegal, chairman of a trading company, who is also a nonvoting delegate of the People's Congress of Yiwu mastering four languages.

Pan Shufa, from Singapore; Ohmine from Sudan, is the general manager of a trading company, holding Ph. D of economics. They have been doing business in Yiwu for many years.

Foreign mediators participating in dispute mediation are good at empathy thinking, providing advice from the aspects of human nature, law, and reason, and formulate a collegiate plan to better open the deadlock and improve the success rate of mediation. Pan Shufa, a Singaporean businessman who has been in business for more than 10 years in Yiwu, has two days a month to go to the People's Mediation Committee of Yiwu Foreign-related Disputes to be on duty to participate in mediation of foreign trade disputes. Many disputes were settled under the mediation of foreign "senior uncle". Sura recalled that once a Sudanese businessman purchased a batch of products worth more than 3 million

---

[1] 吴献华. 世界商贸之都[J]. 人民画报 · 2017 义乌特刊, 2017: 66−67.

yuan in Yiwu, but later he lost contact. Many shop owners in Yiwu market failed to get the payment. After he learned it, he made a special trip to Sudan at his own expense. Through his personal connections in the local area, he tried every means to find the whereabouts of the other party and finally found the businessman himself and recovered the payment in full. The foreign mediators of the Foreign Affairs Commission are employed once every year, without remuneration, but everyone regards this job as a glorious mission in China. Diaro said, "I can participate in people's mediation work, and I can help so many people who do business in China like me." He hopes to learn the essence of Chinese people's mediation and bring it back to his home country.

As of 2016, Yiwu Foreign-related People's Mediation Committee has successfully mediated nearly 300 foreign-related disputes, with a mediation success rate of 96.7% and a total amount of 45, 261, 700 involved in dispute cases, having saved the economic loss 23, 369, 800 yuan for Chinese and foreign merchants. At present, Yiwu City also recruits outstanding foreign businessmen from the countries along "the Belt and Road" and the China-Europe freight train route to join the mediator team to serve the business development and communication.[①]

China-Europe freight train connects not only merchants and commodities, cities and markets, but also countless wealth, life, dreams and future that are related with people. It makes the ancient Chinese civilization constantly meet and collide with the world civilization, respect each other and mutually absorb cultural nutrition. With the increasing number of foreign businessmen, Chinese and foreign cultural exchanges have deepened. This environment has allowed an open and civilized society to form in Yiwu. People from all over the world live in harmony and enjoy the beautiful life of the big family of the world.

Ⅳ. Conclusion

The industrious nature, the tradition of doing business, the mentality of tol-

---

① 吴献华. 世界商贸之都[J].人民画报 · 2017 义乌特刊, 2017: 72-79.

erance, the spirit of innovation, and the courage of the world are characteristics of Yiwu people, which have fully catered to the development concept of "the Belt and Road". The successful case of Yiwu has given us a great inspiration. Through the smooth trade, we have promoted the congeniality of people's aspirations and the world commonwealth.

The small Yiwu, in the great initiative of practicing "the Belt and Road", plays a model role and makes unremitting efforts to realize the bright future of the community of human destiny.

In the process of surveying and collecting research materials, I have further understanding of Yiwu and am deeply inspired. As a native person of Zhejiang, I am proud of the achievements made in Yiwu. "The Belt and Road" is the vision of our country and also direct our future.

Financial Innovation under the Background of "the Belt and Road" Initiative:

A Case Study of the Silk Road Fund

Chen Siyu[1]

Abstract: As an investment institution specially established to serve "the Belt and Road" construction, the Silk Road Fund plays a great role in the implementation of "the Belt and Road" Initiative. Taking the Silk Road Fund as an example, this paper further explains the financial innovation under the background of "The Belt and Road" by elaborating its establishment background and process, positioning, characteristics of various aspects, and its role in solving the funding gap of infrastructure, accelerating China's process of opening to the outside world, and promoting production capacity cooperation between countries.

Key words: "the Belt and Road"　Silk Road Fund　financial innovation

I . Introduction: Proposal of "the Belt and Road" Initiative and establishment of the Silk Road Fund

After the global financial crisis in 2008, the world economy is slowly recovered. In order to get rid of industry hollowing, advanced economies are gradually carrying out "Reindustrialization" to drive national economic development with industrial development. The United States proposed "Revitalizing American Manufacturing", while the European Union has drawn up "Juncker Plan" with a total

---

① Chen Siyu, female, a student of Grade 2 in Ningbo Xiaoshi High School.

scale of 315 billion Euro, and Germany has launched "Industry 4. 0". Developing
countries have also drafted national medium-term and long-term strategies of
economic development for trying to find new engines of economic growth by
accelerating industrialization and urbanization, and diversifying the economic
structure. Kazakhstan launched the Bright Road plan when Indonesia proposed
Global Maritime Fulcrum Strategy, and Poland proposed to build the Amber
Road' etc[1].

From the aspect of resource endowment, countries along "the Belt and
Road" are rich in resources and labor forces, and they are highly complementary
to China; at the same time, most countries still fall behind in infrastructure and
other aspects, thus the market prospects is bright. In terms of natural resources,
Kazakhstan's chromium and uranium, Thailand's antimony, Indonesia's tin,
Turkey's boron, Iran and Russia's oil and gas reserves are among the top three
in the world, and these mineral resources are also relatively scarce in China, so
they can be highly complementary to resources of China. In terms of labor resources, countries along "the Belt and Road" with a total population of more
than 4 billion have a dependency ratio of less than 50%, which means they are in
the crucial demographic dividend period of economic development.[2]
Meanwhile, nearly 500 million people in countries along "the Belt and Road"
have no access to electricity, so there is great space for power infrastructure development in neighboring countries. With the further strengthening of the connectivity between countries along "the Belt and Road" and China, the market
potential of countries along "the Belt and Road" will be further released.

From the perspective of China's domestic economic situation, China's economy is at a critical stage of economic growth transition and transformation of driving forces. On the one hand, traditional industries need de-leverage, cut overca-

---

① 蒲佳琪. 经济全球化的实践困境与 "一带一路" 建设的新引擎[J].现代营销(经营版), 2017
(5): 111.

② 庞超然. 合作逆势升温 "一带一路" 沿线国家发展潜力需深挖[N].中国经济时报, 2017-04-
25.

pacity, transform the mode of economic growth, and explore the international market; on the other hand, high-end manufacturing and advanced technologies shall be introduced to improve the quality of economic growth, cultivate core competitiveness, and promote supply-side structural reform and industrial chain upgrade. [①]

Under this background, in the Autumn of 2013, President Xi Jinping put forward "the Belt and Road" Initiative of jointly building the silk road economic belt and the 21st century maritime silk road in Kazakhstan and Indonesia. Based on the economic development needs of countries, the initiative calls for countries to jointly promote connectivity and production capacity cooperation based on the principle of achieving shared growth through discussion and collaboration to promote connectivity and production capacity cooperation, make respective advantages complementary to each other, and achieve mutual benefit and win-win development. Moreover, countries along "the Belt and Road" route have their own advantages and resource advantages, and they have strong economic complementarity with each other, so there is great potential and space for cooperation among countries. "The Belt and Road" takes five aspects as the main content, including policy communication, infrastructure connectivity, unimpeded trade, accommodation of funds, and people-to-people bond, and focus on them to strengthen cooperation among countries along "the Belt and Road".

Ⅱ. Accommodation of funds and its main content

Capital is an important driving force for economic development. Accommodation of funds is the core content of "the Belt and Road" construction. "The Belt and Road" Initiative involves cross-border investment in infrastructure and industrial projects, and financing bottlenecks are one of the major connectivity challenges. Therefore, building a sustainable and stable financing system for cross-border investment, deepening financial cooperation, and promoting a stable monetary system

---

① 杨捷汉. 丝路基金对推进 "一带一路" 建设的作用[J].区域金融研究, 2017, 537(7): 8-10.

through capital connectivity are important guarantee measures for implementing
"the Belt and Road" Initiative.

The main content of accommodation of funds includes cooperation among
international financial institutions, opening and integration of financial market,
and financial supervision and regulation cooperation. In terms of international
finance cooperation, accommodation of funds could promote the development of
the Asian monetary stability system, investment and financing system and credit
system, and expand the scope and rules of bilateral currency swap and settlement
for countries along "the Belt and Road" ; jointly promote the establishment of
Asian Infrastructure Investment Bank and New Development Bank, deepen practical cooperation between the China-ASEAN interbank association and the interbank association of Shanghai Cooperation Organization, and carry out
multilateral finance cooperation through syndicated loans and bank credit. In
terms of financial market opening and integration, accommodation of funds
could promote the opening and development of Asian bond market; support governments of countries along "the Belt and Road" and enterprises and financial
institutions with high credit ratings in issuing RMB bonds in China; qualified financial institutions and enterprises in China may issue RMB bonds and foreign
currency bonds abroad, and encourage the use of the funds raised in countries
along "the Belt and Road". In terms of financial regulation cooperation, accommodation of funds could facilitate the signing of bilateral memorandums of understanding on regulation cooperation, and gradually establish an efficient regulation coordination mechanism in the region; improve institutional arrangements
for risk response and crisis management, establish a regional financial risk warn-
ing system, and form an exchange and cooperation mechanism for dealing with
cross-border risks and crises; strengthen cross-border exchanges and cooperation
among credit investigation authorities, credit investigation agencies and rating
agencies. The accommodation of funds gives full play to the role of the Silk
Road Fund and sovereign wealth funds of various countries, and guide commercial equity investment funds and private funds to participate in the construction

of key projects of "the Belt and Road".

Since "the Belt and Road" Initiative was put forward, accommodation of funds has been promoted rapidly. Firstly, strategic cooperation between countries has been strengthened. For example, the central bank of China and Egypt signed a bilateral currency settlement agreement at the end of 2016 to facilitate bilateral trade and investment. In October 2018, Bank of China signed a memorandum of agreement with 13 Banks in the Philippines to facilitate direct foreign exchange transactions between RMB and PHP. And the Philippine RMB Trading Community will establish and promote the RMB-PHP market, through which PHP can be directly converted into RMB. Bank of China expects that there will be more than 10 bllion RMB transactions between Filipino and Chinese traders this year. Secondly, several multilateral international financial institutions have been established, such as the Asian Infrastructure Investment Bank established in December 2015 has become an important platform for accommodation of funds. For another example, on May 10, 2019, "the Belt and Road" Financial Cooperation Committee of the Asia Financial Cooperation Association was formally established in Beijing, the aim of which is to better promote the sharing of experience and information among various financial industries and fields in "the Belt and Road" regions, and build an international platform for business exchange and cooperation. Thirdly, international cooperation at the level of financial institutions has accelerated. At present, 11 Chinese-funded bank have set up 71 institutions for joint financing cooperation with international multilateral financial institutions such as the European Bank for Reconstruction and Development, Inter-American Development Bank, and African Development Bank. Foreign Banks also actively cooperate with Chinese-funded banks to participate in "the Belt and Road" project financing, for example, Banque Misr signed multiple loan agreements with China Development Bank.

III. The orientation, characteristics and investment progress of the Silk Road Fund

1. Orientation of the Silk Road Fund

On November 8, 2014, during the APEC meeting in Beijing, President Xi Jinping announced that China would contribute USD 40 billion to establish the Silk Road Fund. Then, on December 29, 2014, the Silk Road Fund Co. , Ltd was registered and officially started to operate in Beijing. Jin Qi, a senior economist, served as the first chairman of the company. The Silk Road Fund is jointly invested by China's foreign exchange reserves, China Investment Corporation, Export-Import Bank of China, and China Development Bank.

The Silk Road Fund is an investment institution specially established to serve the construction of "the Belt and Road". It adheres to the concept of "openness and inclusiveness, mutual benefit and win-win", and provides investment and financing support for economic and trade cooperation as well as bilateral and multilateral connectivity within the framework. The establishment of Silk Road Fund is an important measure for China to promote "the Belt and Road" construction. Meanwhile, it is also a practical action for China to use its own financial strength to directly support "the Belt and Road" construction and actively participate in the global expansion of infrastructure investment and financing and promote the sustainable growth of the world economy.

The Silk Road Fund is a medium and long term development investment fund with a longer investment period than commercial investment funds. It focuses on promoting infrastructure, resource development, industrial cooperation and finance cooperation projects with relevant countries and regions around "the Belt and Road" construction. By focusing on equity investment and comprehensively utilizing various investment and financing methods such as equity and creditor's rights, we will promote the "going global" of domestic high-end technologies and high-quality production capacity to ensure medium and long term financial sustainability and better investment returns.

2. Main feature of the Silk Road Fund

From the perspective of investment mode, the Silk Road Fund flexibly uses equity investment and creditor's right investment mode to participate in overseas projects of enterprises, and it takes enterprises as the main body, reasonable investment returns as the basis of investment, and market-oriented operation as the guarantee of sustainable investment. By the end of August 2018, equity investment accounted for about 70% of the total investment (commitment amount) of the Silk Road Fund. The Silk Road Fund also actively participates in PPP projects to improve project construction and operation efficiency.

From the perspective of investment field, the Silk Road Fund mainly invests in railway, highway, airport, port, municipal official website and other infrastructure construction; support the development of traditional sources of energy, such as oil, gas and minerals, and clean energy, such as hydropower, wind power and nuclear power (in line with the different resources of countries along "the Belt and Road"); provides funds to facilitate industrial and finance cooperation among countries along "the Belt and Road", and takes the synergy of development strategies and industrial plans of countries into special consideration. By the end of August 2018, the Silk Road Fund had invested about 70% of all the promised investment in oil and gas development, energy and power and other infrastructure projects in countries and regions along "the Belt and Road". It has played an important role in promoting economic development and improving people's livelihood in countries along "the Belt and Road".

From the perspective of investment philosophy, "the Belt and Road" Initiative clearly puts forward the idea of "jointly building a green silk road". The countries along "the Belt and Road" are mainly emerging economies and developing countries, most of which are committed to industrialization and urbanization and highly dependent on energy industries such as minerals, therefore, they are faced with the problem of how to balance the social benefits, economic benefits and ecological benefits. At the same time, the central and western regions of countries along "the Belt and Road", foreign regions in the Middle East, central Asia and other areas are facing serious desertification problems. For example, 1/3 of western China is desert, and the desertification of the land is increasing. 66% of Kazakhstan's land is deteriorating, and nearly 1. 8 trillion hectares are being desertification[①]…Desertification seriously threatens the survival, development and security of people in regions along "the Belt and Road" and the successful implementation of "the Belt and Road" Initiative. Therefore, the Silk Road Fund follows international rules and the legal policies and cultural customs of the countries where it invests, advocates the concept of green environmental protection and sustainable development, and implements the concept of green development and green finance.

3. Investment progress of the Silk Road Fund

Since the establishment of the Silk Road Fund, it has played an important role in promoting "the Belt and Road" capital connection, actively participated in transnational project investment and established cooperative partnership with overseas financial institutions, and achieved plentiful achievements.

The first investment project of the Silk Road Fund was the participation of China Three Gorges Corporation in the Camelot Hydropower Station Project in Pakistan in April 2015, which not only strongly supports Pakistan's clean energy development and infrastructure construction, but also promotes the export of Chinese equipment and technology standards. In June 2015, the Silk Road Fund participated in the project of China National Chemical Corporation's acquisition of Italian tire production, which became the first merger and acquisition project of the Silk Road Fund and played an important role in supporting enterprises to introduce advanced technology and management experience from abroad and expand overseas markets.

The Silk Road Fund exploited the advantages of diversified investment and financing cooperation to the full, and invested in the Hassyan Clean Coal Power

---

① 邱淑群 . 美丽中国壮哉中国生态梦[J].华人时刊(上旬刊), 2015(4): 1-3.

Station Project (PPP project) in Dubai. The Hassyan Clean Coal Power Station Project is a PPP greenfield development project and the first clean coal power station construction project in Dubai. The project uses supercritical clean coal technology of international standard, starts the smooth process of energy sector in gulf oil states such as United Arab Emirates, and gradually changes the status quo of local energy structure. At the same time, as a financial investor, the Silk Road Fund jointly provides equity financing with Dubai Water and Electricity Authority (DEWA), electric power operation enterprise ACWA Power (ACWA) with influence in the Middle East, and Harbin Power Equipment Corporation. In addition, the Silk Road Fund joined a consortium of state-owned banks in China and middle eastern banks to address the problem of funding sources for the construction and operation of the project.

Ⅳ. The Role of the Silk Road Fund

1. Solve the infrastructure financing gaps

Sustainable infrastructure is an important driving force for sustainable economic growth and a key investment focus of the Silk Road Fund. The countries and regions covered by "the Belt and Road" Initiative have a high economic scale, the economy is generally in the development period, the demand for infrastructure investment such as transportation is strong. In Asia alone, there is a huge funding gap for infrastructure. According to the estimate of Asian Development Bank, before 2020, the annual infrastructure investment demand in Asia is as high as USD 730 billion, while the world bank and the Asian Development Bank can only provide about USD 20 billion annually to Asian countries, only 40% to 50% (USD 8 Billion to USD 10 billion) of which are spent on infrastructure construction. Infrastructure construction in developing countries along "the Belt and Road" are experiencing financing bottlenecks. It is difficult to effectively match infrastructure projects with market-based financing methods, and infrastructure investment faces a large financing gap. [①]

The Silk Road Fund takes the construction of investment and financing platforms as the starting point to break the funding bottleneck of the connectivity of countries and regions along "the Belt and Road". Through the establishment of infrastructure joint investment platform, industrial manufacturing cooperation between countries along "the Belt and Road" can be strengthened when the economic and trade development can be promoted. At the same time, countries can exploit their enterprise advantages to the full and jointly promote the economic development of their regions. By the end of August 2018, the Silk Road Fund had signed contracts for 25 investment projects, with commitments of over USD 8. 2 billion, and the actual contribution exceeded USD 6. 8 billion. The Silk Road Fund has made flexible use of equity investment and debt investment, designed and matched products mainly with equity investment and supplemented with debt investment, and participated in infrastructure projects. The advantage of equity investment is that it does not increase the debt burden of the host country, but it can play a credit enhancing role in project financing, attract private capital and debt funds to participate in investment, address the funding gap without adding the debt burden to less developed countries.

2. Accelerate China's process of opening up to the outside world

By establishing incentive and restraint mechanism, designing reasonable risk sustained release and compensation mechanism and reasonable exit mechanism, the Silk Road Fund encourages enterprises to go abroad, and help enterprises that have gone abroad to go further. Investment abroad is the important support of "the Belt and Road" construction. Driving high-quality industries and high-end technologies to go abroad through capital means opening to the outside world at high level. The Silk Road Fund uses capital thinking to promote enterprises to go out with capital. It innovates methods of investment and financing,

---

① 曾睿, 唐安冰. 首届中新(重庆)战略性互联互通示范项目金融峰会在渝成功举行服务 "一带一路" 打造中国—东盟金融合作新典范[J].重庆与世界, 2018, 497(21): 20-23.

and comprehensively uses various financing methods and currency combinations to provide strong support for the realization of various projects and enterprises' technologies to go out. For example, China is now leading the world in equipment manufacturing, electronic information, modern agriculture and other technologies, so the silk road fund strongly supports projects that can drive China's superior production capacity to go abroad, including high-speed railway, power and high-end equipment manufacturing.

The Silk Road Fund's participation in international projects will greatly promote the internationalization of RMB. From the perspective of the function of international currency, RMB is mainly used as cross-border trade settlement currency and partial payment currency at present, but it is still in its initial stage as the pricing currency and reserve currency. "The Belt and Road" construction is based on the trade circle and investment circle. While consolidating the monetary foundation of cross-border trade settlement, international investment will boost the development of RMB's international monetary functions such as money of account and reserve currency. With the continuous expansion of the trade circle and investment circle between China and countries along "the Belt and Road", the acceptance, use and circulation of RMB in such regions will continue to improve, and the international influence will continue to expand, and it accordingly opens up an important path for the internationalization of RMB. China has accumulated a large amount of foreign exchange reserves since the reform and opening up, but the capital allocation of foreign exchange reserves is not reasonable and diversified, so it results in excessive low capital utilization efficiency. As an important channel to use foreign exchange reserves for international investment, the Silk Road Fund plays a great role in improving the rate of return on foreign exchange reserves.

3. Promote production capacity cooperation between countries

The Silk Road Fund not only invests in infrastructure construction, but also plays an important role in exploiting the advantages of national resources and promoting win-win cooperation among countries through investment in industrial projects.

Since the Chinese government put forward "the Belt and Road" Initiative in 2013, foreign investment and cooperation of Chinese enterprises have increased rapidly. In 2014, China's investment flows to countries and regions along "the Belt and Road" reached USD13. 66 billion, and the inventory investment reached USD 92. 46 billion at the end of the year. In 2015, Chinese companies invested a total of USD 14. 82 billion in 49 countries related to "the Belt and Road" Initiative, with year-on-year growth of 18. 2%;[1] China has contracted 3, 987 foreign contracted projects in 60 countries, with a total value of USD 92. 64 billion, accounting for 44%[2] of the total value of new contracts signed by China in the same period. By the end of 2015, Chinese companies were promoting a total of 75 cooperation zones, more than half of them are processing and manufacturing parks closely related to production capacity cooperation and with a total investment of USD 7. 05 billion. There were 1, 209 enterprises in the zone. The total output value of the cooperation zone was USD 42. 09 billion, and the taxes and fees paid by the host country were USD 1. 42 billion[3], which drove the transfer of some production capacity of traditional industries such as textile, clothing, light industry and home appliances to overseas countries.

The Silk Road Fund has also made significant contributions to cooperation in production capacity. For example, on December 14, 2015, the Silk Road Fund signed an agreement with the then KAZNEX "Corporation for Export Development and Promotion" (later reorganized as Kazakhstan Investment Corporation). The Silk Road Fund invested USD 2 billion to set up a China-Kazakhstan Pro-

---

① 郭朝先, 刘芳, 皮思明. "一带一路" 倡议与中国国际产能合作[J]. 国际展望, 2016, 8(3): 17–36.

② 马莉, 孙美玲. 习近平 "一带一路" 建设思想的哲学思维论析[J]. 聊城大学学报(社会科学版), 2018.

③ 刘一贺. "一带一路" 倡议与人民币国际化的新思路[J]. 财贸经济, 2018(5): 103.

duction Capacity Cooperation Fund, focusing on supporting production capacity cooperation and related projects between China and Kazakhstan. This is also the first special country fund set up by the Silk Road Fund. Meanwhile, the Silk Road Fund has set up a USD 15 billion of special loan for China-Kazakhstan production capacity cooperation. So far, a number of China-Kazakhstan cooperation projects have been completed and put into production, with a total of 34 projects, such as Aktogay copper concentrator with an annual output of 25 million tons, Pavlodar electrolytic aluminum plant with an annual output of 250, 000 tons, Caspian Sea Asphalt Plant with an annual output of 1 million tons and Menara Cement Plant with a daily output of 3, 000 tons. There are 43 projects are implemented, including Atyrau Refinery Crude Oil Deep Processing Project, Alma-Ata tempered glass factory, 100, 000 tons of large diameter spiral welded steel pipe and other projects, these projects have filled the gaps in Kazakhstan's electrolytic aluminum, copper mining, high-end oil products, special cement and other industries, promoted the industrialization of Kazakhstan, and provided many jobs and promoted local development. Later, in June 2018, the Silk Road Fund signed a memorandum of understanding on strategic partnership with Astana international financial center of Kazakhstan, and purchased part of Astana international exchange through China-Kazakhstan production capacity cooperation fund. Proposed by the Silk Road Fund, China and Kazakhstan have jointly established a working group, establish and maintain business contacts with relevant government departments, embassies and consulates, and large enterprises of the two countries, work closely with each other in terms of project development and policy coordination, and jointly track key projects in the field of China-Kazakhstan production capacity cooperation that have social and economic benefits, so as to promote the fund to better promote China-Kazakhstan production capacity cooperation.

V. Conclusion

This paper expounded the background and process of the establishment of the Silk Road Fund, its positioning, characteristics and role. Taking the Silk Road Fund as an example, this paper described the innovative financial model and international cooperation model under the background of "the Belt and Road". It is not hard to see that since the launch of "the Belt and Road" Initiative, China has increased cooperation with other countries and making constant efforts to build a community of human desting and better life on earth. As high school students, although we are still far from such a high-demand and high-level company as the Silk Road Fund, we are all a member of the global village and member of over one billion Chinese people, and we have the obligation and must contribute to the realization of "the Belt and Road" Initiative.

In December 1953, when Premier Zhou Enlai met with an Indian delegation, he put forward the Five Principles of Peaceful Coexistence for the first time, which is, respect for each other's sovereignty and territorial integrity, mutual nonaggression, mutual non-interference in internal affairs, equality and mutual benefit, and peaceful coexistence. On this basis, "the Belt and Road" follows the principles of wide consultation, joint contribution and shared benefits, that is, upholds opening up and cooperation, harmony, inclusiveness, market principles and mutual benefit. The five principles of peaceful sharing proposed in sixty years ago is an important initiative in the history of international relations. It has made historic contributions to the establishment of a new type of international relations that is just and reasonable. Today, "the Belt and Road" Initiative aims at adding new impetus to common development through this new platform for international cooperation and building "the Belt and Road" into a road of peace, prosperity, openness, green development, innovation and civilization. This initiative not only deeply reflects China's great power spirit, but also will make historic contributions to the whole world. Therefore, We should study hard and practice hard to become a builder of "the Belt and Road" Initiative and the community with shared future for mankind.

Research on Tourism Culture Education for Chinese Youth Based on "the Belt and Road"

Shi Shaojun[①]

Abstract: In the past 40 years since the reform and opening up, with the great development of China's economy, the Chinese people's pockets have been bulging, and the per capita sustainable income of residents has been constantly growing, and more and more Chinese people have gone abroad to travel. With the changes of the times, the tourism industry has changed from the pure sight-seeing to a cultural quality improvement and the embodiment of congeniality of people's aspirations. In the era of pluralism, culture as a soft power has increasingly become an important factor in expanding China's influence. It can be said that cultural strength is another important component of a country's comprehensive strength in addition to traditional political strength, economic strength, military strength and other hard power. With the gradual strengthening of China's hard power, the improvement of soft power has become an unavoidable topic. Therefore, in this article, from the perspective of a young student, the author focuses on the relationship between "the Belt and Road" and tourism culture and starts from the history of "the Belt and Road". By this approach, the author conducted active exploration on many aspects including inheritance and exchange of contemporary tourism culture, the economic significance of tourism industry on the countries along the route of "the Belt and Road" and its impact on the congeniality of people's aspirations, and as well as the impact of tourism

---

① Shi Shaojun, male, a student of Grade 2 of Xingning High School, Ningbo City, Zhejiang Province.

industry on international situation and the vision of the youth. All contemporary Chinese youth have the responsibility and obligation to actively participate in this great practice. The author believes that the promotion of this grand "the Belt and Road" tourism culture strategy and the construction of human destiny complement each other, and the vast majority of young people can grasp this opportunity and accomplish great achievements.

Key words: "the Belt and Road" tourism culture youth exploration accomplish great achievements construction of the community of human destiny

Ⅰ. Introduction

In 2019, President Xi Jinping proposed the initiative to build "the Belt and Road". Looking back the past several years, "the Belt and Road" Initiative, especially the tourism culture, has achieved great achievements. Since 2013, China has signed 24 government documents for setting up cultural centers with 17 countries along the route of "the Belt and Road", and established 16 Chinese Cultural Centers along the route of "the Belt and Road" and also host more than 1600 sessions of Chinese Carnival Cultural Events. Chinese cultural center has been expanding in the circle of friends around the world, with higher and higher gold content and better development prospects. It has become an important platform for young people along the route of "the Belt and Road" to understand Chinese culture and social development in China.

The world today is undergoing complex and profound changes. The in-depth impact of the international financial crisis is still grim, the world economy is recovering slowly, the international investment and trade pattern and multilateral trade rules are brewing profound adjustments. The bottlenecks facing the development of countries still exist, how to adapt the trend of the era of economic globalization has become an unavoidable problem. At present, the construction of "the Belt and Road" tourism culture is in full swing, and young people shoulder the historical responsibility of "the Belt and Road" from concept to action and from vision to reality. Therefore, the author hopes that the youth will actively explore "the Belt and Road" tourism culture and practice with heart and soul, in order to achieve congeniality of people's aspirations, mutual understanding and common development.

Ⅱ. Historical background of "the Belt and Road" Initiative

"The Belt and Road" is enlightened from the ancient Silk Road. As is well known, as early as during the reign of Emperor Wu of the Han Dynasty, Zhang Qian was dispatched to the western regions. The travels along the diplomatic mission route made Zhang Qian realize that this was a new opportunity to promote economic and trade exchanges, achieve congeniality of people's aspirations and ethnic integration. The ancient Silk Road came into being under such a background, and the ancient maritime Silk Road came into being accompanying with the increasingly national power of the Han Dynasty. The ancient Silk Road ran through various countries in the western regions, and then extended to the countries in central Asia, western Asia and Europe. The silk trade and various cultural exchanges to overseas countries made outstanding contributions to the world economy and trade at that time.

The ancient Roman poet Virgil and geographer Ponbonius repeatedly referred to "the Silk Kingdom", and the works *The Travels of Marco Polo* set off the first "China Fever" in Western history. "The Belt and Road" is the innovation and promotion of the spirit of the ancient Silk Road. Silk Road is an important channel for trade between China and the west. Moreover, Silk Road achieved more positive achievements in mutual penetration of culture ranging from business activities to cultural exchanges, creating the plural pattern featured with cultural integration and congeniality of people's aspirations, consolidating the power to open a new era. "The Belt and Road" tourism culture construction provides an opportunity of exchanging and mutual leaning tourism culture for young people from all over the world.

III. Analysis of the current status of tourism culture

"The Belt and Road" Initiative adheres to the cooperation principle of "extensive consultation, joint contribution and shared benefits" and the cooperation principle of "openness, cooperation, harmony and inclusiveness, market operation and mutual benefit and win-win situation". "The Belt and Road" embodies the collective wisdom of the new generation of leaders of the CPC Central Committee with General Secretary Xi Jinping as the core. As a youth of the new era, we should actively respond to acquire the great initiative, inherit and carry forward the spirit of the Silk Road, keep pace with the times and seize the opportunity to accelerate construction of tourism culture together with the people all over the world, in order to benefit people of various countries along the route of "the Belt and Road", this not only conforms to China's national conditions, but also highlights the call of the times.

1. Youth should increase their enthusiasm in understanding "the Belt and Road" Initiative

Many Chinese youth get to know "the Belt and Road" through the media including newspapers, websites, etc. Contemporary youth should strengthen their ideals and beliefs in the process of promoting "the Belt and Road" tourism culture. They must find the target in the depth exploration of the historical footprint of "the Belt and Road", and realize the self-value through "the Belt and Road" tourism culture platform so as to better serve the society and all mankind.

2. Chinese youth should strength their in-depth understanding of "the Belt and Road" initiative

The author once asked his classmates about the specific content of "the Belt and Road", and most of them answered with sentences like "that is just the silk road". When the questions come to which countries "the Belt and Road" passes through, they just can give some simple and rigid answers. The times entrusts the contemporary youth with a glorious historical mission. As an important force for social change, young people should have a strong sense of social responsibility and historical mission. As the most energetic and energetic youth group, we should deeply understand the development strategy of "the Belt and Road", have the courage to innovate and practice, and actively participate in the construction of "the Belt and Road". This great initiative is related to the comprehensive development and success of China's future modernization construction. It plays a significant role and has a far-reaching influence.

3. Chinese Youth should increase their urgency in understanding "the Belt and Road" Initiative

Tourism culture has the characteristics of wide coverage, high relevance and strong driving force. Therefore, we must create a new model of tourism culture and rely on the unique platform of tourism culture to promote the rapid development of the economy of the countries on the route of "the Belt and Road" and the congeniality of people's aspirations. Every country and every nation has its own beautiful cultural traditions. Chinese culture is extensive and profound, but western culture also has many aspects deserving learning. We can also take its essence and learn from the excellent culture of others. In this way, the excellent cultures of various nationalities and countries can be available for mutual inclusion and mutual reference, promoting the integration of the nations and congeniality of people's aspirations.

4. Chinese Youth should lay more emphasis on the importance of understanding "the Belt and Road" Initiative

Tourism culture is an indispensable cultural heritage and soul of China's tourism industry. It is the key to China's tourism industry maintaining its Chinese characteristics and enhancing its international competitiveness. As a tourist, the material needs are lower-level and are easy to be satisfied; while the spiritual and cultural needs are a higher level of demand, which is not easy to be contented but has influence on the overall situation.

If tourism cannot meet tourist's cultural needs, it loses the value for its existence. Culture is characterized by region, nationality, and inheritance. It is often unique to a country and region and is rarely comparable. It is easy to create its unique brand and characteristics. Creating famous brands is a magic weapon in the tourism competition, and it is a winning strategy to promote tourism culture on the road of sustainable development. Therefore, we must attach great importance to the construction of tourism culture, conduct in-depth exploring on the connotation of tourism culture, strive to create a tourism culture atmosphere and establish a tourism culture system with Chinese characteristics. ①

IV. Combination between "The Belt and Road" and tourism culture, diversified and compatible

1. Definition and exploration significance of tourism culture

Encyclopedia of China defines tourism culture as follows: "The so-called tourism culture refers to the unique culture that is embodied the tourism practice process of a certain nationality or a country from generation to generation. Tourism culture includes philosophical concepts, aesthetic habits, customs and humanities that are only unique to this nationality or country. In other words, tourism culture is a special manifestation of a common cultural tradition of a nation in the process of tourism."

Tourism requires culture as its resource, and culture needs tourism to realize and exert its value. The two have a relationship of mutual inclusion, mutual integration and mutual flourishing. According to its basic attributes, tourism resources can be divided into two categories: natural tourism resources and humanities tourism resources. Natural tourism resources include geography, waters, atmosphere and space landscapes, and biological landscapes. Humanistic tourism resources include cultural relics of physical forms, classical gardens and ideology of literature and art, and religious culture.

---

① 汪东亮, 胡世伟, 陆依依, 等. 旅游文化[M] .北京: 清华大学出版社, 2016.

Our daily life is like a circle. We never know what is outside the circle and how big it is, and the same is true for culture. Cultural factors permeate all aspects of modern tourism activities. Tourists' travel behavior is a kind of cultural consumption behavior. The motivation and purpose of traveling abroad is to obtain spiritual enjoyment and psychological satisfaction. Both natural resources and human resources require unique and fascinating national culture to attract and motivate tourists' travel motives. Once they lack the unique cultural heritage of their own nationality, they will lose their characteristics and cannot reflect the unique spiritual connotation of the nationality and consequently will also lose its strong appeal. Practice has shown that "all countries with developed tourism will win with tourism culture".

The year 2018 is the fortieth anniversary of reform and opening up. Standing on such a historical node, it is of great significance for the youth studies and explores "the Belt and Road" tourism culture: We need to "gain new insights through reviewing the old" so as to mutually learn and reference. Only when we know what we have done in the past can we do better in the future. From the ancient Silk Road to "the Belt and Road", we should enable the concept of "extensive consultation, joint contribution and shared benefits" to be deeply rooted in the hearts of the people, making young people become more rational, more practical, have more sense of responsibility and duty so as to actively improve the quality of tourism culture and strive to make tourism culture a national strategic industry in the 21st century.

2. Principles and objectives of exploration on tourism culture

"Every nation develops and expresses its own culture. We should appreciate others' culture and learn from them. In this way, the excellent cultures of various countries are mutually tolerant, so that it can display a colorful world and a diverse culture. " This famous proverb is selected from the keynote speech by the famous sociologist Fei Xiaotong at his 80th birthday party, explaining the principles of how to deal with the relationship between different cultures. We take tourist attractions as an example. Nowadays, it has become a common phenomenon to explore its own cultural heritage in combination with its unique historical heritage. The inseparable relationship between tourism and culture tells us to keep pace with the times in a sense. Only by actively developing and innovating the culture with "the Belt and Road" tourism characteristics can the vitality of tourism culture be highlighted.

The author thinks that with the implementation of "the Belt and Road" and the new breakthrough in the construction of tourism culture in the future, it is bound to break this passive situation. As the saying goes, gold and silver cups are not as good as reputation. As an intangible asset, the tourism culture brand can enhance the awareness of the tourism consumer group in a subtle way. The contemporary youth shoulders the heavy responsibility for "the rejuvenation of the country, and the revitalization of the nationality", the purpose of our exploration on tourism culture is to learn and use relevant theoretical knowledge and employ multiple initiative measures to actively launch the construction of tourism culture brands, bring the historical and cultural treasures of 5000 years of Chinese civilization to the whole world and promote the congeniality of world people's aspirations.

As countries along the route of "the Belt and Road" plan to jointly develop tourism culture, infrastructure construction such as railway transportation will become necessary. It brings unprecedented opportunities for China's high-speed railway to "go global". China's high-speed rail has played an extremely important role in promoting economic exchanges between Asia and Europe and Asia-Africa economic development. According to China News report, in 2018, China Railways opened a total of 6,300 trains in Central Europe, with a year-on-year increase of 72%. In the past few years, the construction of Jakarta-Bandung High-speed Railway and Addis Ababa-Djibouti Railway, as well as Mombasa-Nairobi Standard Gauge Railway (SGR) which is known as the "Century Project" in Kenya have greatly promoted the development of the local economy and tourism culture.

3. The construction of tourism culture is in the ascendant, and it has spawned a mobile payment culture.

Mobile payment tool Alipay and WeChat make it easier and faster for Chinese people to travel abroad. Alipay now has already been used in 33 countries and regions such as Europe, America, Japan, South Korea, Southeast Asia, Hong Kong, Macao and Taiwan, and supports more than 20 kinds of currencies such as US dollars and British pounds, covering nearly all consumer places such as catering and supermarkets, department stores, duty-free shops, theme parks, overseas airports, and tax refunds. According to the latest Tencent report, WeChat payment has also been available in more than 13 countries and regions, covering more than 130, 000 overseas merchants worldwide, supporting the settlement of more than 12 foreign currencies.

Thailand is especially worth mentioning, the whole country uses WeChat for payment, and friends who travel to Thailand can "go and leave" without having to exchange their currencies and no longer have to worry about the cash used for change.

Ⅴ. Fruitful achievements in "the Belt and Road" tourism and cultural exchanges between China and foreign countries

According to the 2017 Cultural Development Statistics Bulletin of the Ministry of Culture and Tourism, China has signed cultural cooperation agreements with 157 countries, and has signed nearly 800 cultural exchange implementation plans, having initially formed an intergovernmental cultural exchange and cooperation network covering major countries and regions in the world. China has vigorously promoted the construction of cultural exchange brands and organized more than ten culture years and tourism years including China-Central and Eastern Europe, China-ASEAN, China-EU.

Since 2015, China has carried out a series of publicity and promotion with the theme of "Beautiful China—Silk Road Tourism Year" for three consecutive years, and successfully created nearly 30 Chinese international cultural and tourism brands, including "Happy Spring Festival" "Silk Road Tour" "Youth Sinology Study Program" "Chinese Culture Lecture Hall" "Millennium Canal" "Tianlu Tour" and "Arab Art Festival". In 2017, "Happy Spring Festival" program held more than 2,000 cultural activities in more than 500 cities in over 140 countries and regions. In addition, Silk Road (Dunhuang) International Cultural Expo (SRDICE), Silk Road International Art Festival, Maritime Silk Road International Art Festival and other comprehensive cultural festivals with the theme of "the Belt and Road" have been successfully held in the world.

Since the implementation of "the Belt and Road" Initiative, China has joined hands with UNESCO to actively build a bridge of youth interaction and friendship among various countries, promote cross-cultural dialogue and exchanges as well as mutual learning and reference, especially the cultural exchanges among young people from all over the world. The cultural exchanges between Chinese and foreign youth held under this theme have been brilliant and wonderful. In December 2017, the Maritime Silk Road Intangible Cultural Heritage Exhibition was held in Quanzhou, Fujian Province, with 117 projects from all over the world. [1]

VI. Looking forward, creating new chapter

1. Deepen traditional friendship and promote cultural exchanges

According to Xinhua News Agency, from March 21 to March 26, 2019, President Xi Jinping paid a state visit to Italy, Monaco and France. As to presenting impressive humanities exchanges, We can see the wonderful "collision" between Chinese Peking Opera and the Italian opera *Turandot*, China's Palace Museum (Forbidden City) Cultural Relics Exhibition and the Monaco Royal Culture Exhibition. Sichuan Zigong Lanterns light up the small town in the south of France... In the harmony between the civilizations from the East and the

---

① 林善传. 海上丝绸之路非物质文化遗产展在泉州举行[DB/OL].新华网, 2017－12－12. http://www. xinhuanet. com//overseas/2017－12/12/c_ 129762662_ 3. htm.

West, world people are more intimate and congenial. The author believes that the development of "the Belt and Road" tourism culture is undoubtedly a fulcrum for China to incite the world. For China's future development, tourism culture can be said that a slight move in one part may affect the situation as a whole. ①

2. Deepen cultivation and extensive promotion, achieving broad prospects

On March 21st 2019, President Xi Jinping published a signed article in Italy entitled *East Meets West – A New Chapter of Sino-Italia Friendship*, and pointed out that the road to humanistic communication between the two countries is becoming broader and wider. As early as over 2,000 years ago, China and ancient Rome, though thousands of miles apart, were already connected by the Silk Road. A signed article by Chinese President Xi Jinping titled "Move Together toward Common Development" was published on March 23, 2019 in leading French newspaper *Le Figaro* ahead of his state visit to the European country. The article pointed out: "I hope our two countries will take bigger strides in our cooperation in culture, tourism, education, sports and youth affairs, and at the subnational level, and hope to see our cooperation play an exemplary role in driving the cultural and people-to-people exchanges between China and the West. "②

Italian Prime Minister Conte also personally participated in the Second "the Belt and Road" Forum for International Cooperation. During the preparation and holding process of the forum, the participants reached 283 pragmatic outcomes. During the forum, the Entrepreneur Conference was held with the participation of many elites from industrial and commercial fields, project cooperation agreement worth more than USMYM 64 billion was successfully signed. These achievements fully demonstrate that the "The Belt and Road" construction should

---

① 习近平. 东西交往传佳话　中意友谊续新篇[N].人民日报, 2019-03-21: 01.

② 习近平. 在共同发展的道路上继续并肩前行[N].光明日报, 2019-03-24.

be in the principle of complying with the tide, winning the hearts of people, bene-fiting people's livelihood, blessing the whole world, and thereby meanwhile pro-mote the construction of tourism culture. ①

3. setting up tourism platform for cultural exchange

If a country's tourism industry lacks its own national traditional culture, it will lose its characteristics and cannot reflect the unique spiritual connotation of its own nation, and also it will lose its strong competitiveness and attractive-ness. Practice has shown that "every country with a prosperous tourism industry win with tourism culture". Therefore, it is the future development direction to establish a tourism culture system with Chinese characteristics, create a tourism culture brand and achieve win-win cooperation.

With the promotion of "the Belt and Road" tourism culture, it will defi-nitely increase the demand for tourism talents. According to the statistics of the Ministry of Education, a total of 489, 200 foreign students came to China's higher education institutions in 2017, with the growth rate remaining above 10% for two consecutive years. China has become the largest destina-tion for studying abroad in Asia, and China's international influence is stead-ily increasing. China has also established 530 Confucius Institutes and 1, 113 Confucius Classrooms in 149 countries and regions around the world. Through the promotion of inter-school friendly cooperation and cul-tural output, China has established the ideological foundation of mutual re-spect and learning, safeguarding justice and common progress in the hearts of young people all over the world. This also promoted cultural exchanges and mutual understanding between the countries. ②

---

① 习近平. 在共同发展的道路上继续并肩前行[N].光明日报, 2019-03-24.
② 牛弹琴. 第二届 "一带一路" 峰会中国取得十大成就[DB/OL] . 新浪网, 2019 - 04 - 28. http: //news. sina. cn/gn/2019-04-28/detail-ihvhiqax5451077. d. html.

Ⅶ. Promoting the construction of tourism culture, Chinese youth have great potential

1. Correctly recognize the relationship between tourism culture and youth

Youth is the future and the hope of a country. Chinese government attaches great importance to the interactive exchanges between Chinese and foreign youth. Youth have their own unique outlook on values, full of vitality, active in thinking, unwilling to stick to the rules, participate in social transformation and innovation in their own unique ways, thus affecting the process and direction of social development and culture development. It is these characteristics of youth that make youth culture rebellious, pluralistic and open. To this end, at the critical moment of reform and opening up, China will develop a healthy and energetic youth tourism culture and maintain the advanced nature of the cultural direction.

Looking at the major domestic problems in China, it is imperative to meet the growing needs of the people for a better life. People have changed from the simple pursuit of material needs (such as food and clothing) to the spiritual needs. Youth have the most dynamic and avant-garde consumption concept, so they are mainstream consumers of domestic commerce ranging from small milk tea shops and creative supplies stores to large-scale online shopping and WeChat business. Therefore, the development focus of "the Belt and Road" tourism culture can give priority to youth, so that young people can become a fresh force to promote the development of "the Belt and Road" tourism culture.

2. Joint contribution and shared benefits, striving to be a tourist culture communicator

The author believes that the revival of Chinese traditional culture must start from ourselves, but also start from the youth all over in the world. Chinese young generation is lucky to catch up with the new era of the great rejuvenation of the Chinese nation. In witness of the new era, every youth should stand on the forefront and strive to be a tourist culture messenger. Culture must be deeply rooted in minds of every Chinese, and must go out to the world and share with the world people and get along with the culture of various counties in the world. [1]

In May 2018, International Youth Forum (IYF): Creativity and Heritage along the Silk Road was held in Changsha and Nanjing. More than 70 youth representatives from 51 countries participated in the forum. Representatives from Hannah Getaqi from Ethiopia wrote to President Xi Jinping to report their feelings of participating in the forum and made suggestions on the construction of "the Belt and Road", China-Africa cooperation and youth exchanges between China and Africa. President Xi Jinping wrote back to the youth representatives in August, emphasizing that the youth are the future of the country and encouraging them to work hard to build a community of human destiny. [2]

VII. Conclusion and reflection

In 1957, former Chairman Mao Zedong gave a speech to students studying in Soviet Union in Moscow: "The world is yours and ours, but in the end it is yours. Your young people are full of vigor and vitality, like the sun at eight to nine o'clock in the morning. Hope is pinned on you. The world belongs to you. The future of China belongs to you." Promoting the construction of tourism culture is undoubtedly a fulcrum for China to incite the world. As a new force and pioneer of this new era, youth shoulders the mission of building "the Belt and Road". The communication and exchange in tourism culture can not only enable mutual inclusive and mutual trust among people in various countries, but also cultivate the youth outlook of values and promote the good atmosphere of society. The development of "the Belt and Road" tourism culture is in line with

---

① 宋德全. 让文化自知成就文化自信 当代青年大有可为[DB/OL]. 中国青年网, 2017 - 12 - 27. http://t. m. youth. cn/transfer/index/qnzz. youth. cn/zhuanti/ggyj/sdq/201712/t20171221_ 11210479. htm.

② 杨俊峰. "一带一路" 五年来 中外文化交流成果丰硕[DB/OL]. 人民网, 2018 - 11 - 27. http://ip. people. com. cn/GB/n/2018/1127/c179663-30423646. html.

China's actual national conditions. It is an important initiative in keeping with the trend of the times. The grand initiative of "the Belt and Road" points out the direction of development and the goal of struggle for our contemporary youth from the national level.

Exchanges and mutual learning make civilization enriched and diversified. As the saying goes, "a river does not choose a small stream, so it can be as deep as it is deep". If the flow of rivers is blocked by human force, even a big sea will also dry up one day. Cultural exchange is a bridge linking people and plays an irreplaceable role in international exchanges. Accordingly, with history as the horizontal axis, with opportunities as vertical axis, on such an intersection point, the author, from a youth's point of view, as a firm belief in the development of "the Belt and Road" tourism culture: believe that numerous youth like author himself will have faith in that continuous promoting the construction of "the Belt and Road" tourism culture will inject momentum for promoting development and prosperity of world civilization, extend vision into the future, create a community of human destiny.

A Brief Analysis of Folk Customs and Cultures of Various Countries along the Silk Road from the Perspective of History

Sha Yuzhou[①]

Abstract: As we all know, "the Belt and Road" initiative originated from the ancient Silk Road. The ancient Silk Road ran for thousands of miles and lasted for thousands of years. It embodied the Silk Road spirit featuring peace, co-operation, openness, inclusiveness, mutual learning and mutual benefit. Over a thousand years ago, Chinese ancestors had already found a way to communicate with other countries along the Silk Road. It was because of the Silk Road that China became a celestial empire and all other countries came to China to offer respects and congratulations. From the perspective of history, the author analyzes the cultural exchanges and economic development on the ancient Silk Road, takes "congeniality of people's aspirations" as the theme, and analyzes the fusion and exchange of folk customs and cultures of various national civilizations in combination with the multi-polarization development of contemporary international society and world, and further discusses how to understand and deal with foreign culture correctly and how to let our culture go out into the world. Cultural construction is an important part of China's political and economic construction and the construction of "the Belt and Road". We should critically introduce and integrate the excellent foreign cultures in the principle of "selecting their essence and discarding their dross". We should not only identify with our own culture, but also respect other ethnic cultures. We should learn from each other, seek common

---

① Sha Yuzhou, male, a student of Grade 1 in Ningbo Xiaoshi High school.

ground while reserving differences, understand each other's individuality, live in harmony, and respect the cultural diversity of the world, so as to jointly promote the prosperity and progress of human civilization.

Key words: "The Belt and Road"　congeniality of people's aspirations cultural force　multi-culture　critical inheritance

Ⅰ. Introduction: the origin of "the Belt and Road" —the ancient Silk Road

Silk Road, which is the most famous channel for foreign exchanges in the history. It is also the pride of the Chinese people. To understand "the Belt and Road" Initiative, we can start from history and see how ancient people interacted with foreign countries.

As early as in the Western Han Dynasty, Zhang Qian set out from Chang'an, although his real purpose was not to communicate with western countries, but Zhang Qian's journey to the west opened up the Silk Road for the first time, which was later called the "farfetched journey". In the Eastern Han Dynasty, Ban Chao set out from Luoyang on another diplomatic mission to the western regions. This time, he arrived in the western regions, while his entourage arrived in Rome, bringing with them many silk products from China, hence the travel route was named as "Silk Road". It is also known as the first dialogue between oriental and occidental civilizations. In addition, in the Eastern Han Dynasty, Indian monks came to Luoyang along the Silk Road, thus Buddhism reached China and enriched the content of the Silk Road again. Later, in the Tang Dynasty, Buddhist master Xuanzang traveled to India along the Silk Road to seek Buddhist scriptures, which promoted the exchanges between Chinese and Indian civilizations. When he came back, he wrote the book *The Great Tang Dynasty Record of the Western Regions*. In the Song Dynasty, China's porcelain was also introduced to many western countries along the Silk Road, which was once called the "Porcelain Road".

In general, the Silk Road starts from China, connects Asia, Africa and Europe and promotes economic and cultural exchanges among countries on the three continents. It can be seen that the ancient people not only brought Chinese goods to the world on the Silk Road, but also brought many things from the west back to China. This is exactly in line with our "going out, bringing in" concept. "The Belt and Road" Initiative, as the development and extension of the ancient Silk Road, naturally adheres to the same concept, so it is bound to require us to strengthen exchanges and cooperation with foreign countries.

Ⅱ. Purpose and significance—starting from history

As our ancestors, they knew the importance of foreign communication long ago. It is because of the development of the Silk Road that the Han Dynasty and Tang Dynasty flourished in history. Looking back the Tang Dynasty, a celestial empire attracting all other countries came to offer respects and congratulations, its capital Chang'an gathered a gear deal of talents and specialists from around the world. On the streets of Chang'an, foreigners can be seen everywhere. Ordinary people are not surprised to see them, and sometimes they will make friendly contact with them, not to mention expelling them. Why is that? In addition to the fact that the common people themselves were quite open and good at accepting new things, the Tang Dynasty implemented enlightened policies which also played a significant influence. The rulers of the Tang Dynasty did not repel the communication between the common people and foreigners, but encouraged them to have more communication with foreigners with an inclusive attitude. It was precisely because the Tang Dynasty was able to carry out close cultural exchanges with foreign countries, making foreigners and local people have "congeniality of people's aspirations", so that the Tang Dynasty became the unique most prosperous country in the world at that time.

Along with the world multi-polarization trend further strengthening and China's comprehensive national strength continuously esclating, we should refer to the template of the ancients to open a new strategic plan "the Belt and Road".

This not only has played a good role in promoting our country's economic development, but also contributed to the common prosperity and development of the world economy and strengthen further in-depth hierarchical relationship between countries in the world.

In order to effectively implement "the Belt and Road" Initiative, it is necessary to give priority to "five links", namely: policy communication, road connection, trade cooperation, currency circulation and congeniality of people's aspirations. In this paper, we will make a detailed study on "congeniality of people's aspirations".

Ⅲ. Language and culture

1. Relationship between language and culture

There are many countries in the world, and the languages of these countries are also different from each other, which manifests the differences between them. As a unique distinction, language is undoubtedly the unique culture of this country. As early as in the 1920s, the American linguist E. Sapir pointed out in his works *Language*: "There is something behind language, and language cannot exist without culture." [①]Linguist Palmer once mentioned in his works *Introduction to Modern Linguistics* that "the history of language and the history of culture go hand in hand, and they can help and inspire each other". [②]Language is regarded as an important component of culture.

In addition, we all know that when we want to have in-depth communication with another country, or understand the culture and language of other countries, language is undoubtedly is a bridge between the two cultures. Language is also the first step to achieve "congeniality of people's aspirations".

---

① [美]萨丕尔. 语言论[M] .北京: 商务印书馆, 2019.
② [英]帕尔默. 现代语言学导论[M] .北京: 商务印书馆, 2019.

2. Ancient people's attitude towards foreign languages

In the Qin and Han Dynasties, some part of the western regions (today's Xinjiang, Qinghai, Tibet, Gansu and other places) were not same to the language of the people living in central plains, even the dialects of different regions in central plains were not the same, so translators became an important role at that time. According to the *Rites of Zhou*, these translators in ancient times were called "tongue people", but their status was not very high. Later, as the territory of China gradually expanded those difficult languages or languages spoken by very few people gradually disappeared. according to the data, there are only dozens of foreign words in the pre-Qin literature, and to the war and peace period of the Han dynasty and Huns, more than 100 Huns words had been introduced into the Chinese, e. g. "单于" (dán yú) and "祁连" (qí lián) were introduced into the Han Dynasty at that time. And we are familiar with the poem "阿爷无大儿" (my father has no elder son), the character "爷" (yé) is originally introduced from Hsien-pei language, and the character "挺" in "挺好" (very good) was introduced from Manchu language. [1]

After the Han and Tang Dynasties, with the prevalence of Buddhism, Sanskrit was gradually introduced into China. It is said that in the Eastern Jin Dynasty, Wang Dao, who "Shared the World" with Sima Rui, Yuan Emperor of the Eastern Jin Dynasty, often dealt with Indian monks and could speak Sanskrit from time to time. Later, Xie Lingyun, a famous litteratrist of the same period, learned Sanskrit better than Wang Dao. It can be seen that the ancients attached great importance to foreign languages.

Learning the languages of ethnic minorities makes the Han nationality and other ethnic groups integrate quickly. Later, Emperor Xiaowen of the Northern Wei Dynasty carried out the reform to advocate Hsien-pei people learn Chinese to change to use Chinese surnames, and encouraged the marriage between Hsien-pei nobles and noble families of Han nationality, making ethnic minorities

---

① 王北静. 古人怎样学外语?[DB/OL].梨视频, 2019-01-24.

and Han people live in harmony and happiness with "congeniality of people's aspirations". Buddhism also spread widely in China with the prevalence of Sanskrit in China. In the Tang Dynasty, people from the grassroots to the royal family and their relatives all could speak a few Sanskrit words, and most of them believed in Buddhism. [1]

3. Foreign countries learn from China

According to news from Russian media: Russia's first set of Chinese textbooks will introduce modern China to Russian students, and Russian middle school students will learn Chinese calligraphy and idioms.

According to the Russian Satellite News Agency on March 7, 2019, Alexandra Xizova, the editor of Russia's first set of Chinese textbooks, said that the Chinese textbooks for middle school students will supplemented some information about modern China.

She said: "This set of Chinese textbooks is adapted for the needs of the 21st century. In short, these books are not only suitable for today, but also for tomorrow. With them, Russian students will learn Chinese language and learn more about the world at the same time. " She pointed out that cultural difference is a major difficulty for Russian students to learn Chinese. Russian students also have difficulty in grasping Chinese characters and pronunciation.

Russian students in Grade 11 of the 2018/19 school year will take the national Chinese language test for the first time, the report said. Chinese has become the fifth foreign language subject to be tested nationwide, following English, German, French and Spanish.

Anzor Muzaev, Deputy Director of the Bureau of Education and Science Supervision of Russian Federation, said that a total of 289 people from 43 regions in Russia have registered for the national Chinese language test. According to the report of Russian Satellite News Agency on March 7, Alexandra Xizova said the Chinese syllabus of Russian middle schools will include

---

[1]　佚名. 大唐时大街上随处可见外国人?唐朝时期经济实力怎么样?[DB/OL]. 百家号.

calligraphy and the basis of idioms.

Xizova said: "Calligraphy is an integral part of Chinese culture. Textbooks, study notes, materials and exercises for teachers' books, and of course including reference materials dedicated for Chinese pictographs which are used to develop and consolidate vocabulary and pictographic skills, learn beautiful calligraphy, and understand the structure, philosophy, and ethics of Chinese pictographs. Russian students in Grade 11 are required to know more than 1,000 Chinese vocabularies, and the syllabus will include modern words and idioms. Chinese idioms, proverbs, sayings, riddles, and idiom stories must be reflected in textbooks, starting in the first stages of language learning. " [①]

To be sure, the above news from Russia reveals an individual case, but it is also evident that the importance of the Chinese language has been growing in the world. Moreover, with the establishment of Confucius Institute in various countries, Chinese has been introduced to the world. According to statistics, more than 100 Confucius classrooms in primary and secondary schools have been set up in more than 50 countries along the route of "the Belt and Road", which has aroused a rush of foreign people to learn Chinese. Against the background of general global economic weakness, the steady and rapid development of China's economy and foreign trade is particularly eye-catching. Under the trend of economic integration, the demand of various countries on technical talents who can understand Chinese has increased significantly. At the same time, along with China's economy going out to the world, Chinese culture is becoming more and more influential, so sinology has become a "Prominent Study". The worldwide "Chinese Fever" has become a common phenomenon in the global language communication system.

And just in last year, Nankai University (NKU) developed Confucius Institute as a bridge of communication between China and Thailand. In addition to

---

① 佚名. 看外国人这么学中文......极度舒适[DB/OL].参考消息网, 2019 – 08 – 19. http://www. xiangyizc. com/xuexijiaocai/1326. html.

courses in Chinese language, folk culture dissemination forms such as Chongqing beloved folk song *Youngest Sister* as well as the famous Sichuan opera play *Face-Changing* was employed to promote the development of the relations between the two countries, this can be regarded as a good example. ①

4. China learns from foreign countries

As we all know, China always adheres to the principle of tolerance and openness when dealing with foreign languages. For example, daily words in our life such as "sofa", "cola" and "coffee" are all derived from foreign words and become part of our language. At the same time, a large number of people in China are also learning foreign languages. For another example, some Chinese high schools offer such courses as German, French and Japanese as elective courses.

However, these situations seem to be good, but in fact not too many people can learn foreign languages well and apply in the work in the future. It can be seen that our attention to language is still not enough, so it is no wonder that there are fewer translators, especially translators of minority languages in China. From the point of view of "the Belt and Road" Initiative, learning a foreign language makes it more convenient for us to communicate with foreigners, while communication with foreigners is indispensable for us today. Only by means of continuous communication and learning can "congeniality of people's aspirations" be achieved, and thereby we can understand their and our common interests and promote mutual cooperation. Of course, we can also use their languages to have a glimpse of their local customs. Therefore, the author thinks that we must pay attention to foreign language training and have a persistent willing to study foreign languages. With regards to the national level, the author hopes that the country can focus on supporting people's learning of foreign languages, and also attach importance to the profession of "translation" to provide support,

---

① 史欣. 从孔子学院到孔子课堂, 西南大学搭建中泰友谊桥梁[DB/OL].百家号西南大学, 2018, 279(900) .

so that more and more people have confidence in the prospect of this profession.

Finally, under the tide of globalization, international communication is getting closer and closer, and language is the very bridge of communication. A foreign language will widen our vision. It is also a great opportunity for us to look internationally. We must recognize the cultural diversity of the world and respect the cultures of different ethnic groups. We must follow the principle that all ethnic cultures are equal. In cultural exchanges, we should respect differences, understand individuality, live in harmony and jointly promote cultural exchanges and prosperity of the world.

IV. Food culture — taking Malaysia and Italy as examples

(1) Malaysia: Malaysian cuisine is generally prepared with four spices, including Tomyam, Assam, Tapai and curry, and is mainly made with sour and spicy taste, presenting bright and colorful. Due to the abundance of local coconut trees, coconut juice is commonly used in dishes, which is the main ingredient in Malaysian food. Famous dishes are Tomyam Soup with Seafood, Assam Curry Fish Head and so on. [1]Malaysia is a pluralistic society, which is also evident in food and other aspects. Malaysian food also brings together different food from Malaysian native ethnic groups, China, India and western countries, making a variety of cuisines dazzling. Similar to China, the principal food of Malaysians is rice, but noodles are also quite common.

(2) Italy: Italian cuisine is very rich with numerous dishes. Italian food has a long history and has a profound impact on the catering of European and American countries. Italian cuisine has also derived into French cuisine, American cuisine and other cuisines, thus gaining the reputation of "mother of western food". It is generally prepared with the spices such as green pepper,

---

[1]　李丽. 马来西亚的三大菜系[DB/OL] .新浪博客, 2017−02−08. http://blog. sina. cn/dpool/blog/ s/blog_ 13812b3250102zxjwm. html.

chives, etc. Its cooking method usually consists of frying, sauteing, frying, boiling, sauced braising with garlic and dried chilli, which are slightly spicy and attach great importance to the lingering taste in mouth and lips, and the food that is slightly stiff and elastic is all the more preferred. Famous dishes with Fiorentina Steak, the Devil Chicken, Baked Lobster Naples, Barry Turtle, Ausbok Beef, Ma Gelong Salad, Mered Macaroni, meat sauce with eggs, white bean salad with meat, braised chicken with green pepper, Braised Prawns, Braised fish, cold stewed chicken, white bean soup, ham with cutting noodles and other delicious food, this also makes the visitors from all over the world came here in an endless stream and linger for satisfying their appetites.

(3) China: Chinese cuisine covers many types and varieties of dishes. Just because of the differences in regions and nationalities, many kinds of dishes are derived. Moreover, the processing and cooking methods of each dish are also different. China is a multi-ethnic country, due to the differences in geography, culture, belief, and climate and so on, the types and flavors of dishes vary greatly and derive into many schools. There have been four major cuisines and eight major cuisines in the folk since ancient times. Chinese cooking is not only exquisite in skills, but also pays attention to the taste of the dishes, food color, aroma, and the harmony between taste and shape. The appearance of dishes is embodied in various ways, whether it is a carrot or a cabbage heart, a proficient cook can carve them into a variety of shapes, develop a unique style and thereby achieve the harmony of color, aroma, taste, form, give people a special enjoyment in sight and taste. [1]

It can be seen that there are many differences between Malaysian cuisine, Italian cuisine and Chinese cuisine. Apart from regional differences, cultural differences hold a dominant position. Malaysia is located in the low-latitude region, which is mainly of tropical rainforest climate with high temperature and

---

[1] 高小秋 . 欧洲美食巡游记: 意大利篇 [DB/OL] . 2018 – 10 – 22. http: //m. jieju. cn/News/ 20181022/Detail 8070b/. shtml.

abundant rain throughout the year. It is very suitable for the development of rice cultivation and aquaculture. Coconut trees are also a common local plant. Since most local people believe in Islam, Nasi Kandar is a popular Islamic dish. It is a dish of chicken, fish and meat cooked in a rich curry sauce.

Italy is situated on the coast of the Mediterranean Sea, so there are abundant varieties of seafood. In addition, with Mediterranean climate, Italy is suitable for developing Mediterranean type agriculture by giving priority to planting fruit, flowers and vegetable. In addition, wheat and barley are also planted, which are not only exported to other countries, but also used as fodder for livestock. Therefore, Italy has well developed animal husbandry, with abundant sources of beef, mutton and pork. As we all know, Rome, the capital of Italy, has been the center of western civilization for centuries, absorbing a large number of cultures from different countries, which is reflected in the diversity of dishes and characteristics. The "western" food in Italy is completely different from that in Malaysia and China, which reflects the rich and colorful culture of each country.

However, China has a vast territory, with a diversifed type of climates, environments and folk customs also vary in different regions, inevitably there will be differences in food and dishes. Chinese cuisine pays attention to color, aroma, taste, shape and utensils.

The food culture of three countries are all featured with diversity. However, the diversity of Malaysia and Italy cuisines is due to their close communication with neighboring countries and absorption of diverse cultures of various countries into their own food culture, which is reflected in the diversity of their food culture. The diversity of Chinese cuisine, on the other hand, absorbs abundant domestic cuisine due to its vast territory.

Malaysia is an island country, but it pays attention to inclusiveness and openness. Food from all over the world is gathered in Malaysia. Italy absorbs the diverse cultures of other countries, which laid the foundation for the important position of ancient Rome and Italy in the world. Of course, since the reform and opening up, China has never been more open to the outside world.

As a saying goes: "to grasp a man's heart, you have to grasp his stomach first", when we can seek common points while reserving difference in terms of food and promote integration of different countries, we have become much closer to "congeniality of people's aspirations". First of all, this can promote the sense of belonging of the foreigners. Secondly, when a country's diet goes out to the world and can be accepted by most people, which can promote the identity between people from different countries. For example, when Chinese people fall in love with Italian food, they will certainly gain good impression on Italy, and also can let Chinese people know more about Italy. At the same time, the study on food also facilitates our study on local culture.

V. Conclusion: the power of folk customs and culture

With the development of economic globalization, the integration and exchange of folk customs and cultures of various national civilizations have been made available. Due to the diversified cultural patterns and distinct cultures of different regions, we are inevitably required to know how to properly deal with foreign cultures and how to let our own culture go out to the world.

A culture is determined by a certain economy and politics, and reacts on a certain politics and economy, exerting a significant influence on politics and economy, while an advanced and healthy culture will promote the development of society. In today's world, with increasingly fierce competition in overall national strength, culture has become an increasingly important source of national cohesion and creativity, an increasingly important support for economic and social development and also an increasingly important factor in competition in overall national strength. Therefore, for China, cultural construction is an important part of our political and economic construction, as well as an important part of "the Belt and Road". So we should critically introduce and integrate foreign excellent culture by "taking the essence and discarding the dregs". We should not only identify with our own culture, but also respect the cultures of other ethnic groups. We should learn from each other, seek common ground while reserving differences, understand each other's individuality and live in harmony. We should respect the cultural diversity of the world and work together to promote the prosperity and progress of human civilization.

Rethinking the Development of Ningbo Cultural Tourism Industry under the Background of "the Belt and Road" Initiative

Hu Yiyang[①]

Abstract: In 2013, Chinese President Xi Jinping put forward "the Belt and the Road" Initiative, that is, the Silk Road Economic Belt and 21st Century Maritime Silk Road. Tourism, as an open and comprehensive industry, has unique advantages in "the Belt and Road" Initiative. "The Belt and Road" Initiative has become a new engine of China's tourism development and injected new vitality into the transformation and upgrading of China's tourism industry. In this context, as one of the starting ports of the Maritime Silk Road, Ningbo, should explore the strategic thinking of the development of Ningbo's cultural tourism industry on the premise of understanding and analyzing the current situation and existing problems of Ningbo's cultural development, centering on impact of "the Belt and Road" development strategy, clearly improving platform for "going global" of cultural tourism industry in Ningbo, take advantage of opportunities to get to the point of "come in", so as to realize the development goal and the benefit of cultural tourism industry in Ningbo.

Key words: "the Belt and Road"　Ningbo　cultural tourism

Ⅰ. Introduction

"The Belt and Road" construction is a major strategic measure for China to cultivate new competitive advantages in the country under the new historical con-

---

① Hu Yiyany, male, a student of class 109 Yinzhou High School, Ningbo city.

ditions, to create a new pattern of opening up, and to find new impetus for regional economic development. Through "the Belt and Road" construction, there will be a large-scale three-dimensional Eurasian sea and land transportation channel spanning the east and west and connecting the north and south. This will certainly promote the development of China's foreign trade and deepen our cultural and tourism exchanges. Located in the prime location of "the Belt and Road" strategy, Ningbo is the original port of origin of the ancient Maritime Silk Road. It is known as the "living stone of the ancient Silk Road" and has the advantage of developing cultural tourism. Under the background of the deep development of "the Belt and Road", how to develop the cultural tourism industry with its own advantages, and drive and promote the comprehensive improvement of Ningbo's social economy with the development of the cultural tourism industry. Through field investigation and interview, I have put forward some ideas on the status quo, characteristics, problems and countermeasures of the development of Ningbo's cultural tourism industry.

II. The Development Status and Characteristics of Ningbo Cultural Tourism Industry

I. The development status of Ningbo cultural tourism industry

—In 2018, Ningbo received a total of 125 million tourists in the whole year, with a year-on-year increase of 13. 76%. The total tourism revenue was RMB 200. 571 billion, with a year-on-year increase of 19. 7%.

—In 2017, the city received 1, 869, 100 inbound tourists and realized foreign exchange income of USD 990 million.

—In 2017, there are more than 100 scenic spots in Ningbo, 52 among which are A-level tourist areas, including 1 5A-level tourist area, 32 4A-level tourist areas, 19 3A-level tourist areas and 3 2A-level tourist areas.

—The investment in key tourism projects is accelerating. In 2017, Ningbo has built 191 tourism projects in the library. The total planned investment was

RMB 211. 669 billion, the actual investment was RMB 16. 432 billion, and tourism projects accounted for 3. 28% of the city's fixed asset investment.

—The development of seaport tourism was rapid. In 2017, the number of seaport tourists was more than 1, 200, and the total income reached more than 25 billion yuan. Among them, Xiangshan County received 7. 3 million tourists and the tourism income was 7. 6 billion yuan.

2. Characteristics of Ningbo cultural tourism industry

"Rich in culture and an important trading port's the city image of Ningbo, and it is also the most vivid description of the characteristics of Ningbo City. Long history and culture, superior geographical location endows Ningbo with distinctive characteristics of tourism culture.

(1)Ancient architecture highlights the charm of Ningbo as a famous historical city

Built in the reign of Emperor Xianfeng of the Qing Dynasty, the Drum Tower is a symbol of the official establishment of the state and the city in the history of Ningbo. It is one of the ancient buildings under national protection. The Old Bund is located on the north bank of the Sanjiangkou in Ningbo, 20 years earlier than the Shanghai Bund. It is one of the few remaining Bunds in the country with a hundred years of history. Lined up along the edge of the Yongjiang River, foreign consulates, Catholic churches, banks, shipping docks, the Old Bund records Ningbo's whole history of opening as a commercial port. First Hall Under Heaven is the earliest existing private library in China, the oldest library in Asia and one of the three largest family libraries in the world, and its library culture is famous throughout the country. With Qin's ancestral hall and garden of southern Yangtze River Delta, it is a masterpiece of residential buildings in Ningbo. Founded in the Eastern Han Dynasty, developed in the Tang Dynasty, and prosperous in the Northern Song Dynasty, the great Buddha's hall of Baoguo Temple is "No bird inhabits, no insect enters, no spider spins, and no dust on the beam". After thousands of years of vicissitudes of wind and rain, the temple is just as good as when it was newly built. Regions south of the Yangtze River are moist and with frequent typhoons, so this is indeed a miracle. Founded in 1233 A. D. and located in the southwest of Ninghai County, Qiantong Town, covering an area of 68 square kilometers, is an ancient town with a long history, profound cultural accumulation and unique geographical location in the south of Yangtze River. After more than 760 years of development, the ancient buildings of the Ming Dynasty and the Qing Dynasty remain intact. The Cicheng Ancient Building Complex around Ningbo, Chiang Kai-shek's former residence also left too many heritage treasures. With the polishing of the wind and rain, the city is even more shining.

(2) Yangyang Oriental Port highlights the bright spot of Ningbo's marine culture

Beilun Port, as a world-class deep-water port, was once famous for the continuous export of silk and porcelain by sea in history. Now, as the starting point of the new Maritime Silk Road, it has endowed Ningbo with an opportunity for the development of marine culture and a new highlight of Ningbo's tourism culture. The marine culture of Ningbo is with a long history and abundant connotation. Marine folk culture, marine biological culture, marine fishery culture, marine celebrity culture, marine commercial culture, marine film and television culture, coastal defense culture, maritime culture, and port culture constitute the marine culture tourism resources with Ningbo characteristics.

(3) Unique local delicious food highlights the unique style of Ningbo food culture

Food is the paramount necessity of the people, while food is the first factor to consider in travel. Among the six elements of tourism in "food, housing, travel, tourism, shopping, and entertainment", food is at the top of the list. This is not only because food is indispensable in tourism, but also because food culture has the potential to promote tourism in multiple ways. Seafood products, Ningbo dishes, Ningbo pastry, snacks, constitute a good basis for Ningbo food culture tourism resources. Ningbo Cuisine is also known as Yongbang Dish, it is an important branch of Zhejiang cuisine, one of the eight major Chinese cuisines, so it is long-standing and well-established. Known as the East China Sea big yellow croaker and the swimming crab, the Song Dynasty poet Su Dongpo has a poem for the Ningbo shuttle crab: "The crab roe under the shell is appropriate to be served with liquor, while the white meat in the pincers could increase people's appetite. " Ningbo sweet soup balls made by Ningbo traditional craft, boiled glutinous rice balls in fermented glutinous rice, yellow colored glutinous rice cake, Cicheng rice cakes, crystalline steamed stuffed bun, Xikou multi-layer steamed bread, eight-treasure rice pudding with sweetened bean paste, stuffed lard and sesame dumplings, Ningbo fried dough twist, and crisp bean candy are well received by visitors. Ningbo Nantang Old Street, Town God's Temple, the Old Bund of Ningbo and other street features also reflect the unique style of Ningbo food culture.

(4) The integration of culture and tourism highlights the unique characteristics of ningbo's tourism culture

Tourism theme of Ningbo history and culture: cultural tour with First Hall Under Heaven as the theme, historical and cultural tour with Hemudu as the theme, port culture tour with the theme of Orient Port, historical architectural tour with Cicheng Ancient Town as the theme, meditation tour with Tiantong Temple and Ashoka Temple as the theme, the Republic of China customs tour with Chiang Kai-shek's Former Residence as theme, the red culture tour with the theme of Siming Mountain Base, cultural tour of the sea with the theme of Shipu Fishing port, red dowry tour with the theme of red dowry culture, and commercial culture tour with the theme of Ningbo Confraternity. These tourism and cultural themes reflect the deep integration of Ningbo tourism and culture, make full use of and in-depth development, and determine that Ningbo's tourism economic development brings vitality.

Ⅲ. Advantages of Ningbo cultural tourism industry

Ningbo has prominent regional advantages and strong driving force for tourism development. Ningbo is the economic center of the southern wing of the Yangtze River Delta region and an emerging tourist destination in the region. Among the highway skeletons that have been built or under construction in Ningbo, there are obvious "cross" shapes, one is Huangshan from Anhui to Hangzhou via Ningbo and Hangzhou, and the other is the coastal passage from Shanghai and Suzhou across the bridge. Ningbo is at the intersection of the two expressways. It connects east China and south China, the two largest sources of tourists, and connects Jiangxi and Anhui from east to west, expanding the tourism hinterland. In addition, the completion of Hangzhou Bay Bridge has connected Shanghai with Hangzhou and Shanghai-Ningbo expressway, transforming the former Yangtze River Delta tourism traffic "One way leads to the end" into the tourism traffic "triangle loop", and Ningbo officially entered the Yangtze River Delta 2-hour traffic circle with Shanghai as the core, so it is with very convenient railway, highway, aviation and other traffic. This location condition has positive significance for Ningbo tourism development.

Ningbo Municipal Government attaches great importance to the construction of city image and brand and the promotion of tourism image is supported. From the early establishment of city trees and flowers to the global collection of city image slogan ten years ago, from the "love city" "civilized city" "smart city" to the current stage of the "famous city", city international image positioning, Ningbo has always paid more attention to the construction of city image. There is a symbiotic relationship between city brand and tourism image, so a healthy and good city image is bound to bring a positive impact on the shaping and dissemination of tourism image.

Policy support from the Ningbo Municipal Government has always taken culture as an important resource to develop tourism industry and cultivate new economic growth point of tourism. In national economic and social development plan for the 11th five-year of Ningbo, the municipal government proposed to develop tourism resource with high starting point and high grade, explore and enhance the cultural connotation of Xikou in Fenghua, Hemudu in Yuyao, Collection of Books in First Hall Under Heaven, Yuehu Culture and other tourism resources, improve and upgrade a number of scenic spots and tourist resorts with high cultural status and great influence. All these have provided strong policy support for the development of cultural tourism industry.

IV. Problems Existing in Ningbo's Cultural Tourism Industry

1. Ningbo tourism is not deeply integrated with Ningbo characteristic culture

Ningbo is a famous historical city with rich tourism as well as cultural resources and numerous and high level historical and cultural relics, the prehistoric culture of all ages can be found here. However, in the process of reservation or development and construction, the tourism resources are lack of deep excavation based on cultural connotation, and tourist attractions is not deeply integrated with historic culture, resulting in the obvious lack of historical depth of Ningbo's tourism image. Historical sites such as the Old Bund, the Town God's Temple, the Drum Tower and Chiang Kai-shek's Former Residence have been occupied by a strong commercial atmosphere, lacking a sense of historical tradition and culture, and the historical heritage has been damaged to varying degrees, and the value of cultural tourism is lacking.

2. There is a certain deviation in the value orientation of the development and construction of Ningbo ancient cultural relics

Ningbo ancient cultural relics occupy a large share of tourism and cultural resources. The early cultural relics, such as Hemudu Site with more than 7000 years of history, Historical Site of the Butterfly Lover, Qingjian Kiln Site of Shanglinhu Lake, Tianfeng Pagoda, Baoguo Temple and a number of ancient temples, are all true depictions of Ningbo's long history and cultural city. However, there are deviation of value orientation in the development and management of cultural tourism, such as Hemudu Site and Historical Site of the Butterfly Lover. The discovery of the former site proves that the Yangtze River basin and the

Yellow River basin are both the birthplace of the ancient culture of China. However, such a birthplace of ancient culture is with rare tourists during the peak season, and tourists during the tourist off-season is even less. On the contrary, because of the widely-spread love story of butterfly lovers, large-scale activities such as Butterfly Lovers Cultural Festival and Blind Date Party are held every year. It is understandable to hold these activities. There is nothing wrong with holding these activities, but is there some prejudice against the birthplace of ancient culture?

3. Ningbo marine culture has not played its inherent advantages and effects

The main city of Ningbo is far away from the sea, and the environment of coastal tourism is obviously insufficient. There are many ports and hinterlands used for industrial development, and few are really used for tourism development and construction. In addition to bathing spots and a few coastal defense sites, there are few tourist attractions with marine culture as the theme, which is not consistent with the status of Oriental Port and coastal city. It is a defect in the strategy of developing the city of port economy with paying attention to the development of port economy, but neglecting the development and construction of cultural tourism.

4. Lack of clear image positioning and core concept

Although Ningbo has rich tourism and cultural resources, it lacks clear image positioning and core concepts. This is related to the fact that the image of Ningbo city has not been clearly defined and the core concept has not been recognized. From Four Business Cards to Credit Ningbo, Smart City, Beautiful Ningbo, Civilized City, and to the International Port City, Capital of Oriental Civilization, the city image and concept are not clear, so the tourism image is also naturally affected.

5. Lack of systematic and continuous brand establishment

A tourism brand IP image including tourism propaganda slogan, tourism image logo, tourism theme brand series, and it is a systematic project. In recent years, the tourism slogan of Ningbo has been changed many times, and the supporting facility is deficient.

6. Lack of high-level professional planning team and effective media communication

In order to achieve the desired effect, the shaping and spread of cultural tourism image must rely on high level professional planning team or institutions. At present, the organization responsible for image building and promotion of Ningbo cultural tourism lacks a high-level professional planning team. In addition, Ningbo's local tourism media lack effective integration and planning, and cannot achieve the desired communication effect.

V. The Significance of "the Belt and Road" Initiative to the Development of Ningbo Cultural Tourism

"The Belt and Road" is short for Silk Road Economic Belt and 21st Century Maritime Silk Road. In September and October 2013, Xi Jinping put forward the strategic ideas of building New Silk Road Economic Belt and 21st Century Maritime Silk Road respectively. "The Belt and Road" is a concept and initiative of cooperative development. It relies on existing bilateral and multilateral mechanisms and effective regional cooperation platforms between China and relevant countries. It aims to use the historical symbol of the ancient silk road, hold high the banner of peaceful development, actively develop economic cooperation partnerships with countries along "the Belt and Road", and jointly build community of shared interests, community of common future, and community of responsibility with political mutual trust, economic integration and cultural tolerance.

On March 28, 2015, authorized by the State Council, the National Development and Reform Commission, the Ministry of Foreign Affairs and the Ministry of Commerce jointly issued the Vision and Action on Promoting the Joint Construction of the Silk Road Economic Belt and the 21st Century Maritime Silk Road. The article clearly put forward these ideas: strengthen tourism cooperation, expand the scale of tourism, and hold tourism promotion week, publicity month and other activities in each other's country. Jointly build international quality tourist routes and tourism product with features of the Silk Road, and improve convenience of visa application for tourists from countries along "the Belt and Road". Promote cooperation on cruise tourism along the 21st Century Maritime Silk Road; at the same time, the article points out that "grab the key passages, key nodes and key projects of the transportation infrastructure, give priority to the lack of road sections, smooth the bottleneck sections, and improve the road safety protection facilities and traffic management facilities to improve the road access level. "

On May 14, 2017, at the opening ceremony of "the Belt and Road" Forum for International Cooperation, President Xi Jinping pointed out that ancient ports in Ningbo and other places are "living fossils" which record the history of the ancient Silk Road. This conclusion highly appraises Ningbo's historical status, and it is also a good opportunity for Ningbo to improve its cultural tourism image.

The conclusion of "living fossil" of the ancient Silk Road provides a new way to explore Ningbo's cultural tourism. Under the background of "the Belt and Road" construction, through deeply exploring and systematically arranging the connotation of the "living fossil" of the ancient Silk Road to integrate the profound Maritime Silk Road culture with modern urban culture, to enrich the connotation of Ningbo tourism culture, and to clarify the image of tourism culture. This provides a favorable opportunity and rich connotation for improving Ningbo's cultural tourism image.

The construction of "the Belt and Road" hub city provides new impetus for the improvement of Ningbo's cultural tourism image. At present, Ningbo is actively planning to give full play to the regional advantages of "the Belt and Road" and the Yangtze River Economic Zone, accelerate the construction of a modern international port city, and strive to occupy a favorable position in the new round of international competition. This provides a strong impetus to improve the image of Ningbo's cultural tourism.

The promotion of city-wide tourism provides new support for improving Ningbo's cultural tourism image. In December 2017, Ningbo Municipal Party Committee and the Municipal Government issued *Several Opinions on Promoting the Reform and Development of Regional Tourism*. It points out that the reform and development of tourism should be integrated into the overall situation of the city, gradually form the development pattern of regional tourism, and strive to cultivate tourism into the engine industry of modern service industry in Ningbo. The related measures brought by this document provide a strong support for the promotion of Ningbo's cultural tourism image.

Ⅵ. Suggestions on the development of Ningbo Cultural Tourism Industry under the Background of "the Belt and Road" Initiative

The development of "the Belt and Road" Initiative is integrated with the international market. The innovation of various theories provides brand-new innovative ideas for the development of Ningbo's cultural tourism industry in the new period, so as to promote the development of innovative theories under the strategic background of "the Belt and Road". Through the analysis of the integration of Ningbo cultural tourism industry, it is concluded that the development of Ningbo cultural tourism industry should focus on the innovation of the development model.

1. Government

(1) Strengthen regulation and seize the opportunity to boost policy

First of all, employ high-quality tourism personnel, and the relevant tourism personnel training institutions should also vigorously cultivate high-quality practitioners; secondly, the national tourism administration department shall strictly manage the relevant professional qualification examination, improve the quality of practitioners and managers in scenic area, and strengthen the operation and management ability of scenic area, so as to improve the comprehensive attraction of scenic area; thirdly, strengthen supervision, and severely punish unlicensed tour guides and other acts that disturb the order of the tourism market.

(2) Integrate resources, realize multi-Product strategy, and develop characteristic cultural tourism brand projects

It is necessary to systematically integrate Ningbo's tourism resources, focus on developing and protecting existing tourist attractions, and exploit the unique characteristics of Ningbo tourism resources. Profoundly explore the excellent regional cultures such as oceanic culture, religious culture, love culture of butterfly lovers, business gang culture and folk culture, explore, enhance and realize the cultural added value of Ningbo tourism through the characteristic culture productization and the marketization reorganization, and further build a brand of cultural tourism characteristics of the project.

① Marine tourism culture. Use marine fishery resources and fishery products resources, etc to open up tourist space where tourists can experience oceanic culture, sightseeing, and entertainment, plan and design a number of related theme activities, such as the construction of Elephant Hill, Daxie Island and other attractions of marine recreational fishing culture and food culture tourism projects.

② Urban cultural tourism. The urban tourism circle formed by relying on famous historical and cultural cities and international port cities is the core of Ningbo's urban cultural tourism. For example, Dongqian Lake can be used to build a national first-class tourist resort with natural landscape; extend the cultural corridor of three rivers, form a hundred-mile landscape belt, and focus on shaping the product image of Ningbo urban recreation business district and recreation culture belt.

③ Buddhist cultural tourism. Ningbo has Tiantong Temple, Baoguo Temple, Ashoka Temple, Xuedou Temple and other Buddhist tourism resources. In addition to opening up special cultural tourism routes such as pilgrimage tour for Buddhists, various Buddhist cultural activities can also be held for more ordinary tourists to enhance the interest and knowledge of Buddhism tourism, so as to further explore the cultural connotation of these Buddhism tourism resources.

④Ancient town and village cultural tourism. Ningbo has famous village and ancient towns with profound historical and cultural deposits and distinctive characteristics. In the development of cultural tourism products, these ancient towns and famous villages should pay attention to the participation, strengthen the cultural experience of tourists, and make tourists change their role from spectator to active participant. For example, fishing culture and farming culture of famous villages and ancient towns are organically integrated into modern leisure tourism products, allowing tourists to participate in fishing or farming activities in ancient towns; fully explore the folk culture of famous villages and ancient towns to deepen tourists' understanding of them and to shape the unique image of the ancient town.

(3) Build bases for eco-tourism and the Silk Road cultural industry

The development of eco-tourism is a powerful way to develop tourism economy. The establishment of ecological tourism needs to strengthen the environmental protection of Ningbo eco-tourism area, so the government's responsibility is indispensable. The government and relevant departments need to formulate relevant laws and regulations to strengthen people's awareness of environmental protection in eco-tourism areas, and properly complete the publicity and education of employees and tourists, so as to minimize the damage to the ecological environment while developing the tourism industry. Meanwhile, take the opportunity of the New Silk Road Economic Belt to build a new starting point of the Silk Road cultural tourism center. By virtue of its unique tourism resources, it can explore traditions and historical culture, promote the transformation of industrial structure from humanistic to landscape and sightseeing to leisure, and create an industrial base by gathering culture in Ningbo.

(4) Strengthen exchanges between countries and regions along the Silk

Road and create new forms of regional cooperation

On the one hand, it is necessary to strengthen tourism cooperation with the cities inside and outside the province along the Silk Road and establish tourism cooperation institutions or organizations related to the Silk Road. For example, Ningbo can jointly build a horizontal regional tourism circle with neighboring Hangzhou and Suzhou, so as to drive the development of regional linkage, jointly build the Silk Road cultural heritage tourism corridor and expand the tourism market. On the other hand, strengthen tourism cooperation with Southeast Asian countries, promote the healthy development of inbound and out-bound tourism, actively promote the open development strategy of "going out and coming in", and accelerate the development of the international tourism market by setting up overseas offices and simplifying the procedures of applying for inbound and outbound tourist visas.

2. Tourism Enterprise

(1) Make full use of resources to build quality international tourism brands

Firstly, tourism enterprises should make full use of existing tourism re-sources, develop tourism products according to local conditions, and highlight the superiority and uniqueness of Ningbo tourism resources; secondly, it is nec-essary to strengthen the exchange and cooperation of information, experience and resources among the peers to form a good competitive environment and pro-mote the ecological development of the whole tourism industry; thirdly, building an international tourism brand needs to study the demands of tourists, for exam-ple, certain brands of restaurants, theme hotels, etc. By grasping the consumer psychology and purchase demand of tourists, the level of various products and services under the tourism brand can be adjusted, so as to explore and promote Ningbo's potential international tourism market.

(2) Optimize the tourism industry cluster and enhance the view of social re-sponsibility

Tourism enterprises need to fulfill their social responsibilities consciously, improve the tourism industry cluster system and establish a good international image. For Ningbo, tourism enterprises should integrate the awareness of social responsibility into their daily management, refine the responsibility to individuals, and add the route of Ningbo tourism scenic spot to the characteristics of the silk road and re-plan it; at the same time, the company should establish a corresponding evaluation system linked with performance to let every employee can realize the importance of fulfilling social responsibility, so as to form an effective corporate social responsibility management and implementation system and improve the performance of tourism enterprises. In addition, high-quality tourism industry cluster will also promote the improvement of the overall quality of tourism, and form benign competition among individual tourism enterprises, so as to develop more innovative tourism routes and products, and eventually drive the qualitative leap of Ningbo tourism.

(3) Strengthen marketing and publicity of the Silk Road tourism and development of tourism products

First of all, Ningbo tourism enterprises can enhance the publicity of Silk Road tourism by participating in various domestic and foreign tourism trade fairs or expos, and organize special discount tour groups to carry out targeted and main promotion in some major tourist sources at home and abroad. Secondly, it is necessary to strengthen communication and cooperation with surrounding tourist hot cities and port cities, build new ideas to develop high-quality tourism routes and new tourism special projects, etc. Thirdly, Ningbo Silk Road cultural tourism image and tourism products are fully publicized by the media to further promote the silk road tourism. Fourthly, different types of tour-themed promotional activities should be made for different tourist source markets, such as historical and cultural tours, religious and cultural tours, silk road cultural tours, etc. , so that different audiences can understand the significance of Ningbo cultural tourism.

3. Media

(1) Correctly transmit information and improve the image of Ningbo tourism

media

Media publicity is an important factor influencing tourists' travel decisions. Expression of media, the application and publicity of news structure elements will directly affect the public's cognition, therefore, the image of tourist attractions and the authenticity and reliability of tourist information disseminated by media are quite important. Ningbo's tourist attractions are numerous, scenic spot order and environmental maintenance also needs more energy to manage. Firstly, the media should not deliberately distort and fabricate facts to pursue economic benefits and attract the attention of the audience; secondly, the media needs to correct the excessive reports on a certain aspect of a certain thing for a long time, and provide fair and objective news reports so as to avoid wrong data of multiple media communication, and get rid of the "stereotyped image" of Ningbo tourism in the eyes of the public due to the interaction of political, economic, social and cultural factors. In addition, great efforts are made to select correct and appropriate methods and approaches to actively guide the public's cognition of Ningbo, give full play to the guiding role of the media, and establish an accurate international media image.

(2) Actively build cultural discourse rights and promote international cultural exchanges

With the rapid development of modern information and communication technology and electronic media, it is possible to spread cultural discourse in a large scale across countries and internationally. Therefore, under "the Belt and Road" Initiative, media communication is essential to enhance the discourse power of Chinese culture and promote international cultural exchanges. However, enhancing the discourse power of Chinese culture is a challenge that cannot be underestimated in today's cultural globalization. First of all, media communication needs to abandon the rigid narrative mode, analyze the problem from the public point of view, and enhance communication effectiveness and attractiveness. Secondly, the propagation mode of media should be changed more effectively and appropriately, so as to guide the values and behaviors of social members. Thirdly, the mode of communication in China is too conceptual and mechanical, so that domestic and foreign audiences are of aesthetic fatigue.

Ⅶ. Conclusion

Ningbo cultural tourism industry has broad prospects, and it is a sunrise industry with huge development potential. In order to accelerate the development of the cultural and tourism industry, it is essential to stimulate the development of the tertiary industry, promote economic restructuring, promote the transformation of the development model, promote the new urbanization process, expand the opening up, create a livable and suitable living environment, and improve the city's image and competitiveness. Under the guidance of the concept of regional tourism, the whole society should make efforts to improve the image of Ningbo's cultural tourism. Under the background of "the Belt and Road", Ningbo should firmly grasp the historical opportunity provided by the new era and develop several routes simultaneously. The planning of urban public space should give full consideration to the shaping of the image of urban cultural tourism, and make use of the Old Bund, Qing'an Guild Hall, Korean Embassy, Yongfeng Storage Site and other sea silk sites to build a vivid and rich tourism spatial pattern. For example, in order to develop the "Living Fossil of Maritime Silk Road" tourism route, on the one hand, the relics of Maritime Silk Road should be connected with other tourism resources to launch the theme route; on the other hand, media resources should be integrated for marketing. For example, the establishment of the Maritime Silk Road expert think-tank provided publicity materials for "Living Fossil of Maritime Silk Road" and so on. Therefore, we must unify our thought, clarify ideas, seize opportunities and build on the momentum, and constantly improve the experience and participation of Ningbo's cultural tourism activities, so as to make Ningbo's cultural tourism industry go out of China and into the world.

Study on the Ways of Grassroots Silk Road Culture Construction under "the Belt and Road" Initiative

Zhang Yimeng[①]

Abstract: "the Belt and Road" contains rich Chinese ideas and Chinese wisdom, while steady and step-by-step construction of "the Belt and Road" must be based on a broad, deep and solid public foundation. From the perspective of "congeniality of the people's minds", the author stands at three different levels i. e. the country, the media and the masses, to profoundly explain the reasons, problems and solutions to the problem of the construction of grassroots Silk Road culture.

Key words: "The Belt and Road"　grassroots Silk Road culture construction　cause　problem　countermeasure

I . Introduction

In May 2017, the Ministry of Environmental Protection, the Ministry of Foreign Affairs, State Development and Reform Commission, and the Ministry of Commerce jointly issued *Guiding Opinions on Promoting the Construction of the Green Belt and Road*, systematically expounding the significance of building a "Green Belt and Road" and promoting in an all-round way the green-oriented process of "policy communication" "facilities connectivity" "smooth trade", fund circulation" and "congeniality of the people's minds". And to promote the long-term maintenance of "the Belt and Road" construc-

---

①　Zhang Yimeng, female, is currently a student of Grade Two at No. 1 High School of Luanping County, Henan Province.

tion, "the people's hearts and minds" can be described as important. In order to promote long-term maintenance, "congeniality of the people's minds" is very important. Cultural development at the grassroots level is the primary task to achieve congeniality of the people's minds. Only promoting it to all aspects of social life and subtly influencing the social practice and life of grassroots people, can we lay a solid foundation for the promotion of "the Belt and Road" construction and make "the Belt and Road" truly become the "basic state policy" in the new era. To achieve the commonwealth of the people, grassroots cultural construction is the primary task. Only by letting the Silk Road culture be ubiquitous and ubiquitous, pushing it to all aspects of social life, subtly affecting the social practice and life of the grassroots people, can lay a solid foundation for the construction of "the Belt and Road". As a youth, the author believes that we should focus our attention on the people around us, that is, thousands of grassroots people. This is not only because we are one of them, but also because "the Belt and Road" is a national initiative. Everyone, whether it is a national leader or a government official, whether it is a grassroots cadre or an ordinary people, whether it is a first-tier city or a small county or town, you are qualified and obligated to really understand "the Belt and Road" and contribute a little bit of your power. Therefore, this article focuses on a study on the ways of grassroots Silk Road culture construction under "the Belt and Road" Initiative.

Ⅱ. The necessity of grassroots Silk Road culture construction

As for the necessity of the grassroots Silk Road culture construction in "the Belt and the Road" Initiative, we can roughly analogize this as the importance of grassroots cadres in the development of the country as compare. In history, Zheng Banqiao of the Qing Dynasty wrote in his works *Poem Inscribed for Ink Bamboo Painting* that "although we are only small officials in the state and county, the people's every little thing is affecting our feelings". Although the grassroots cadres are at the grassroots level, they bear important responsibility. Especially nowadays, from agricultural subsidies to special poverty alleviation, further to land acquisition and demolition and project construction, the responsibilities of grassroots cadres are more closely related to the interests of the masses. The working attitude of grassroots cadres directly affects the development of grassroots work and the protection of the rights and interests of the common people. At that time, thanks to the persistence and dedication of the old branch secretary Huang Dafa, Caowangba Village of Zunyi, Guizhou Province spent more than 30 years to cut through the "life channel" on the cliff and thereby ended the long history of water shortage. Only by means of pressing forward in the same direction, the grassroots cadres and the masses can be continuously drawn closer to each other and the strength for starting entrepreneurship can be united together. General Secretary Xi Jinping said: "The cadres should go deep into the grassroots level, go deep into reality, and go deep into the masses. Cadres should temper qualities and improve abilities in the main battlefield of reform and development, front line of stability maintenance and the forefront of serving the masses. " The grassroots level is an inexhaustible resource, and it provides us with a broad stage for the entrepreneurship. The grassroots cadres can do a great job and will create marvelous achievements. Hundreds of hundreds of boats compete, the one striving to oar takes the first. The vast number of grassroots cadres should emancipate their minds, raise demanding standards strive for the first, emulate advanced figures and perform their duties, adding new impetus and injecting positive energy to the grassroots work in the new era. The same is true for the grassroots Silk Road culture construction. It is not only conducive to meeting the growing spiritual and cultural needs of the people, but also plays a pivotal role in promoting the construction of "the Belt and Road".

Ⅲ. Achievment and inadequacies in the construction of grassroots Silk Road culture

China has made in economic and trade cooperation with other countries since the implementation of "the Belt and Road" Initiative:

(1) As of June 2018, China's trade in goods with countries along the route totaled more than USMYM 5. 5 trillion, with an average annual growth rate of 1. 1%. China has become the largest trading partner of 25 countries along the route.

(2) Foreign direct investment exceeded USMYM 70 billion, with an average annual growth rate of 7. 2%. The contract value of newly signed foreign contracted projects in the countries along the route exceeded USMYM 500 billion, with an average annual growth rate of 19. 2%.

(3) Chinese enterprises have built 82 overseas economic and trade cooperation zones in the countries along the route, with a total investment of USMYM 28. 9 billion, 3, 995 enterprises getting settled in the zone, and the collected host country's taxes and fees totaled USMYM 2. 01 billion, creating 244, 000 job posts for the local area. At present, Chinese enterprises have explored the third-party market cooperation in the construction of "the Belt and Road". China has also continued to relax foreign investment access, create a high standard of business environment so as to attract countries along the route to invest in China.

(4) China has accelerated the construction of free trade zones with countries along the route. China has signed or upgraded five free trade agreements with 13 countries along the route. The high-standard free trade network based on the surrounding areas and covering "the Belt and Road" and facing the world has been under accelerated construction. China has also signed an economic and trade cooperation agreement with the Eurasian Economic Union and completed a joint feasibility study with Russia on the Eurasian Economic Partnership Agreement.

(5) In November 2018, China actively held The First China International

Import Expo, with 172 countries, regions and international organizations participating in the conference, more than 3, 600 companies participating in the exhibition, and more than 400, 000 domestic and foreign buyers attending the conference for negotiation and purchase. According to statistics, among the millions of pieces of information displayed by Baidu Encyclopedia Search "the Belt and Road", 70% are related to the economy. It can be seen that "the Belt and Road" Initiative at the national level is more often implemented as an economic strategy.

From a domestic perspective, the relevant measures of "the Belt and Road" construction in various provinces and regions are too independent, lacking division of labor and cooperation, and lacking local characteristics and explosiveness. Compared with the embarrassing situation of some tourist attractions in previous years, this phenomenon is nothing but blindly following the trend, drifting with the flow, they failed in finding respective development positioning and goal orientation.

IV. The ways of grassroots Silk Road culture construction

1. The government level

The first is to strengthen cultural exchanges and cooperation between the countries along the route in the construction of "the Belt and Road". To interpret "the Belt and Road" Initiative with cultural achievements is not just a simple economic strategy, but a comprehensive strategy with long-term goals and aimed at the development of politics, economy, military and diplomacy and other aspects on the basis of cultural exchanges. We should give the strongest proof with practical action. The second is to implement the "one province, one country and one emphasis" strategy, namely "1 + 1 + 1" strategy. One province and one country: This strategy is aimed at those provinces that have direct geographic links with countries along the Silk Road, such as Inner Mongolia, Xinjiang, and Heilongjiang. In April 2015, Heilongjiang Province issued *Implementation Opinions on the Planning and Construction of China-Mongolia-Russia Economic*

Corridor Heilongjiang Land and Maritime Silk Road Economic Belt, Heilongjiang is adjacent to Mongolia and Russia, and enjoys an advantageous geographical position, leveraging "the Belt and Road" Initiative to promote the provincial economic development pace. By this way, Heilongjiang Province make up for its geographical disadvantages relative to the eastern coastal provinces and regions and turn its weaknesses into strength and closely follow the tide of the Belt and Road, it is worth learning. Similar to this, Tibet Autonomous Region promulgated *Construction Planning for the Important Channels for Tibet Opening to South Asia* in 2017; in 2014, Inner Mongolia Autonomous Region successively issued the *Implementation Plan for the Cooperation Mechanism between Inner Mongolia Autonomous Region and Russia and Mongolia* and *Planning Outline for Inner Mongolia Autonomous Region Deepening Comprehensive Cooperation with Mongolia*. All these are based on fully utilizing favorable climatic, geographical and human conditions. Provinces and regions that "the Belt and Road" passes through, such as Shanxi, Shaanxi, Inner Mongolia, Ningxia, Xinjiang and Tibet on the route of land silk road, and Jiangsu, Zhejiang, Shandong, Fujian, Guangdong on the Maritime Silk Road, these provinces and regions and areas directly related to "the Belt and Road" can take advantage of its geographical location and actively integrate into the construction of "the Belt and Road". For example, Henan Province is located in the central plains. Zhengzhou, the provincial capital, is located in the center of China's traffic cross. Beijing-Guangzhou Railway and Lanzhou-Lianyungang Railway intersect here, the newly-built Beijing-Zhuhai Expressway, Lianyungang-Khorgas Expressway and National Highway 107 and 310 pass through the city. 4E Xinzheng International Airport is open to navigation in more than 30 cities both at home and abroad. In addition, Zhengzhou has the largest train marshalling station in Asia and the largest LTL cargo intermodal station in the country. It has built air ports, railway ports and highway ports with complete equipment, sound mechanism, advanced management and high throughput. Cargos can be jointly inspected and sealed in Zhengzhou and directly shipped to overseas. It can be said that its

traffic position is a powerful boost to its integration into "the Belt and Road".
Therefore, in September 2017, Henan Province issued the *Construction Plan for
Promoting Zhengzhou-Luxembourg Aerial Silk Road.* Therefore, "1 + 1 + 1"
strategy can give full play to the advantages of various provinces and regions,
strengthen the division of labor and cooperation among provinces, enhance
internal cohesiveness, and jointly promote the steady and step-by-step construction
of "the Belt and Road".

2. Media level

The mass media must break the bottleneck of the publicity and promotion
of "the Belt and Road", there are three ways as follows.

The first is to set up "the Belt and Road" node spokesperson. As a product
of economic marketization, celebrity endorsement is an inevitable trend. In
2017, the World Health Organization invited three young Chinese artists to act
as advocates of tobacco control in China. In 2019, the Chinese youth artist Jack-
son Yee was invited to attend the UN Youth Forum as a special health envoy of
China, with the popularity on the whole internet once maintaining high. Therefore, the so-called "influencing ability" of celebrities and artists is not only
applied to commercial publicity, but also can be upgraded a high level to be
applied in national strategic publicity and promotion, making the national guide-
lines and policies that are beyond the reach of the people be really down to the
earth in a way that the masses love. The "node spokesperson" mechanism is to
set up "Silk Road Spokesperson" at all important nodes along the "Silk Road",
and use the star effect to enhance the public's attention and enthusiasm for "the
Belt and Road", thereby enhancing participation and improving the national consciousness. Moreover, "dual-generation mode" can be adopted in the choice of
"node spokesperson", i. e. , separately setting up "node spokespersons" for the
adolescents and middle-aged groups according to the age of the audience in order
to achieve better publicizing effect.

The second is the production of large-scale TV dramas of "Revisiting the

Belt and Road". The popularity and wide audience of TV dramas is undoubted, its cultural dissemination in the artistic display method is also more easily penetrated into the hearts of the people and more intimate to masses than the high-end documentaries. The production of "Revisit the Belt and Road" TV series should be detached from the traditional documentary model, no longer use the official obscure language to introduce "the Belt and Road", but choose the artistic expression methods to truly reproduce the folk customs and culture on the way to the Silk Road. It should be easy to understand and close to life. Specific contents of the TV dramas can be divided according to the regional classification, and the historical origins between each piece of land and the Silk Road can be deeply explored. From ancient times to today, parallel time-space shooting techniques can be used to make the plots more subtle and more deeply impressed the audience. Thereby, people will unconsciously have long-lasting in-depth recognition of "the Belt and Road".

The third is to develop the mobile phone software for "the Belt and Road" Cultural Exchange. The software is designed with various kinds of sectors according to different countries and different regions, and releases official information in a timely manner; set up a "Opinion Collection Platform" to collect public opinions and criticisms on "the Belt and Road" Initiative through the Internet, expand channels for public opinions collection, and ensure fairness and justice; and implement a reward system to stimulate public enthusiasm in participation. For the problem of software download, you can cooperate with the mobile phone manufacturers and sellers, set the software to the factory-owned mode.

3. The mass level

The author believes that the publicity and promotion of "the Belt and Road" initiative should be based on Chinese youth. There are three reasons:

Firstly, the phenomenon of "Amusing Ourselves to Death" is more common among adolescents, but has relatively small proportion in middle-aged and older people group;

Secondly, adolescents are staying in an important period of forming world outlook, outlook on life and values. Publicity and education of positive energy have a greater and longer-lasting impact on them;

Thirdly, adolescents are the pillars of the country in the future. They are the active leaders and practitioners of the construction of "the Belt and Road". The road to the future needs to be escorted by them. But how to make "the Belt and Road" deeply rooted in the hearts of adolescents and inspire them to contribute to the construction of "the Belt and Road" ?Firstly, set up "the Belt and Road" research organizations in each elementary and secondary school, and hold knowledge contests on a regular basis. The score of the competition is included into students' credit. As an important place for students to entertain at school, setting up "the Belt and Road" research organizations can not only satisfy the students' entertainment mentality but also gain knowledge and influence from entertainment. In the short term, students may just hold the mentality of "look and see". However, with the advancement of research and deepening of under-standing, students will gradually change their mentality and correct their attitudes from simple entertainment to purposeful and focused studying. Knowl-edge contest and credit system can undoubtedly stimulate the enthusiasm of some "score-based" students, and attracted more students to participate. Secondly, carry out the activity "the Belt and Road into Campus". The extensive imple-mentation of "drama into the campus" is the best example. Its publicity forms include opera performance, opera knowledge popularization, the study and understanding of opera characters and opera costumes, and the school can organ-ize teachers and students to carry out opera performance by themselves under the guidance of professional opera actors. This approach is undoubtedly more practical, more appealing and has higher participation degree. "The Belt and Road into Campus" can display the achievements made in the construction of "the Belt and Road" by means of showing the digital silk roads to all primary and middle school students through the mode of touring show, and regularly organizeoutstanding students to visit the historical site of "Ancient Silk Road", and visit the countries along the Silk Road to learn about local humanities and geography, thus stimulating their cohesion and centripetal force.

V. Conclusion

As the steersman, implementer and spokesperson of the construction of "The Belt and Road", grassroots Silk Road culture construction progress is directly linked to the social conditions and public opinions, related to the Silk Road cultural exchange and associated to the steady and step-by-step publicity and promotion of "the Belt and Road" construction. Silk Road culture is the spiritual guarantee for the development of "the Belt and Road" and is the basis for enhancing the ideological identity of the countries and people along the route of "the Belt and Road". As the main body of social history and the main body of social practice, the construction of grassroots culture occupies an irreplaceable position in the publicity and promotion of Silk Road culture. Culture comes from the people and in return serves the people and benefits the people. Therefore, as a new generation of young people, what we should do is to learn and actively promote the achievements of "the Belt and Road" through our own efforts, enhance the consensus of the world people and promote the dissemination of Silk Road culture. Thereby, we can make our own contribution in composing the new chapter of the great process of "the Belt and Road", only in this way can we live up to our country's cultivation.

Postscript

Time flies, it seems like yesterday that I made the opening report in the High School Affiliated to Renmin University of China on December 31, 2018. "We are determined to do some great things". Under the call of President Xi Jinping, eight middle school students were going through a busy period of high school study, and meanwhile they seized every minute and second to finish the research of *The Belt and Road Initiative: A Bridge to the Future (II)*. It lasted nearly a year and came to a successful conclusion. We snatched a little leisure from "Practice for exams" and finished our tasks of research respectively. This is a big deal for all the members of the research team. It should be said that research is a matter of our life. I believe that the students who participated in this research will benefit greatly from it. While completing their independent studies, we participated in the whole research process, mastered the methods, and understood the society and the world.

Here, we would like to express our gratitude to the education and training of the school, and to the community for their attention and support; to the High School Affiliated to Renmin University of China, The National Centre for Communication Innovation Studies, Communication University of China, Ningbo Sub-center of Beijing Youth Leadership Culture Development Center for jointly approving our research project; grateful to the academic support of Chinese Education Society; grateful to the National Centre for Communication Innovation Studies, Communication University of China, Social Development Division of the National Development and Reform Commission, the office of the Education Supervision Committee of the State Council, Center of Ministry of Education, Committee of Social Science of Ministry of Education, Global Governance Research Center of Peking University, Institute for Philanthropy Tsinghua University, China Railway Construction Corporation Limited, China Galaxy Securities Co. , Ltd. , Global Energy Interconnection Development and Cooperation Organization, and China Aerospace Science and Industrial Corporation for their support; to leaders and experts from higher education institutions including the High School Affiliated to Renmin University of China, PLA Academy of Military Sciences, Tsinghua University of South Korea, Zhejiang University, School of Journalism of Renmin University of China, The Institute of Public Administration of Tsinghua University, Capital Normal University, China University of Political Science and Law, Zhejiang Wanli University, China Agricultural University, Zhengzhou University, Inha University of South Korea, Peking University, Beijing University of Posts and Telecommunications and central enterprises including China Railway Construction Corporation Limited: He Lei, Ou Xiaoli, Di Xiaoning, Wang Lisheng, Zheng Baowei, Fan Deshang, Deng Guosheng, Miao Baojin, Li Chunxia, Zhang Lei, Su Shangfeng, Gao Qiuming, Yan Guoqing, Chen Xiaofei, Cui Junjian, Ning Ye, Wang Weiwei, Su Mier, Chen Gang, Du Yongmei, Liu Wei, thank them for their lectures and guidance; our special gratitude shall go to professor Li Chunxia for her guidance and coordination; at the same time, to our parents for their great support; and we would also like to express our gratitude to the media and all sectors of society for their attention and support, including Xinhuanet, people. com. cn, China News, Kwangmyong, Jurisprudence Daily, China Education Daily, China Educational Television and The UK Chinese Journal. we would like to express our gratitude to our project sponsor: Li Xushuang, student of Professor Luo Weidong (Vice President of Zhejiang University), from Chu Kochen Honors College, Zhejiang University. Li Xushuang has published two monographs when carrying out research in the High School Affiliated to Renmin University of China, among which the project *The Belt and Road Initiative: A Bridge to the Future*(bilingual edition in Chinese and English) presided over by her was published by the commercial press, recognized and accepted by the relevant leaders of the National

People's Congress, the main leaders of the National Development and Reform Commission, and the main leaders of Ministry of Education and Publicity Department of the Communist Party of China, and reported in front-page by People's Daily propaganda report When studying in the university, Li Xushuang actively participated in social practice activities and published papers in national core journals, served as the interpreter for Chairman of the National Party of New Zealand, and the former Minister of Immigration and other officials of New Zealand while visiting China, and served as the leader of the visiting team of Cambridge University during the winter vacation and achieved good results. We will study harder, follow the example of our predecessors, strive to repay families, schools and society with the best results, and contribute youth and wisdom to the future construction of "the Belt and Road".

Due to the love for "Family, Country, and the World", we work hard for our dreams with great aspiration, in order to "make the society better and the world more peaceful", we fight for the future with lofty spirit and soaring determination. The saying "Youth should be fearless and high-hearted, why are you unable to recover after the comedown" has inspired young souls of generation after generation. We are a responsible new generation. The dream is still far away, but the pace must start at the moment, so we have started the journey to "the Belt and Road" construction. When make the summary and review, I hope to have more power injection, and then continue to move forward, until to the ideal destination.

At the moment when this collection of essays is to be published, we would like to join hands with the youth of the world to forge ahead. Take "the Belt and Road" as an opportunity, and with the fearless ambition, we believe the bright future is not far away from us.

Group Leader: Dong Xuhan, Zhang Siqi, Song Zhenghan

August 1, 2019